D0254125

I Must Fly!

1) apologize it you're running late.

2) make patient feel he (she) the only one you have

3) give a gift (flowers

4) greet everyone with a smile & introduce yourself.

5) call patient the evening after procedure or at least next day

6) have staff in waiting room that they call rescheduled if they've waited longer than

7) take phone calls immediately

To Robert Collins
INSTRUCTOR PILOT!
Best regards ~

I Must Fly!

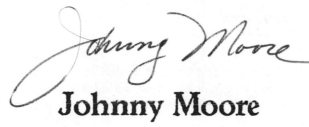

Johnny Moore

July 1, 2012

Sugarpine Aviators
Quincy, California

©1998 by Johnny Moore
All rights reserved.

Published by Sugarpine Aviators
P.O. Box 1450 • Quincy, CA 95971

Library of Congress Catalog Number 97-068741
Cover design and typography by BookWorld Press, Inc.
Manufactured in the United States of America

Quality Books, Inc. has catalogued this edition as follows:

Moore, Johnny, 1940-
    I must fly! / by Johnny Moore. -- 1st ed.
    p. cm.
    ISBN: 0-9658720-5-X

    1. Moore, Johnny, 1940- 2. Air pilots' writings, American. 3.
Air pilots--Biography. I. Title.

TL540.M66A3 1997   629.13'092 [B]
                            QBI97-40810

I dedicate this book to my wife, Judy,
who let me be me.

TABLE OF CONTENTS

ABOUT THE AUTHOR

On April 3, 1940, Johnny Moore was born into a family that included authors, composers, generals, surgeons and scientists. More importantly, it included pilots. It is not surprising that he insisted that his destiny was to fly. As a youth, every airplane he saw flying overhead prompted feelings of frustration because he was not in the cockpit.

Johnny holds a Master's Degree in Anthropology and lifetime adult teaching credentials in the fields of Anthropology and Aviation. He has published articles in internationally read aviation magazines. His practical experience spans a wide range of flight activities, over twenty-two thousand hours as a pilot including, Alaskan bush flying, firebombing, cropdusting and movie stunts. He is also an Inspection Authorized Aircraft and Powerplant mechanic, FAA Designated Pilot Examiner and an aviation Fixed Based Operator.

ACKNOWLEDGMENTS

Thanks so much to my wonderful grandparents, Dave and Edith Rogers, for raising me in spite of the hell I caused them. Thanks too, for keeping my parents' "V" war mail so that I would better understand their love for each other and for me, since they could not be here to explain those things themselves.

I must thank my loving wife, Judy, for helping me write this book and for putting up with the antics that appear in these pages.

Thanks go to all the crazy characters who appear herein. Especially Al Ewald! Thanks to Jim Magoffin, Paul Harris, Pat Morrow, Larry Parker, Ran Slaten, Scott Kerr, Gary Hendrickson, Art Lawhern, and the others who suffered through various rough drafts of this manuscript in order to give me advice. Thanks also to Ruth Jackson, who plowed through many corrections in the story and insisted that I clean it up a little.

In view of how much it costs to produce a book, I must confess that I have not told the entire truth. I have deliberately left out huge chunks of gut-wrenching conflict with certain government agencies and individuals and have, instead, concentrated on the aviation experience.

I appreciate the fates that allowed me to spend my life doing what I love to do, that is—fly!

FOREWORD

My earliest memories were of flying with Mom before I was four. I remember the sound and smell of the airplane and the image of the sunlight reflecting off the instruments. I also remember how she uttered a squeal of delight when she let me have the yoke of the Taylorcraft. I pushed forward as hard as I could and loved the floating sensation.

The first chapter is a dialogue of World War II "V" mail. That is, photocopied and censored wartime correspondences that open up a little window into my mom and dad's time to reveal their passion for aviation. At that time, when faced with the common cause to win the War, people were fiercely patriotic. Dad left a successful medical practice and volunteered to help with the war effort as a flight surgeon. They left behind a little boy who just had to fly.

As for myself, this is *not* a weepy-eyed story about the thrill and grandeur of flight. It is, rather, a down-to-earth tale about making a living in aviation. It is filled with episodes both good and bad, sometimes hilarious, sometimes deadly. The stories of many wonderful, not so wonderful, and downright weird characters traipse through these pages, and I have learned from all of them. This *is* a story of the development of a child into an adult, of a student into a journeyman, of a hotshot flying enthusiast into a humble and wiser pilot and person. The story is sometimes introspective and personal, sometimes instructive and political. It is often humorous. Anyone who likes to fly as a pilot can relate to, and learn from, these flight experiences. Those interested in the aviation industry, and the business of it, will alternately grit their teeth and heave sighs of relief along with me. This is real life, human drama. This is my search for the "promised land," of finding fulfillment as a pilot and a person. I'll tell you right now—if any of this stuff gets me in trouble, I'll deny every word!

Part I
THE SEARCH

Chapter 1
Mom & Dad

TO: JOHN W. MOORE, CAPT. M. C.
FROM: GAIL ROGERS MOORE

ST. PATRICK'S DAY
March 17, 1944
Spring has sprung in Quincy today. Gave me the itch to go up to
Gold Lake—I suppose I won't get up there this year, they've cut
us down to two gallons now and I can't go to the airport and
Gold Lake too. I got up early this morning and flew to Susanville
with Barbara Baldwin in Draper's Luscombe. It was her first cross
country. She did OK. She'll make a good pilot. We took some
instruments over for Harry Alley to put in C.A.'s ship—if and
when it gets put together again.

March 20, 1944
Saturday night we were invited up to Bill Bailey's—we had quite
a time. What a bull session. Bill provided ample liquid and the
party just went on and on. I spent most of the evening trying to
get a job running shuttle service for Draper between here and

Reno. Course that would necessitate my getting a C ticket, but I guess that it could be done. C. A. was very much opposed to my doing it, saying that I didn't have to do such things, that I could get in all the flying that I wanted to. But fooey Honey, I'd like to do something on my own just once.

Yesterday, Sunday, Barbara B. and I went out and took a cross-country to Beckwith. We got out real early and it was beautiful! She did all of the flying and I did all the looking. I flew for a while with Floyd (he still hasn't gotten his written OK from Washington for his solo). Then Draper asked me if I would check a fellow out for him. The fellow had been instructing at Basic somewhere down the line. Did I feel silly! Anyhow, I checked him out—did he ever tromp on those rudders. He certainly seemed jittery as the dickens. When he landed, it was on one wheel. I jumped the right rudder and hauled the stick clear back and he didn't even know I'd touched it. Fine pilot. He did all right the second time around—I turned him loose, cause he could fly the thing, so he took a passenger and cruised around the valley about 3,000 feet. These valley cats don't like the mountains.

(This was the day the B-25 that my dad was riding in as a passenger was shot down near Papua, New Guinea. All aboard perished. Wes was 36.)

March 26, 1944
I spent most of the afternoon out at the airport and got a ride with Bill Bailey. He doesn't get out very often but when he does he certainly wrings that poor little Aeronca out. It got pretty gusty by the time we got down and it felt as though we were getting spanked in the pants. Bill made a lousy landing but his air work was swell. A B-T came in just as we got out of the ship—it was from Chico. It didn't use any more of the field than

the Cubs do. I've been trying to wrangle a ride in it but I'm not making much progress. Guess even up here in the sticks they are afraid to break the rules. Oh well, maybe after the war I'll get a ride in something more than a 65. (A 65 horsepowered airplane.)

April 1, 1944
Boy! Am I green over that ride you had. I'd probably been sick as a goose, but I'd certainly love to get a chance to do that! (Wes logged stick time in a P-38 fighter while sitting on the pilot's lap—a Flight Surgeon's prerogative.) Best I could do was to go up with Al Classen today after he got his Commercial and sit there while he tried everything he'd ever heard of a light plane doing. By the way, Quincy scored 100% on tests with the CAA. Irene got her Private, Floyd passed his check for his hand, Al got his Commercial and so did Peter Mingrone. Quincy is turning out pilots at a good rate! Aren't you proud? Our runway is dry as a bone and Beckwith is under three feet of snow. They have tried skis up there but I don't think they did very well because there were holes in the snow. Can you imagine that!

FEATHER RIVER BULLETIN
April 6, 1944
Little John David Moore's birthday is April 3, and a party had been planned for him at the Quincy Forest Service campgrounds Sunday. It was held, because his daddy would have preferred it that way.

At the height of the birthday party, an Army training plane zoomed into Quincy Sky Harbor. Aboard it was Mrs. Moore's brother and Lt. David H. Rogers of Luke Field, Phoenix (Flight Instructor). His mother had telephoned the news to him Sunday morning and he obtained permission to fly here at once.

"ROTARY ROOTER"
VOL. 14 NO. 15
EDITOR: LINK PECKENPAH
April 10, 1944

Wes (Dr. John Wesley Moore) became a member of this club during 1936 shortly after establishing himself as physician and surgeon and the head of Quincy's Industrial Hospital. He was elected a Director of the Club in 1940 and served as the Club's Vice President in 1941. Most outstanding of Wes' accomplishments was the establishment of an airport for this community. We are all rather proud of Quincy Sky Harbor and we have it because of Wes Moore's leadership and untiring efforts. Wes' dream of a standard size fully equipped airport in American Valley will become a reality in the not-too-distant future if we carry on. When that airfield is established, it should be dedicated to the memory of this fellow who with courage, foresight and enthusiasm sold the importance of aviation to the community.

FEATHER RIVER BULLETIN
December 14, 1944

Gail Rogers Moore, a prominent Quincy woman, was instantly killed late Tuesday when the ship in which she was flying with Edward R. Hansen of Quincy crashed following a take off from Quincy Sky Harbor. Experienced flyers who arrived at the scene of the accident were certain that the plane's motor went dead allowing it to fall in a nose dive without sufficient elevation for pulling it out. Mrs. Moore has been one of Quincy's most enthusiastic boosters for aviation and learned to fly under the training of her husband, who ranked high among the local flyers. Quincy Sky Harbor owes its start to the hard work and far-sightedness of the late Dr. Moore and it is ironical that the first fatal accident should take the life of its founder's wife.

Note: The accident occurred the day before Mom was to take the test for her Commercial Pilot License. She was 29.

The task of raising little Johnny fell upon Grandpa and Grandma Rogers. Grandpa retired as U. S. Forest Service Supervisor in 1946. Through his efforts at that time, the Gansner family donated the land to build a safer airport that became known as "Gansner Airfield." By 1948 I was eight years old and I remember Grandpa, the first "Airport Committee Chairman," walking alongside the grader making sure they did this airport job right.

The Sky Harbor was abandoned but not before it had accrued a short but colorful history. For example, picture the owner of the Stone House bar located some half mile distant taxiing his biplane down the road from its hangar to the airport. In those days they still ran cattle down Main Street, too. In my childhood memory, I see a blood-red triplane taxiing up to the fence. As it got closer I could see the guns mounted up front. I remember crawling through a wrecked airplane stashed out behind the office shack. I was pretending that I could fly. The newspaper wrote about a time when two guys in a BT-13 were lost over Quincy and their airplane circled and circled. A telephone operator started jammin' jacks and called all the folks she knew to get out there and surround the strip with their lights on. Sure enough it worked and the low-winged military trainer landed safely. They pronounced loudly to the throng, "You folks saved our lives!" Now that was community involvement!

Chapter 2
Grow Up Kid!

Ken Metzker was my dad's best man at his wedding. When I was a young boy my grandparents would take me over to Ken and Helen's vacation home on the west side of Lake Tahoe. They had a boat house that stood about twenty feet above the sparkling waters and I loved to run as fast as I could on top of the roof and sail out over the water. I spread my arms and pretended that I could fly! Mary Lee was wondering how the family should address her younger brother John and me so that we didn't both answer at once. She decided to call me "Johnny" and the name stuck. One day John and I decided we would try to fly. I just knew I could! We jumped off the garage roof holding hands. He, being a year older, survived unscathed, but I broke my arm and found out something about flying!

I became the kid peering through the fence watching the airplanes, not because I wanted to steal something, but because I wanted to fly. So one way or another, fly I did. I hung out at the airport and begged rides and saved up my money and paid Lorraine Wardman to take me up in her Luscombe and do loops and rolls.

Mine was the classic mistake that so many high school kids make; that is, managing to get good grades, usually without studying, or sometimes doing poorly in a class because you didn't like the teacher. In junior high I hated the math teacher.

I tried my hand at college and majored in failure. The culture shock of moving from the remoteness of Plumas County and stepping into the party life of San Jose State College was too much. I had a wonderful time, but they kicked me out. I have to say that it didn't help when, just before finals, I made chlorine gas in chemistry and got a good whiff of it. Yep, it was deadly chlorine gas all right! I stumbled from the lab choking and made my way down the damp San Jose streets to the cold rooming house where I stayed. Upstairs in my room the bed consisted of a mattress on a wooden floor. I could think only of sleeping because my throat was painfully sore. I customarily slept naked, so I stripped down and flopped on the chilly mattress and stretched out. Suddenly I was jolted with a white pain and then everything went black. An electrical plug had been pulled out of the wall leaving the two prongs in the socket. As the base of my head touched the two charged prongs I was electrocuted! I was found by a housemate the next morning lying naked on the uncarpeted floor apparently sleeping. I had contracted a terrible cold and was bedridden for the critical weeks during finals.

It was summertime and school was out and I was going to fly come hell or high water! I practically camped at the airport at Quincy. Herb and Lorraine Wardman lived in a tiny trailer behind the administration building and used the county's building as part of their home. There was a little bar with six or seven stools where Lorraine would whip me up a "vegaburger" for lunch. Over the large south-facing windows hung pieces of shirts taken from students on their first solo. Lorraine would cut them up so they looked like little short pants. When the solo students earned their Private Ticket she would stick a gold star on the pants. You got a gold star for each additional certificate that you earned (such as a Commercial). I wanted lots of gold stars so that I could be proud of my "pants." While working for flying time, I planted rosebushes by the beams on the front porch. My favorite was a climbing white rose, a healthy and vigorous plant indeed. I hoped that it and I would both live long and well!

Herb and Lorraine ran a "Mom and Pop" business. Herb was the Airport Manager appointed by the Plumas County Supervisors. One of his jobs was to sell avgas for the county. Being strict Seventh Day Adventists the Wardmans would leave a note on the fuel pumps on their mandatory Saturday day off, "Help yourself, leave money inside or mail it." The Manager/Fixed Based Operator arrangement worked well. The county needed someone to pump gas, plow snow and fix things. The FBO needed help getting through the winter in order to continue providing services such as charter, Forest Service fire reconnaissance, flight training and aircraft rentals. Herb would do aircraft inspection and repair work too.

One evening I rode up to Bucks Lake with friends in their car to take part in a secret teenage beer bust. Bucks Lake is nestled in the mountains above the five thousand foot level, eighteen winding road miles from Quincy. It was several more miles around to the dam once you arrived at the lake. The main party instigator was the daughter of the owners of Haskins, one of the three resorts located at the lake. The party and bonfire were going good in the gathering darkness. "Daughter" and I were in her car engaging in activities not usually condoned by parents when suddenly her mother roared her Jeep into the fire light circle. Murder gleamed from her eyes. Following her were several local sheriff's deputies. I reacted with "pilot-like" lightning reflexes and dove away into the underbrush. I hid under a log and a deputy jumped right over me. All the kids complained loudly as the cops hauled them off to jail. Pretty soon an officer said, "Aah hell with him. I guess he got away." I gloated at my successful escape as they drove away and silence settled onto the dark scene. It was chilly and very dark, and I had to jog to keep from freezing. Suddenly feeling the cold I thought, "I really am alone with no wheels and it's twenty-some miles to town!" My clothing was thin. I set off down the lonely mountain road uncertain as to who had out smarted whom. Dawn came as I dragged myself to the airport just in time to go to work at my new job on the Borate Crew; both shoes had holes worn in the soles.

The borate mixing tank was set up by the Forest Service at the Quincy airport. It was handy to be able to keep taking flying lessons, plus I got to know the crazy pilots who flew the fire-fighting biplanes. I flew almost every day, alternating between a 1941 Luscombe and a 1946 Cessna 120. I was in the 120 the day Lorraine told me to take it up alone. I kept my eye on the barn roof off the end of the runway and added power. My heart was in my throat as I left the ground. "Wheee! I'm actually flying alone." Suddenly, the inside of the airplane looked a lot bigger without Lorraine in the right seat.

My first solo flight was behind me and I became determined to become either a professional pilot, or a rock n' roll star. The decision was made when I took a thrilling (and dangerous) ride with Herb. I was in the back seat observing his technique of rolling back and forth down Bear Creek Canyon to Dead Man Springs and into the bottom of the huge Middle Fork canyon. It was breathtaking and I admired Herb's skill and his mission of looking for a lost hiker.

I almost quit flying in frustration with the paperwork. The test questions were a closely guarded FAA secret. Herb suggested that I try the written exam just to see what was on it. Of course, I flunked the test and remembered nothing. I finally passed it on the fourth try and wondered if I really had the brains for this sort of thing.

Fall came and I returned to Sacramento, this time to try the Aviation course at the college. An acquaintance who was also living at the "J" Street rooming house introduced me to *big* bikes. He was the proud owner of a Triumph T-110, a 650 cc engined limy machine. I cracked open the throttle and to my surprise the sudden acceleration jerked me backward and, while hanging on, the handlebar throttle was forced to the wide-open position. I tried to make the turn at the end of the block but the foot peg struck the pavement and the bike flipped, sending me flying over the handlebars. I hit, rolled, and came up on my feet facing the machine as its engine screamed at high rpm, its throttle still stuck open. I ran over and shut it down as its owner ran around the corner in a panic. I was bloody on one side from head to toe. Boy, what a thrill! I just *had* to have a big bike.

The Aeronautics Department at Sacramento City College had a club consisting mostly of tandem-seated and tail wheel-equipped Aeronca Champs. The little ragwings didn't have starters or electrical systems. I was hand propping an Aeronca by myself and suddenly it roared to life! Because I had set the throttle too far forward, it roared a little too loudly. A link parted on the little restraining chain that was holding the tail wheel and the now bellowing Aeronca lunged forward. I dove left away from the flashing prop. Then, as the wing strut flashed over me, I sprang backward into the open door and pulled the throttle back, my heels making twin drag-marks in the dirt. We were heading for a line of planes and if I had missed that lever it would have been a major disaster. The whirling propeller would have chewed up who knows how many airplanes! Fortunately, nobody saw the incident and it remained my secret.

After soloing the last summer, I had also completed solo cross-country flights to several high altitude airports in California and Nevada. Nevertheless, the Aero Club instructors had banned all flight out of the valley because they considered flying in the mountains too dangerous. Their Cessna 120 had recently been transported out of the High Sierras in a basket. The cabin heater was leaking carbon monoxide and knocked out the pilot who also came out in a basket. The room that I had taken at the rooming house on "J" Street was the very one he had vacated due to his death. His bereaved widow was there moving his things out when I moved in. It was a good thing that I wasn't superstitious.

My instructor, Mr. Lincoln, used a "gossport" to communicate with me in the Aeronca. A gossport is a horn connected to a tube where the instructor injects his voice into the student's ear. The student can't talk back. Sometimes communications weren't so good. I thought my flying was just fine. From about thirty yards away, Mr. Lincoln made a circle in the air with his finger as I was taxiing back to the hangar after fueling. I thought that meant take it around the pattern, so I confidently motored over to the runway and took off. That's what the sign meant in Quincy. After a couple of touch-and-go's I wondered why Mr. Lincoln was standing next to the strip jumping up and down and waving his arms. After I landed, he informed me, red faced, that the hand signal he had given earlier meant that he had wanted me to taxi around the row of hangars and park it, not to fly solo. Consequently, he grounded me. My plaintive explanations fell on deaf ears. Mr. Lincoln wanted a letter from my former instructor describing my previous deportment as an airman. Herb wrote him back a scathing accusation that he should make his orders clear and that I was the best student he had ever had. (I'll be forever grateful for that letter.) Since Mr. Lincoln's and my relations remained strained, I took a check ride with the other instructor, Mr. Waters, who turned me loose to soar with the eagles again!

The 1960 college session was out and I was back in Quincy and continuing my flight training. I must say, learning to fly under Lorraine was fun. She liked stalls and spins and so did I. Sometimes she allowed the spin to get so close to the ground it scared me. She just laughed when she knew she'd gotten my attention. She was also once a World Champion acrobatic motorcycle rider. She once had performed in her own show in San Carlos and could ride a Harley backwards. She taught me to ride my Triumph TR-6 motorcycle backwards, too. The learning was painful sometimes. I vividly recall the time I wandered out into the loose gravel and the 380-pound bike fell over on the back of my bare leg, its red hot, high rising exhaust pipes burning my flesh. It took a frantic effort to get it off me since I was facing away from the machine.

I finally earned my Private Ticket and nobody could tell me what to do anymore. I was now *Pilot-In-Command!* Before the certificate was signed and sealed, however, I was cut down a notch. In order to attain the coveted Pilot-In-Command status it was necessary to take a flight test with Mary Barr, the Designated Pilot Examiner located at the Susanville Airport. Mary laughed when I opened up the cowling of the Cessna 120 to check the oil before our check flight and found the oil cap sitting on the battery box!

Late one afternoon I was flying back from Susanville in the 120 when I spied a white "X" on top of a hill. Everybody knew a distress signal when they saw one. As I roared by (too low and too fast to really see anything), I was certain that I saw a figure moving across the clearing where the big white "X" lay. That was enough for me. After landing at Quincy I visited the Sheriff's

Office and told them, "Somebody was in trouble out there; who knows, maybe a plane crash!" It was late in the day and the site was a good twenty-five miles from town. Everyone would have preferred to go home to dinner, but I persisted. Finally the sheriff agreed to take a rescue team out there right away, provided that I went along and showed them the spot. I agreed, and the group bounced up the dusty, double wheel track road to the point where we would have to cross Indian Creek on foot and scramble up the hill. I gulped, looking from the ground; that was no hill with a gentle slope, that was a mountain with a steep, rocky face choked with trees and brush. Besides that, it was already twilight. I charged on, leading the group up that dirty, dusty SOB until we finally arrived at the top as darkness closed in on the north-facing Sierra slopes. I looked around the clearing in the twilight and spotted the "X." It was constructed of white sheet-like material with rocks scattered around it to hold it down. Upon close examination, it appeared to be pretty weather-beaten. A short snag was standing nearby. An experienced Search-and-Rescue Team member laughed and said, "This is an old aerial survey marker! Where the hell are the people that you claim you saw moving around here?" I looked at the short snag and realized that my relative movement in the airplane must have made the rotted wooden sentinel appear to be someone moving across the clearing! I quietly took the last position in the struggle back down the slope in the darkness. I suspected that some of the curses floating through the dusty evening air were being directed at me!

I returned to the Forest Service Borate Crew, this time as the straw boss. The operation had moved to the Beckwourth Airport. Sometimes fellow student Bill Holland and I would commute some eighteen minutes to the Beckwourth Airport in formation in Wardman's Luscombe and Cessna 120. Not very bright financially; but we had to fly, didn't we?

The air tankers of the day were 600 horsepower Stearmans and Navy N-3-Ns. Their pilots were the likes of "Wild" Bill Whitfield, Lee Sherwood, Frank Michaud and Neal Wade, all crop dusters; these individuals were a combination of serious businessmen and "nut cases." This air tanker stuff was a picnic compared to the brutally difficult and dangerous agricultural flying. The end of a good day of fire fighting usually brought a great show from the tanker pilots. They would perform a low pass followed by a landing right out of a hair-raising pull up. This was where the three-ring circuses really began. This was the first year that the little 600 horsepower biplanes and crop duster pilots were mixing in with the big Grumman TBM 1,200 horsepower torpedo bombers. The Avenger pilots usually had radically different backgrounds from the ag pilots. One thing they all had in common, though, was the urge to have fun in their airplanes. There were few rules that were enforced. The pilots were the kings. At the end of a long, hard day of fire fighting, those fliers felt like warriors returning from battle and, by God, it was time to celebrate. The TBMs piloted by Don Orinbomb, Dick Douglas and Frank Kunke, bellowed by on a showboat pass so low lizards cringed. An empty TBM going as fast as it can was impressive as it pulled up in a steep climbing turn, lowered its landing gear and flaps and landed after reversing directions. Bill Whitfield in his N-3-N would perform multiple loops, gaining altitude with each maneuver. Neal Wade in his Stearman approached the airport crop duster-style, no light between his wheels and the sage brush, and just barely bumping up over low fences. Other aircraft entered the show, such as Stevenson with his fast, powerful, and gorgeous F7F fighter-bomber. That twin-engine "Tigercat" was impressive just sitting there! The U. S. Forest Service also had their TBMs and T34 Mentor lead planes.

Imagine a huge forest fire on the edge of the high desert in the mountains that rise up very close to the airport. Picture a fire that is powerful enough to create its own thunderstorm-like weather. See the heat and smoke punching up through the cool upper air layers to create strong winds which in turn suck masses of air into the seething heart of the monster and out its top. The parcel of air condenses and creates a true cloud called an "ice cap." The winds created weird conditions at the airport, dangerous even to us on the ground. Once a strong gust caught me standing on the top of a slippery slurry tank and knocked me in, sinking over my head. Borate is a slippery, slimy, itchy mess and turns crusty when it dries and there were no showers at this airport! Thunderstorms were dangerous, too. One time, a sudden thunderstorm blew through, and full barrels of oil rolled around on the ramp in the raging wind. It started to rain buckets and big hail stones. I saw a high-winged Pacer wildly gyrating in its traces and I knew that, without assistance, it would be blown away in the powerful gusts. I ran out between the rolling oil drums with the lightning flashing and thunder cracking, and grabbed the aircraft's strut, but found myself with my feet off the ground. I'm sure that the wing and I would have taken flight together if help had not arrived. One of the huge TBM dive-bombers spun around in the tremendous gusts even though it sat loaded with the heavy borate slurry and its tail wheel was locked!

Pilots didn't like it when they were denied their flying time. Once, just as Dick, nicknamed "Mr. Couth," taxied out for takeoff, the fire dispatch was canceled. Radio calls were directed at him but, mysteriously, the radio reception became garbled. I was ordered to run out next to the runway and stop the takeoff. Fat chance! As the heavy TBM roared by, its landing gear was retracting. Douglas's head was cocked ninety degrees to the runway looking right at me instead of where he was going. He had a big toothy grin and his third finger sticking up conveying a fairly obvious message. The aircraft's borate-coated belly just did clear the fence as he staggered into the hot air bent on making some $$s.

These pilots played as hard as they worked. I should say they worked hard *when* they worked. The guys were all in town at a local celebration drinking and carousing. The usual procedure was to party all night and sleep all day at the tanker base. They became local legends and folk heroes of sorts. They were aggressive and fun loving by nature. Most of the tanker pilots couldn't keep their hands off the local females. Orinbomb got in big trouble fooling around with the wife of a champion archer. He kept his pistol handy in case the guy showed up at the tanker base to surprise him with his bow and arrows. The Avenger pilots all grew handlebar mustaches to set themselves apart from mere crop dusters.

One day there was great excitement over the Forest Service radio. Bob Schacht's twin Beech was losing power over the middle fork of the Yuba River. Don Orinbomb was in the area in his TBM when both engines of Schact's twin went silent. There was no silence on the radio, however. With Orinbomb diving ahead of Schact, he said, "How 'bout this spot," referring to a section of the river. Schact would reply, "No, shit no, there's not enough room!" Schact was out of fuel and incredibly he found the only deep-water hole in Yuba River that existed at this time of year. Every other area bristled with deadly bedrock moistened by only a trickle of water. Bob, the lucky bastard, was standing on the wing of his downed Beech waving "OK" and "THANKS" signals as Orinbaumb circled.

Don Acres was a tall, blond, good looking guy and possibly the only pilot who didn't philander and booze all night. He had a young family waiting at home. Just out of the Air Force, he was flying a TBM for the Forest Service. One hot, smoky day he didn't come back. They say he struck a snag with a wing as he made a run on the fire, into the sun, following a Forest Service T-34 lead plane. Somehow it didn't seem right. I realized that sudden death could be just around the corner for these pilots. It really wasn't all fun and games.

One pilot had a pet raven. The critter was wild but it took to the guys at the tanker base. It liked to land on your shoulder and pull at your ear while begging for a trinket. When the buzzer sounded announcing a fire dispatch, the pilot ran and the raven flew to the three-blade propeller-equipped TBM parked nearby. The pilot would climb into the cockpit while the raven awaited the action perched on the highest prop blade. As the starter whined and the heavy propeller turned over, the raven would fly away and eventually return when things settled down, ready to repeat the routine.

I asked a Forest Service T-34 lead pilot for some advice on loading a TBM. The day was heating up and the pilots were complaining about the density altitude caused by the 4,900-foot elevation. He thrust his sunburned face close to mine and the order was, "Ah bullshit; fill 'em up! They're always whining about something." On the next takeoff it looked like the TBM was going to take out the fence at the end of the runway, as well as the power lines down the road, also, some jack rabbits farther out into the valley who were scattering in fright. Circling with gentle banks over Sierra Valley, the thundering Avenger finally gained enough altitude to proceed to the fire and disgorge its slimy burden.

Upon his return, the pilot's tight, tan Levi's were covered with grease and sweat, and his shiny Wellington boots became dustier with each stomp. He strode up to me and yelled, "What the hell do you think you're doing? You damn near got me killed!" I lamely replied that a lead plane pilot ordered me to do it.

To the west, a Forest Service lead plane bellied in on the

grassy field next to the runway at Quincy. According to Herb, they jacked the airplane up, replaced the propeller, lowered its gear, switched to the full fuel tank and flew it away! (The implication was that the pilot panicked when the tank ran out of fuel and forgot that he had another tank full of fuel.) Herb always told the story with a sneer. He never did like Forest Service pilots, nor anyone else who carried a mantle of authority.

Ran Slaten arrived at the job shortly after I had left for greener pastures. He described to me a scene that he could never forget. Seven TBMs were out at twilight, which was unusual because they were not supposed to fly after dark. Ran squinted into the strong orange glow to the west created by the setting sun and thought he saw something. Everyone else was sitting around bored. One worker stood on top of the borate tank staring in the opposite direction. Suddenly, there they were, all seven of them in tight formation. They popped out from behind a ridge, rattled the roofs of the little village of Beckwourth just a scant mile away and suddenly were only inches above the crew. The man on the borate tank fell eight feet to the ground as if hit by a lightning bolt. The noise was horrific. The big-bellied, mid-winged monsters peeled off one by one, pitched up, dropped their landing gears and landed in perfect sequence. Each pilot was grinning like the little kid that he was at that moment!

Chapter 3
Commercial Pilot

I had earned my Commercial Pilot Certificate, quit the Forest Service and had gone to work for Wardman. I flew their co-op fire patrol, putting to use all the "good" examples I had learned from the tanker pilots. I couldn't believe that I was actually getting paid to fly (minimum wage, of course). I took off at 5:30 every afternoon in Wardman's yellow Luscombe for the two-and-a-half hour sortie. The mission called for a systematic search at low level for smokes that could erupt into forest fires. I communicated with the lookouts via the Forest Net battery pack radio. Flying near the ground and circling Soper Wheeler's log landings was interesting. It was here the logs were loaded onto the trucks that hauled them to the mills. There were often whole loads consisting of only a couple of logs. Where the cats were skidding the logs into the landing, I could actually smell the sharp scent of fresh cut timber and the musty odor of soil that had been disturbed after lying quietly for thousands of years. I couldn't help feel some pangs of regret as I watched the old trees go down, not to be replaced even in several lifetimes.

I used the job to teach myself low-level antics. At the bottom of the Middle Fork of the Feather River, I was expected to check out a road under construction at Milsap Bar. If I couldn't turn around, I had to fly for miles through Baldrock Canyon at very low levels before reversing course. To avoid, this I taught myself to do a "vertical reverse." This risky aerobatic maneuver was accomplished by pulling up into a vertical half of a snap roll, thereby reversing course without producing any turn radius. A snap roll is executed with a quick full up elevator motion and full rudder, and stopped with the reverse motion. In this case, full throttle should be used. The snap roll is sort of a horizontal spin while a vertical reverse is half of a snap roll going straight up. The other half of the maneuver is the completion of the last half of a loop. I had to be careful to remain oriented in the tightly enclosed area of Baldrock Canyon!

The last checkpoint of the day was Argentine Lookout which perched on top of a massive rock that dropped off thousands of feet to the timberlands below. It was the only lookout not equipped with a radio and had only a telephone for communication. Every day at the same time I would fly close to the roof and pull up into a triple snap roll. On the final roll the nose would be pointed about thirty degrees down. One wrong move and I could easily split S right into the mountain. A "split S" is half of a snap roll. You stop the snap roll upside down and reverse course in the last half of a loop, a nice maneuver if there is nothing in your way as you pull out. It was all worth it to impress the woman on the catwalk. I always ended the patrol with a low pass down runway six, a steep pitch up and turn-around into the wind for a landing on two four. Lorraine would say in her distinctive high-pitched voice, "Oh my, that was pretty!" She was not one to squelch my "creativity."

At night I would often practice with our band that roved around the area plying rock n' roll and cross-over country. Our singer, Larry Crayton, was the idol of hundreds of teens and young adults. He was a combination of black and Cherokee blood lines and sang Little Richard and Elvis. We had fun in the local bars, just the two of us, doing troubadour rounds and singing old favorites for drinks and kicks, with me playing the guitar.

I rode my motorcycle down to San Francisco and took a battery of tests for the Veterans Administration. The purpose was to determine what sort of career they thought I might be suited for. I was quite a sight walking through the door in my black motorcycle leathers, covered with road grime and hair windblown. I rang the scoring bell in something called "abstract reasoning," but was woefully low in math and mechanics. The Ph.D. in the white coat accused me of cheating on the tests. He said that the last thing I had any aptitude for was aviation and he wasn't giving me a damned dime for flight training! We almost had a fistfight and I told him to take his money and shove it!

I was twenty when I bought 1177 Bravo. Its former owner asked if I wouldn't like a check out. Its new owner assured him that he was a master Luscombe pilot and proceeded to take off. I didn't know immediately what was wrong. The former owner must have gained grim satisfaction as he saw his beautiful red and white bird dribble down the runway and stagger into the air like a salmon struggling upstream, its smart-assed pilot struggling for control. I couldn't understand what the hell was going on until I spotted the pitch trim set in the full up position. I learned that it was stupid to turn down a free check ride. The lessons came rapidly. For example, Dick was *the* high school quarterback and all-around athlete, and when I took him for his first airplane ride in my new airplane I just knew he would love it. I said, "Watch this, Dick," and executed a perfect snap roll and the horizon revolved around the nose like a pinwheel. I looked over expecting to see a gleeful grin of wonderment at the exciting maneuver, but instead I saw confusion and nausea. We landed right away and I learned that not everyone delighted in that kind of flying. I hoped that I hadn't ruined him for flying, period, and I resolved not to do it to anyone else.

It was January, 1961, in Sacramento. The fog had lain in for many gloomy weeks and "me and my Luscombe" had the blues. With my Commercial ticket burning a hole in my pocket and my twenty-first birthday rapidly approaching, I was tortured with the restlessness of youth.

Hanging around crop duster and pioneer aerial firefighter, "Red" Jensen, had its ups and downs. The up part was being around real pilots like Bob Schact, the same Bob who ran his Twin Beech out of fuel on a firebombing run. Bob was helping to "fix up" a TBM for the coming fire season. He was a handsome guy with wavy hair, and I can still see him rummaging around Charlie's huge pile of parts looking for some piece of hardware to fit his project. He was the "knock-around-the-world" kind of guy I thought I wanted to be. Jensen's tiny Sacramento airstrip was crammed with helicopters, World War II Dive Bombers, and lots of crop dusters. Charlie (Red) was kind of a sourpuss, but his true colors showed through in 1956 when he spent many hours in his helicopter plucking people off their rooftops during the "Great Flood." He never accepted a dime in payment for those rescues. The down part of hangin' with Charlie was when he made you work like a dog for room and board. He also made sure that you knew how lucky you were that he didn't charge you to "teach you the business." It didn't help matters when my good buddy John Field lied so I could stay in Charlie's bunkhouse. He bragged, telling him that I was an expert electrician and could rewire his house for him. I eventually confessed that I didn't know doodley about electricity.

It was Annual Inspection time for my little Luscombe so I went at it myself to save money and to learn a little more about the business. Red's top dog, Johnny Anoy, "the Inspector," was not impressed with my mechanical aptitude. He was outraged when, in frustration, I snipped off the capillary tube that attaches to the oil temperature bulb (which causes the oil temperature gauge to operate), thus allowing easier access to the oil screen nut! Of course, I had to buy a whole new gauge and capillary tube since it was all one piece. The time came for the flight test, and Inspector Johnny wasn't about to risk his Inspection Authorization by signing off this FAA required "owner assisted" Annual Inspection until it had actually flown. The fifty-foot power lines at the end of the short sod strip flashed under me, and the two-hundred foot gray fog base pressed down. The Sacramento Executive tower seemed far away, but was really looming up within only a mile. OOPS! Engine missing something awful! Swallowing my panic, I staggered around Jensen Field for a short approach. Once again Johnny remained unimpressed as he pointed out the spark plug lying in the bottom of the cowling and the empty threaded hole in one of the cylinders. For a time I was the goat around Jensen's place and I was ready to leave. Jim, a young duster pilot, offered to buy my fuel in exchange for a lift to his hometown of Greely. I jumped at the chance. Besides, I needed to build time in order to make it in the business. Jim and I, a big box of tools (too big and too heavy) and a sleeping bag strained the climb abilities of the little four-banger as we staggered over the wires and east into the unknown. No radio aboard, but Red had talked to the feds and got us a special VFR clearance out of the Control Zone. Anything to get rid of us, I think.

Little shafts of sun lit up the bright green grass on the edge of the fog where the valley rose into the base of the Sierras. Got it made now—POW! Engine running really crappy again, like only three cylinders are firing. Sounds just like the last time, but this time I'm a lot heavier with a corresponding inability to hold altitude. Shoulda' checked ALL the spark plugs again.

With the sun heating the ground near Grass Valley, vertical air currents were created. I considered putting the wounded bird into a field if only I could find one, but where there were updrafts, there was hope! It seemed that the alternative was probably injury and death during an attempted landing! Jim's eyeballs were rolling around, and mine too. I was breathing hard and thinking fast. The Loma Rica Airport was just a little higher in the hills than our present altitude and a little to the east of our present position. Right Jim? Check that chart—gotta' catch just the right updraft and go for it, go baby, go, bump! Full stall right on the very end of the uphill strip. After cracking a few jokes at our expense, Stevenson, the airport operator, gave us an old used spark plug to fill the empty hole. Yep, it was the same Stevenson that I had met with his F7F Tigercat last year while working on the borate crew at Beckwourth. With hearty thanks to Stevenson, Jim and I took off and flew over Donner Pass and on to Reno without incident. We had expectations of a fine night on the town, and after winning at cards, and probably we'd get invited home by some beautiful babes. No such luck. We ended up flopping in a cheap hotel.

The next day it was eastbound and finally, after a long day of flying, we dropped into Tooele, Utah. With Reno some five-hundred miles behind us, darkness was closing in. Trudging up the road into the cold Mormon mining town we endured stares from behind window curtains and catcalls from "car borne" teenagers. It was easy to see that there was a wariness for strangers. Could it have been our cigarettes and requests for directions to the nearest bar?

After Tooele, the next high point in the trip was freezing our tootsies off navigating across the backbone of the Rockies through Medicine Bow Pass, and then on to Greeley.

After dropping Jim off in Colorado, I was off to see the world and try to score a flying job. After all, *I'm a Commercial Pilot!* With memories of nearly freezing to death in the Luscombe with its ineffective heater, I headed south. It was so windy in Colorado Springs that after I landed, almost in my tracks, a couple of line boys wing-walked me to the fuel pumps. After topping off, they walked me back out to the runway for takeoff. (In this case, "wing walking" means that one line boy hung on to each wing helping to discourage the little airplane from flipping over in the wind.) The takeoff was like operating an elevator; that is, when I faced into the howling wind and pushed the throttle forward, the Luscombe and its surprised pilot went straight up. Then, the blazing ground speed took my breath away when I turned downwind. Wow! That's what I was looking for on this little transcontinental sortie—experience!

Soon after my takeoff from windy Lamar, a town located on the high plains near the Kansas border, I was introduced to a new and unfamiliar danger. Except for a lot of wind (which didn't bother me because I was *a Commercial Pilot*), everything was fine. Overhead floated scattered clouds, and straight ahead was the Arkansas River that I had planned to follow east to Dodge City. The powerful wind was out of the north and my wet compass was swinging and jumping in the turbulence. Down low there was dust everywhere and it was starting to obscure my forward visibility. It was becoming difficult to tell the sky from the ground. "I'd better climb," I told myself, thinking that the visibility would improve with altitude. Gradually the turn needle, the slip/skid ball, airspeed indicator and the compass became the focus of my attention. Without those instruments there could be no hope of maintaining control of the airplane. The turn needle is an electrically-powered gyroscope that tells you whether you are turning or not, and the magnetic compass indicates in what direction you are pointed. The "wet" compass is plagued with a number of inherent errors. (It is called wet because it is immersed in white gas to dampen its oscillations.) The slip/skid ball tells you if the rate of turn is appropriate for the angle of bank. There was no natural horizon outside, and no attitude gyro instrument with which to determine an artificial horizon inside. Furthermore, I did not have a radio to contact the outside world for assistance. Midwest dust storms weren't included in my west coast training; but thankfully, partial panel instrument flying had been. I had taught myself how to do loops with reference to only the turn/ball indicator and the airspeed gauge, none of which will tumble while flying in unusual attitudes. Practicing loops on instruments alone without reference to the outside horizon gave me some basis to believe that I could control the airplane in this ugly stuff. Those maneuvers were definitely not part of most schools' training curriculum. Then again, neither was this particular emergency.

"Guess I'll keep climbing and try to hold my easterly heading," I thought while I quelled the rising panic. I assumed that panic was not appropriate behavior for a *Commercial Pilot!* I struggled to remember the inherent errors of the magnetic compass. In order to defeat the northerly turning error, you must roll out of your turn thirty degrees early when turning toward the north, and vice versa toward the south. The accelerate/decelerate errors must be dealt with as well; the compass will swing one way or the other depending whether you are facing east or west.

The little Continental engine kept running hard despite the dirt accumulating in its air cleaner. Finally I could see pale blue sky as I struggled through an indicated nine-thousand-five hundred feet. The thick dun-colored stuff seemed to go on forever—and forever was well beyond the range of my fourteen-gallon gas tank. The ugly storm towered way above me, too. Looking back in the direction that I had just come from I saw scary looking black clouds.

Logic based upon my vast aviation background (after all, *I am a Commercial pilot*) suggested a way out of this predicament. Since I had planned to follow the east-west river and was now maintaining a spiral in a north wind, I must be drifting south. "No problem," I thought calmly, "I'll just spiral down, acquire visual contact with the ground and then turn north to the river." It wasn't going to be as easy as I had hoped, though. I remained calm because of a baseless assumption that a dust storm would have a base. It is easier to be calm when you don't understand the gravity of the situation. Telephone poles and fence lines rushed up as I leveled the wings and pulled back hard on the stick. Immediately a vertical air current thrust the Luscombe and its Commercial Pilot back into the blinding dust. Remembering the inherent errors in the magnetic compass, I concentrated on the instruments and turned north while attempting a controlled descent. I knew my only hope was to encounter the river and try to avoid the power lines that criss crossed my intended path. I found myself gasping again. With a sudden down draft I had visual contact with the ground, right over a farmer plowing a field. "Eeech," I cursed as I saw all the loose soil rising up to join me. I shook my fist at the idiot in his tractor as I bumped past and pulled up over a power line. The tractor driver looked up in amazement at the idiot flying a tiny red airplane in a dust storm. Of course, I found the river and followed it back to a safe landing at Lamar, or I wouldn't be writing this. The kid in me grinned at the Indiana Jones-like adventure I had survived, while the proto man growled, "You stupid, lucky bastard!" That night it snowed in Lamar and I was happy to be in a warm, safe hotel room.

"Ouch!" My fingers were freezing in the cold Colorado morning as I attempted to scrape the frost from the wings. "Heck," I reasoned, "A little smoothing of the frost on the leading edge should do the job with this frigid, dense air to fly in." During takeoff, I screamed mentally as the end of the runway rushed at me and the tail wouldn't respond to my urgent forward pressure on the control stick. At the last moment, with a crow hop, I was just barely able to get airborne. The ground whizzing by remained very close. I learned that there existed a fine line between flying and not flying with the Luscombe's long, thin wing. With frost on the wings and tail surfaces, that tenuous division between flying/not flying occurs at much higher indicated air speeds. According to the accepted theory of flight, as the air flows smoothly over the top surface of the wing at a higher velocity (because of its greater curvature than the flatter bottom side), lift is produced. When a rough surface such as frost is present, the air becomes disturbed and lift is lost. As I struggled higher into the cold stable air, because of a temperature inversion the air became warmer and I could feel the lift improve dramatically as the frost burned off. I now better understood the term, "hanging by a thread" and the "theory of flight" stuff I'd been studying.

The Amarillo Tradewinds Airport seemed like a friendly place. They probably wouldn't be so friendly when they discovered that I had left with one of their fancy tiedown clips. I noticed it myself when I hit the first bump of the day and was startled by a bang, bang, whackety whack sound! At first I feared engine trouble. As it turned out it was only that heavy tiedown clip trying to beat a hole in my metal wing. I guess I unclipped the chain end instead of the airplane end. I was a good twenty minutes east of Amarillo and there was no obvious place to land. "Wait,"

I thought as I spied a wrecked airplane at the end of a field adjacent to a small town. The strip didn't look like much, but what the hell, "Isn't it sensible to risk a wrecked airplane and/or death to save a few dents in the wing?" Of course not! My risk management was flawed, but I managed to land safely anyway.

I was standing waist deep in grass with the engine ticking over and removing the heavy tiedown clip when I heard a commotion. A large group of people from town was running toward me and yelling. I could imagine them carrying pitchforks and other midwestern weapons, although I didn't actually see them. Who knows what they had on their minds—lynching? For all I knew landing in someone's field in Texas was a serious offense. Rather than commit my aircraft and myself to the grasp and control of the unknown, I jumped in, spun around and took off, blasting dirt and grass in the citizens' faces. No doubt more than one fist was raised in the universal sign of anger as the little red two-seater staggered over the fence and off into the Texas sky. The tiedown clip was now safely stowed in the baggage compartment.

Jasper is located in Texas bayou country near the Louisiana border. I could have traveled on, since the day was still young, but I was curious to see what a really Deep South community was like. After fueling up, I secured old 77B and hitchhiked into the small community with expectations of making new friends. I found out that northern strangers with no knowledge of local customs that hitchhike into small southern towns can run into trouble. I watched a high school basketball game and rooted for the home team. I "BS'ed" a few girls at a hamburger stand and then decided to go to a movie. While standing in the line in front of the theater, a police car screeched to a stop and I wondered who they were after. It was me they were after! "Hands behind your head, kid. Spread 'em, kid!"

Varooom! We were off to the interrogation room. Talk about bright lights, these were the classic brain piercing, hot lights you see in the movies. The sheriff was saying, "Where you been this past week, boy?" It seems they'd had a rash of burglaries and that my sworn testimony as to my whereabouts recently didn't ring true for them. The claim of traveling from California to the Louisiana border in a few days while flying my own plane was a little hard to swallow.

Finally, with a few phone calls my story was corroborated and the Judge himself took me to a local hotel and said, "Stay!" True to his word, the next day he drove me to the airport and personally observed my departure.

C.A. King was a multimillionaire and an old family friend who owned a big chunk of the city of Lake Charles, Louisiana. I decided to stop and say "Hi." When I alighted at the Lake Charles airport I looked a mess. Along with my dirty airplane, my appearance in dirty old clothes and needing a shave was that of a drifter. The proprietor laughed in my face when I asked him if he knew C.A. and where I could get in touch with him. I laughed right back when C.A. roared up in his big white Cadillac within a few minutes after my call. We went to the Charleston Hotel, which he owned. After calling Grandpa and Grandma to tell them where I was, he put me up in one of his best suites for a couple of days rest. I got the grand tour of the town, but soon my desire to see more country and find a flying job urged me onward toward the bright lights.

On a left downwind for landing at the New Orleans Lakefront Airport, the foggy sky and Lake Pontchartrain suddenly appeared to merge in a classic whiteout! In a panic I looked back toward the shoreline. The problem was resolved with the view of the coastline and the runway. I regained my bearings and confidence. There were a lot of airplanes both in front of me and behind practicing in the pattern. I wondered if there was anyone in the tower, because without a radio I was at a disadvantage. With all the traffic, it seemed to me that if I attempted to make a full stop on the runway I would force at least one aircraft to go around. Worse, maybe I would get landed on. There was no sign of life in the tower. It showed no signs of activity: no green light, and no red light either. "Heck, with no feds around I'll just land on that adjacent taxiway and save everyone a lot of trouble; safer too."I smirked, "Ho hum, my usual perfect landing." (If I could have reached I would have patted myself on the back.) "But wait," my heart stopped, "what's that red light pointed at me from the tower?"

Later in the FAA interrogation room I answered a question. "Yes sir," I asserted with the conviction of youth, "I thought it was the safe thing to do at the time. No sir, I didn't know it was a violation. Yes sir, it was just a mistake." My assurance was fading as I realized that my coveted Commercial License was about to fly away. (I decided to take an old timer's advice and handle them this way.) Hanging my head I said, "I guess I really ssscrewed up. No, Sir, it will *never* happen again. Thank you sir!" Yep, the humility act worked every time.

With the certain knowledge of how valuable I must be (you know, possessing a Commercial ticket and all), I checked with a local Fixed Base Operator. I said that a job as a line boy would be just fine to start. He replied, "No chance kid, you'd always be pestering me to fly."

It had been foggy and gloomy for days, and so with nothing better to do, I took a tour of Moisant Air Traffic Control Center. A long time controller of Deep South heritage pointed out to me the heavy sails created by the echoes from concentrations of moisture. Years later I realized that "sails" was southern for "cells."

I was tired of wearing out the leather couch at the airport where I had been waiting for the fog to lift. And, too, I was sure the folks around there were becoming weary of this eager, job-hunting Commercial Pilot. It was time to trade the couch and leather jacket for a hotel room and a shower. I had thought about sneaking out under the fog but the feds suggested that would be stupid. They didn't know I was already a seasoned veteran fog flyer. Anyhow, what they said about radio towers with guy wires waiting to entangle the unwary low flier made sense. I relented and headed for town to have a little fun.

Nice bars on Canal Street. Beautiful girl, a little heavy on the makeup, though. I said again, "No sweetheart, I can not afford to buy you a couple of drinks." Several drinks later, the big man behind the bar had his hand out. "Bartender," I said, "I told this lady I was not buying!" Pound, pound, pound, the pavement flashed under my feet. I had always been fast in a short race. Good thing, too! The two bruisers were lost in the crowd behind me. My heart was racing and I thought, "Hope I didn't splinter the doors on the way out!" I resolved to return to my airplane and pursue a career in aviation right after the Mardi Gras. I reasoned that surely someone somewhere would give a young Commercial Pilot a break.

It was back to Sac City College again. I received some advice from Jackie Bender (Sacramento Sky Ranch's resident airport and parts store manager) when I had complained to her that the elevator control in the Luscombe was getting sloppy. She suggested I open some inspection plates and have a look, which I did. Yep, there was a turnbuckle on the elevator cable unwinding and ready to come apart. The safety wire was broken. She mumbled something about, "Damn do-it-your-selfers." I didn't tell her that I had been practicing snap rolls all the way from Quincy to Sacramento, a maneuver that would have put considerable amount of strain on everything involved with the elevator!

I met Judy. The romance started out shaky. When I flew the Luscombe from Sacramento to Reno on a charter to bring her down to college, she didn't show up at the appointed time. I waited a little too long and finally departed Reno, climbing west over the mountains into the setting sun. On the way over the Sierras, I could see the lighted beacons every so often that marked the airline route from Sacramento to Reno. I had badly missed my departure time in order to arrive in Sacramento before dark. Bucking a strong headwind, the miles dragged by slowly. I knew that, at least, there would be no fog with all this wind. Arriving in total darkness with no lights on the airplane, I wondered if I could slip into Sacramento Executive without the tower noticing. "Better try Sky Ranch first," I reasoned. The only problem was that it was unlighted and surrounded by power lines.

I circled the dark, dirt strip a few times and suddenly a set of car lights flashed a couple of times and then stayed on steadily. It was John Field, a buddy who was also taking Aeronautics at City College. He knew that I was supposed to land here and was attempting to light up the end of the strip. I lined up, dropped over the invisible, deadly wires and flared out in the glare of the headlights. I discovered that the headlights behind me didn't really illuminate much. Although I could see the ground, I couldn't tell if I was aimed in the right direction to keep on the little strip. I touched down with the elevator stick all the way back and aimed for a distant city light to keep straight, and was grateful when I stopped, still on the narrow gravel strip. John raced up in his car and guided the way to the tiedowns. I didn't get away scot free; Jackie Bender stormed out and threatened to turn me into the FAA. She softened somewhat when I told her of my dilemma, and accepted my promise that it would never happen again. The humility act worked again!

I let John Field talk me into skipping school and flying over to land in Loren Craner's hay field. John swore he had walked the whole area and it was OK to land there. That poor Luscombe took a hell of a beating during the landing, but at least the gear was intact and it didn't turn over. Next he conned me into landing on a city street near his dad's salvage plant. He assured me that "they" landed there all the time. The south end of the block-long street had a power pole positioned dead center where the blacktop terminated and the north end was blocked by power lines and a busy highway. Both sides of the street had piles of lumber and equipment so "ya better keep it straight." I lined up carefully and skidded around the pole, touching down in a picture perfect three-point landing. A skid is a turn without a bank that forces the aircraft to move sideways. A skid was necessary because that close to the ground there was no room to create a turn with a bank and the road was too short to approach from a higher angle. I had to apply a little brake because I was closing in fast on the crossroads with its heavy traffic. It was a "piece of cake" until a brake failed and I needed power to keep the Luscombe straight ahead. Just before I would have entered the intersection, I stopped by spinning around in a ground loop. Fortunately nothing was hurt. I shuddered, remembering the lumber piles on each side flying close by me on the narrow city street. Luscombes should have their brake cables examined before every flight, especially where they attach to the brake lever at the wheel; and some Luscombe pilots should have their heads examined.

You would think I would learn after a while, but I went along on yet another of John Field's deals. I'd already put in a hard day's flying at Quincy for Wardman on this November day. In the evening I took the Feather River Fliers Club Cessna 172 down to Grass Valley, picked John up and headed for Mexico. The

Sacramento Valley was plagued with its miserable tule fog but it was clear overhead. You could navigate easily since the city lights glowed through the thick stuff. It was dark and there was no place to land if the engine had trouble. In addition, I also hoped the forecast for clear skies in Fresno held. Halfway to Fresno John confided that he had forgotten his wallet and that I would have to handle all the expenses. "Trust me, I'll pay you back with interest," he assured me. The next morning we were inbound to Tijuana. I called and called the tower but received no response so I went ahead and landed anyway. There was a grassy area that looked like a taxiway and I rolled onto it, but then a thickly-accented voice blared over the radio, "6634A. Do not taxi on grass!" They charged me eighty-eight cents for tower assistance!

Touring the town and hitting the bars was an expensive experience. In one dimly lit watering hole the resident "professional ladies" crawled under the bar and fondled us in a variety of illicit attempts to convince us to join them in "the room." John and I laughed heartily and enjoyed our drinks! At any rate, we spent too much of my money and I couldn't pay off the cab driver who drove us to the airport. I wanted to go out to the airplane to get my checkbook, but the cabby and I argued about it until darkness settled in. At that point the airport authorities wouldn't allow us to go out to the airplane and we didn't have any money for a bribe. So there we sat on hard airport benches all night long while the cabby slept in his comfy cab. The next morning I bought our freedom with a twenty-dollar check and all the clothes we had packed in the airplane.

On the return trip to Grass Valley, we were high over the Sierras. The night was cold and starry. You could look down from fourteen-thousand feet and the valley fog looked very close, but a VOR cross check showed us to be somewhere out in Nevada. I refused to believe that we were that far off course. I knew we were definitely not on course to Grass Valley when the familiar lights of the Slide Mountain ski area went by. I decided to land at Reno and have a cup of coffee. We fueled up and I finally dropped John off at Grass Valley and returned to Quincy, dog tired.

I now stayed in Wardman's old trailer behind the lounge at the airport. About dawn the first eager student would roll me out of the sack. To regain consciousness I drank a concoction of lemon juice and well water that Lorraine had shown me. The well water in the trailer and office was so full of minerals you had to do something with it in order to gag it down. Then it was one flight after another interspersed with other odd jobs. Finally, at about two or three in the afternoon I would take time to wolf down the first meal of the day.

Greg and I had gone through Quincy High School together. I taught him to fly in my Luscombe just for the practice before I actually had an instructor rating. When I finally got the certificate, he soloed with only one official hour in his logbook. Sometimes we'd light the fireplace in the pilot lounge and watch the firelight and shadows dance on the open beams and knotty pine walls. Old overstuffed chairs and a couch sat comfortably around the cozy room. Over the large south-facing windows hung pieces of shirts scissored from off the student's backs after they accomplished their first solos.

One early morning Greg was taxiing out for a local practice flight in my '46 Luscombe, and I was close behind him in Wardman's '41 Luscombe with a student. The instructor's side in a Luscombe has no brakes, so time must be spent on the ground teaching the student to use them properly. I was busy with my student and didn't see Greg's takeoff, and so wasn't ready for what was about to happen. At Quincy there is a rare and short-lived condition that occurs when the cooler air near the ground is extremely stable and a warm, powerful wind exists above it.

The combination creates dangerous wind shears at the air masses' interface. On the ground the air is perfectly calm, but after climbing a couple of hundred feet up all hell breaks loose! Typically, this condition descends to the ground in ten to twenty minutes and the windsock goes crazy!

I lifted off and almost immediately had to take the controls. We were being rocked and rolled like I couldn't believe. I felt a sudden fear; "Greg is up here in this severe turbulence in my airplane!" Looking around for my red and white airplane, I noticed the wind was now whipping up fast-moving clouds of dust while the windsock was alternately hanging limp and stretched straight out. This was an instructor's nightmare. Greg began his approach bravely, struggling with the vicious wind shear and crosswinds. He battled the downdrafts and updrafts with the throttle and elevator. While I circled overhead, I could see him gallop down the runway and finally go around, just barely clearing the trees off the west end of the runway. He stuck to the plan I had taught him. He completed an 80-degree turn to the right and a 260-degree turn to the left and avoided being trapped in the narrowing canyon to the west. The second landing attempt was successful. I followed him in with a high speed wheel landing. We parked next to his aircraft. After shutting down, I jumped out and yelled to him as he strolled nonchalantly toward the office. "Hey Greg, how'd you like that?"

He replied, "Aww, it was no biggie."

The wind was howling and gusting and I laughed, "Then how come you only tied down one wing?"

Joe was a good student and learned quickly. Why not, since I was using all very excellent and realistic techniques such as practicing needle-ball and airspeed instrument flying in the clouds when the bases were at least five-hundred feet above the mountains? Also, there were the actual emergencies, such as the time when we took off in the Cessna 120 and suddenly the engine quit cold. In this case, there was enough runway to stop before skidding off the end. I didn't have a clue as to what the problem could be. Suddenly, I remembered Herb had said that the carburetor was leaking and he didn't have time to fix it, so the procedure was to turn the fuel selector from "ON" to "OFF" after a flight. No more leak problem, except that there was just enough fuel in the lines to taxi out on the ramp, perform a runup and begin a takeoff.

It was October of 1961, and Judy and I were cruising down the Feather River Canyon in my cool '58 Ford. We were on our way to get married in Sacramento and I was celebrating with a quart bottle of beer wrapped in a brown paper bag. Being twenty-one years of age I could drink legally, but Judy couldn't, at only nineteen, so I told her she could help me celebrate by throwing the empty bottle out the window. (In those days young folks didn't pay much attention to the environment.) We were motoring down Goat Hill when Judy remembered the fifty-five-gallon trash barrel sitting next to the drinking fountain just off the highway. Making a game of it I said, "Let's see if you can hit the barrel," and I slowed down to a slower pace of forty-five mph. She cocked her arm as the green barrel hurtled closer; and as she tensed to throw I noticed a California Highway Patrol vehicle *right behind me!* I started to yell a warning at Judy to stop, but it ended in a strangle as she tossed the bottle wrapped in the bag. It seemed like slow motion as we watched the bagged object arc and tumble through the air and drill the center of that barrel. I glanced in the rear-view mirror in time to see the patrol officer throw up his hands in amazement. He was still cracking up as he floorboarded his big black and white cruiser and roared past us in search of some other victim. This was indeed a fine day!

I used my Luscombe and student pilot Ron Taunt supplied

the gas. We tossed in our sleeping bags and launched on a seven-thousand-mile quest for adventure and that all-important flying time. Don Luscombe didn't design his airplanes for comfort, but they were aerobatic, could do ninety mph and carried fourteen gallons of fuel. Fourteen gallons amounted to three hours at cruise power before the engine quit. My little airplane now boasted a transmitter with four frequencies and a tunable receiver powered by a wind-driven generator. It was necessary to reduce rpm to hear the low frequency receiver over the spark plug-induced static. In other words, every time you transmitted to the tower, you had to pull the throttle off to hear the answer! The wet compass and chart were the only tools available for navigation.

After I completed a full day's flying, Ron and I took off from Quincy and slept in Reno on the floor the Weather Bureau Office. Beginning at dawn, we stared down the sun for awhile, and finally evening found us in Gallup, New Mexico, and it was Saturday night. While trying to hitch a ride into town, we were picked up, instead, by a couple of Navajo cops who suggested that we get a motel and stay there. Hell, I was twenty-one and tough! I had my rights. So did Ronnie—that is, we thought so, until we walked into a bar and the noisy conversations became silent and all the brown eyes were upon us. We decided to eat instead of drinking. As we were sitting down at a cafe booth next to a rowdy bunch of cowhands, I saw a callused hand sneak out and pinch the large buttocks of the waitress. She swung a frying pan on that poor bastard and nearly knocked his brains out. He was soon lying in the gutter in front of the restaurant. She turned and faced us, head on, with frying pan in hand and said, "Now what the hell can I get for you?" Right after dinner we retired to our hotel room.

New Mexico was a fascinating area with its sheer cliffs, mountains and deserts. We saw Indian hogans with TV antennas sticking out of the rain barrel architecture, and cars and pickups parked all around, making a startling contrast between old and new ways of life.

As I said, our aircraft communications left a lot to be desired. While we were trying to understand taxi instructions from Wichita Falls tower for a night departure, the tower finally turned off all the taxi lights except those that we were using. Later in that leg of our flight, our lights and radio completely failed so we landed at a small, lighted strip and rolled out the sleeping bags. The next morning we discovered that the generator was hooked up backwards.

In Madison, Mississippi, we made friends with workers at the airport and they let us sleep in the attic of a hangar in about three inches of dust. In the morning before leaving I stuck my head in the owner's office to thank him and was shocked at what I saw. The rest of the place was dilapidated or in ruins, but that office was luxurious with a black "shoot on" ceiling complete with "sparkelies." The polished oak desk was huge, and the carpet felt many inches thick. A full wet bar covered the far wall. It seemed that this trip was full of little surprises!

In Meridian, where we made a stop for fuel, a note on the door said "for service call such-and-such a number." It must have been a joke, because the phone was locked up in the office. We saw houses across the countryside and decided to take a shortcut. After hours of crawling around in the Mississippi underbrush and slapping mosquitoes, we finally found a house with a telephone. Lucky we weren't shot.

Motoring along over Florida, we observed the lush tropical growth, coral reefs and blue-green lagoons. There were inland canals with exclusive houses built on them so their owners could dock their expensive boats right in their front yards. The waters around the Keys teemed with shark, barracuda, and stingrays. I had a pair of Polarized glasses and could see beneath the water quite well. When we noticed large numbers of sharks, I pictured our little engine quitting and maybe getting cut in the ditching. I could imagine the sharks noting the splash and smelling blood. I visualized triangular fins coming at us from all directions as the Luscombe sank. With all that in mind, I suggested that Ronnie fly a little closer to the overseas highway that connected the Keys with the rest of Florida.

From the mainland to the island of Marathon, it was necessary to file a flight plan because of the touchy Cuban situation. In Marathon I was offered a job for next season flying an Aero Commander to Cuba on a regular basis. (Who knows what the cargo really was.) I was pleased at this opportunity to become a multi-engine pilot flying out of this paradise! Of course that idea had to be scratched when the Bay of Pigs occurred soon after our visit.

On the way back north from Key West, thunderstorms gathered, and the little Continental engine shuddered and shook as it acquired carburetor ice in spite of the warm weather. The carburetor heat control pulled right out of the panel. Apparently, the wire had broken at the attach point on the carburetor. I could only maintain maximum available power and hold the nose as high as I could without stalling, hoping to create as much heat in the engine as possible and burn the ice out. It worked, and the carburetor throat stayed more-or-less clear of ice. We continued on in that configuration and proceeded to our next stop in Tamiami where I figured out a "Rube" Goldberg fix on the problem, and then we continued north. We avoided the Lake Okeechobee area where several large forest fires were burning.

We flew at treetop level, cruising by Florida communities like Naples America, Sarasota and Crystal River. In the topography there were many deep limestone sinkholes with incredibly clear water. One of them had a sign we could read saying, "Weeki Wachee Springs." It was so beautiful that I suspected that many an underwater motion picture had been, or would be, filmed there.

We fueled at Hattesburg, Monroe, and later, at Shreveport. The next day we stopped in an uncontrolled airport near Dallas where I traded dual instruction with a fellow who owned a Beechcraft T-34 Mentor. He checked me out and we proceeded to have fun at the apparently deserted airstrip. We took off on one runway and landed on the cross runway. Afterward, when I slid the canopy open, there stood a grim-looking person who said he was the Airport Manager. I was going to receive a violation from the FAA for my runway swapping antics. I worried for the longest time that they would find me even though I gave him the wrong address.

After leaving Dallas, Ft.Worth, Mineral Wells, Sweetwater, Midland and Pecos seemed to crawl by under us as we bucked a strong headwind. Ron and I were bushed, it was night and the chart said that Van Horn had lights. We finally arrived over the airport and observed the so-called "airport lighting." The perimeter of the airport property was surrounded by lights and both thresholds were lighted, but not a twinkle on the runway! I lined up the threshold lights as best I could and executed a glassy-water landing since the Luscombe had no landing lights. This maneuver was probably invented by float plane pilots. The procedure is to set up a nose-high descent at a decreased power setting and at an acceptable vertical speed and then just let it hit the ground. After bouncing to a halt, the next task was to find a parking place. Ronnie had to walk ahead of me with the flashlight until we groped our way to a tiedown. We finally located a telephone with the telephone number of a hotel that would come and pick us up. The old pickup bounced its way through the ruts into Van Horn. Our driver was a huge, unshaven individual who stunk of whisky. Bottles rolled around on the floorboard and Ronnie's and my eyes rolled at each other, wondering what we were doing here. In the dim lights of the hotel lobby, we could see big, black circles around our chauffeur's eyes as he peered out from under a Texas-style hat. The whole place reminded me of the Adams Family mansion. A woman with lots of lipstick and a low-cut dress leered at me from the stairway. A ragged-looking parrot shouted epithets at us as we dragged ourselves up to our room. I hoped that we would survive the night. Sleep came hard with the nonstop party going on downstairs at the piano bar. Apparently our chauffeur didn't sleep much, because he drove us back to the airport still stinking of whisky, and dawn had not yet arrived. Oh well! I shouldn't complain. We weren't charged for the rides.

We embarked on one of the longest flights you can imagine, hurtling through the sky at ninety mph, but into a headwind. It was light when we made Fabens, New Mexico, and thereafter fuel stops at the airports of Deming, Cochise County, Gila Bend, Yuma, Thermal, Palmdale, Bakersfield and finally after dark, Fresno Air Terminal. The air terminal was still in the construction process and lights weren't available on the taxiways. We still had miles to taxi to the tiedown area and I asked the tower if we could just park here and throw out our sleeping bags. After all, we had just flown fifteen hours! Permission was granted. We spotted an old, abandoned bus next to the fence and crawled in it for the night with all hopes of dinner and a shower gone. Besides, who had the money for a cab and a motel?

The next day, after two more fuel stops, the good old hometown came into view as the little Luscombe with its tired crew dropped over a ridge just southwest of the airport. After landing, I asked Ron for his Student Pilot Certificate so I could endorse the part that said it was OK for him to fly cross-country solo. Ninety hours in thirteen days of flying back and forth across the continent should be enough dual instruction, don't you think?

Judge Bert and I had a standing inside joke. I had really worked him over in his Cessna 120. I'd tried to help him keep his landings straight and he had done pretty well. One day, while he was practicing touch-and-goes solo, the wind came up suddenly. I saw him get blown off the runway and take a sojourn out through the hay field before yanking the plane back into the air. He came around for a successful landing the next time and quietly taxied to his hangar thinking no one had seen his near disaster. Later I asked him how his landings went, and he shrugged and replied, "OK I guess."

I laughed and asked him, "Then how come you have all that grass hanging from your wheels?"

Frank Nervino asked me to fly his Cessna 180 from Beckwourth, an elevation of 4,900 feet msl to Chester, elevation 4,525 feet msl to pick up a patient, and after flying over 8,000-foot mountains, deliver him to Novato, elevation 01 foot msl. So who gives a damn about the elevations in November, you ask; certainly density altitude was no problem? That's true, but my head cold was plenty of trouble. I can't remember the last 500 feet to touchdown at Novato, nor do I recall any pain. All I know is that suddenly I was aware that the 180 was galloping down the grass runway and people were dashing around in a panic. I quickly brought the tail dragger under control and parked. I had momentarily lost consciousness because of sinus pressure and now knew just how deadly a head cold could be when flying.

I found more instruction work with Al Butler at the Vista Airport in Sparks, Nevada. Most prospective bosses want to give you a check ride, and Al was no different. We flew across the lower mountains south to Minden in the Skylane. Al told me to hold a particular altitude and heading, which I did. I grinned when after a while the altimeter remained precisely where he requested, but the wheels were almost touching the top of a mountain. Finally, Al said I could change altitude and heading if I wanted to; all the while I'm sure he was thinking what a smart-ass I was.

Al taught me an excellent teaching technique for around the pattern. Instead of "pitch, power and trim," such as when you level off enroute, leave the nose up and throttle back so you won't have to trim. Use your throttle for pitch trim control. This technique works like a charm in the faster aircraft which tend to build a lot of unwanted speed in a small pattern. I also learned more about carburetor heat one time when, at high altitude in a Cessna 150, I pulled the heat on because the engine was running rough. The carburetor heat made it run worse, so I enriched the mixture, which made it almost quit. I immediately realized what the problem was, and leaned out the fuel mixture. Of course, the hot air entering the carburetor was thinner and therefore required less fuel for the proper ratio of fuel-to-oxygen. Not using high altitude leaning techniques correctly can embarrass you even if you don't have a carburetor. One time I landed at Lake Tahoe (6,200 foot elevation) in a Cessna 210 with the mixture full rich and the engine wound down to a stop while rolling out because of the excessively rich mixture. There was simply too much fuel in the cylinders for the amount of oxygen present to provide for decent combustion.

One day I received a call from the Pacific Air Lines personnel manager in San Francisco. He said that I had been highly recommended to them and asked would I be interested in a copilot job. When could I come down and talk to them? I said "yes," and "now!" I jumped in my Cessna 180 and hauled ass to San Francisco International. (In those days you could actually pull a single-engine airplane up close to the airline terminals.) I jumped out and trotted up the stairs with high spirits.

The personnel person was typical of their kind, suit and tie, skin that almost never sees the sun, and cold eyes. His smile seemed warm enough, and with a flourish that he obviously enjoyed, he swept his arm toward the window. "That's a Martin 404; how do you think you would fit in its copilot seat?" I could only nod in my excitement, already imagining how it would be to raise the gear for the captain in preparation for the day when I would be in charge.

The manager said that I was to go downstairs and visit the Chief Pilot to settle things. I was almost bolting for the door when he said, "But first you should take this little quiz." He made it sound like an insignificant thing and didn't explain the rules except that there was a time limit, but he didn't say how long. There were fifty questions and I could see that there were plenty of easy ones, but I didn't want to skip around. I guessed that these guys probably wanted a steady type of guy, so I went through the questions one at time, in order. At question number twenty-three, he breezed through the door saying, "time's up" and snatched the test away. Quickly buzzing through the test with an answer sheet, he frowned, "You only got twenty-three questions right; our standards require that you get twenty-five."

I pleaded, "But every one that I answered, I got right. Can I take another test?"

While flying home, his answer reverberated in my mind, "Sorry!" I had learned another simple, but hard, lesson. You *must* prepare for a test! Later I was to realize that you can't compete with other people who study the exact test before taking it, or with someone who at least knows enough to do the easy ones first!

Herb Wardman had been using Denny Mansell's Navajo for charters. On a charter to Las Vegas, he disappeared for days without warning and the furious customers had to take the airlines home. This unfortunate maneuver had political repercussions since those former customers were active in community politics. Eventually things really went to hell for Herb and Lorraine, each taking the money themselves for flights because they knew they were headed for divorce. Herb refused to fuel Lorraine. One day she ran out of gas in the Luscombe just short of the Beckwourth Airport. She and her student were not injured. Another day, soon after, in the Cessna 120, Lorraine and the same student lost control and ended up on their back in the field next to the runway at Gansner. The student lost interest in continuing his flight training after that. Since I was working for them I was caught right in the middle, much to my discomfort.

Chapter 4
Ukiah

Meta Pool was the second female boss I'd flown for so far. She ruled her business with an iron hand on one side and showed great humor on the other. She was a ferry command pilot during the war. When baby Teri, Judy, and I first arrived in Ukiah, she treated us to a fine bash up in her hilltop home that overlooked the airport. Meta was good at telling jolly stories. We met her sons, Oscar and Marty, who she said slept outside on the porch come rain or shine. Both boys flew in the business. When the cat walked across the tablecloth she said not to worry about it, it had been turned over five or six times already! She and her former husband, Lonnie, used to have a fabric-covered Aeronca for student training. She told how it had gotten so rotten that one time Lonnie's feet fell through the floor and dragged on the taxiway. More recently, she had bought a Cessna 182 and "a bill of goods" with it. Supposedly, it had been overhauled by a Greely company, but Dumont Watson, Pool's Air Services' alcoholic ace mechanic, said the engine case had never been broken open. He called it a "Tijuana overhaul."

Dumont had been a crop duster and he was determined to show me how it was done. We flew my Luscombe over to a spit of land extending out a quarter of a mile on Lake Mendocino where orchards grew, and proceeded to buzz the place with a vengeance. Dumont stalled out of every turnaround, and I was just able to grab the controls and save us from disaster. He was unaware that anything was out of the ordinary. By the time we returned to the airport, there were telephone complaints flooding into the airport office.

Meta had enough influence to get the state and the feds to tailor the fire reconnaissance aircraft requirements to exactly what she had, which was a high wing Cessna 182 with 230 horsepower. She was wishing I was Instrument Rated and qualified to fly recon, because the Forest Service observer was reluctant to fly with another pilot that filled in during the summer. The pilot showed him how "safe" the 182 was by shutting off the magnetos and stopping the prop while pulling up into a stall over forbidding mountain territory.

One day I took off in the Cessna 210 and the window suddenly became covered with oil. I could only see out the side window. I executed one of those crop duster turnarounds and landed back the opposite direction, remembering to check that the landing gear was down and locked. I was in the process of dressing down the gas boy who had failed to put the oil cap back on when Meta intervened. She made a strong point when she said, "You are pilot-in-command and it is your responsibility to check the oil cap. Don't ever blame someone else!"

While parked at the privately-owned airstrip called Bonny Doon, northwest of Santa Cruz, I had neglected to shut off the fuel selector to stop the ever present fuel drip. A helpful tire kicker said, "Ya oughta get that fixed. The needle valve is stickin' in the carburetor."

Of course the 210 was fuel injected and didn't have a carburetor. That 210 was always leaking fuel out of the bottom of the cowling. "No problem," Dumont said, "just turn the fuel selector off when you park." Only problem was I forgot it once, (like the time in Wardman's Cessna 120) and the engine quit while taxiing out with a charter passenger at Cloverdale. A little rattled, I restarted and took off.

About an hour after takeoff the passenger remarked, "I thought this was a retractable gear airplane." Sheepishly I pulled the gear lever out and up and heard all the usual satisfactory retraction sounds. After takeoff, having been distracted, I had pulled the lever out and down instead of up which produced a cycle of hydraulic sounds, just not the right ones. Anyway, the word got back to Meta and according to my passenger the engine had quit on takeoff and we had almost skidded off the runway and of course it was all my fault!

The coastal mountains had some strips that could "bite" the unwary. I found out one dark night that although Covelo's one-way strip boasted of lights, only one side worked at a time. The trick was to guess which side of the lights the runway lay on. If you went too far into that dark hole, you didn't go around either, if you knew what was good for you. Near Covelo, the Eel River winds its way through deep coast range gorges to the ocean. About fifty miles due east from the ocean shore nestled the isolated village of Fort Seward where Lindrith Timber Products was headquartered. The village boasted of an 800-foot-long landing strip with a cliff at each end where the river winds around it. There was a tree in the way on the south end of the runway that you must slip around. Dropping deep into the gorge, I followed the river around. I configured the 210 with landing gear down, prop full increase, mixture full rich, and half flaps. Then, left turn, full flaps, power off, skid right, slip left and hit the ground. The landing was made with room to spare. Early model 210s are good at slow flight. Good thing!

One of the stops that day with two of the elders of the company was at Hoopa, an Indian reservation on the Klamath River. A flood had wiped out some of the runway's blacktop and the sun was baking what was left. The 1960 model 210 has tiny wheels that are not good at all in ruts, mud, or soft asphalt. When no amount of power would get us moving in the hot blacktop, the rotund president of the company volunteered to get out and push, so I let him! There he was red-faced, huffing and puffing, with tie flying wildly and white shirt getting dirty. We began to roll and he dove into the back seat while the front passenger slammed and locked the door. We staggered down the rugged canyon, the president struggling with his seat belt. I flew them home with the gear extended just in case the gooey stuff stuck to the tire. The sticky sludge could cause problems with the gear system.

I got a lot of action as an instructor at Ukiah. Judy soloed in our Luscombe. She did a perfect three-point landing on the very end of the long Ukiah runway, and had to taxi quite a way to the first turnoff. I asked her, "Why so short?" She replied, "I didn't want to go around." Judy gave up actively pursuing a Private Pilot Certificate because my grandparents couldn't bear the possibility of history repeating itself.

Frank wanted to go to Arizona and look at a sawmill to purchase and I agreed to give him dual instruction in the 210. He was a difficult student because he didn't trust his instructor. We departed Palm Springs before dawn because of the heat, and to attempt to avoid afternoon thunderstorms. Frank was uneasy in the dark and insisted that we return. We started again when it was light, but had lost a lot of time. Afternoon near the Mogollon Rim usually produces thunderstorms, and today was no exception. Dodging clouds, twiddling VORs, and reading WAC charts in the turbulence was a chore. We saw an airport and decided that this must be our destination, St. Johns. I landed myself because it looked kinda tight. I'll say it was tight, weaving between lumber piles and bouncing over large rocks. The altimeter said we were within a hundred feet of the right elevation, but something didn't feel right. We looked around for a way into town and finally found a sign indicating that we had landed at Snowflake, Arizona, elevation 5,600 feet. Our planned destination, St. Johns, was still thirty-some miles to the east. Chagrined, I flew us to the right airport, my student thinking less of me all the time.

I had to resist the urging of a drunken bunch of passengers from Ft. Bragg to penetrate thunderstorms on the way to Reno. The most obnoxious one claimed he was a former Navy aviator and that I was taking too long by going around the anvil-topped monsters. Once, at Reno, they said, "We'll only be a couple of hours." About eight or ten hours later they staggered into the terminal, and after that I insisted that in the future they get me a motel. Even that wasn't too great. You didn't have to watch television to see crime scenes in progress across the street.

The seasonal job in Ukiah at Pool's Air Service was over and it was back to Plumas County where the only work was "pulling chain" in a saw mill. I kept my Luscombe parked at the sawmill strip next to Indian Creek. One night, a big storm broke and I rushed out to drag the craft to higher ground to escape the now raging river. Good thing, because that airplane would have ended up in Sacramento without burning a drop of gas! Later, I cut out a picture in the newspaper of the little airplane lashed to a barbed wire fence, its tail under the muddy water.

It was time to continue the quest for flight ratings. More and more I realized that I needed an Instrument Rating to find a decent flying job. I took dual instruction from Herb, but I really needed a more focused program. Acme School of Aeronautics was a progressive ground school and I didn't want to mess around with failing more tests. The fact that the classroom was halfway across the United States didn't matter. Without a lot of forethought, Judy and I, and baby Teri hopped in the car and blasted off for Fort Worth.

The ground school was downstairs and the FAA testing room was upstairs. Students took continuous individual ground school until the instructors felt certain that you could pass the test, then you hopped upstairs to gave it a try. Immediately after the test, the student was grilled for any information that Acme might be missing. Since they didn't have an Instrument Instructor test exam yet, I helped them write one. If you failed, you had the option to take more instruction.

A rodeo was in town the day before I was to take my exam. The young cowboys interfered with my sleep. They partied all night long at the motel and swam in the pool in freezing temperatures. It was hilarious to see them siting on the edge of the pool soaking wet, clad in nothing but underpants and cowboy hats. You could hear them coughing as they lit up. The rumpus room was directly below us and the juke box tended to get stuck, playing, "From A Jack To A King," and "The Night Has A Thousand Eyes," over and over again.

I took instrument flight instruction in a Cessna 170, and gave primary instruction to Acme students to help work off my expenses. It could very easily have turned into a career, but I didn't like the flat Midwest with its unfamiliar racial problems that made separate bathrooms and drinking fountains necessary. Strangely, one county was dry and just across the border you could drive up and get a beer with your hamburger. We returned to California with my written exams successfully completed, and I continued taking dual instruction in Quincy and Sacramento.

The big day came and I marched into the Reno FAA office

and faced Inspector Culliton for the Instrument and Instrument Instructor flight tests. I was nervous and the oral didn't go particularly well, but we flew anyhow. The flying went very well. Culliton seemed relaxed, while I kept busy determining intersections with my "coffee grinder" Narco radio. On the VOR approach he asked me if I wanted a cigarette. I said, "Sure." One didn't turn down a cigarette when offered by an FAA Inspector, did one?

We talked about everything but what I was doing, and after a particularly jolly joke, his voice suddenly became cold and hard, "How long until missed approach?"

I immediately retorted, "Twenty-three seconds!" He laughed and was satisfied with my performance. God help me if I hadn't been ready for that question. At any rate, my hot new tickets opened the door to work for Bridgeford Flying Service.

Chapter 5
Tahoe

It was spring of '63 and Judy was very pregnant with Jack. We were at the Napa airport and I was talking like a Dutch uncle to Jack Bergan, one of the owners of Bridgeford Flying Service. BFS had locations at Napa, Stockton, and South Shore Lake Tahoe. Since I was rated as an CFII, (Certified Flight Instructor-Instrument) I could "do it all." When Jack called Bob Barton, the straw boss at the lake, I felt a little uneasy when I was referred to as "the answer." He requested that I drive from Napa to Tahoe and interview with Mr. Barton. Although we had already been to Stockton that day I needed to work and we drove up the mountain. The interview went well enough, so we moved to the place where the bright lights meet the wilderness.

The Tahoe Valley Airport was laid out north and south with a field elevation of over six thousand feet. During summertime the temperature rises and the density altitude becomes dangerous to unwary pilots. To the north was the dazzling blue lake and to the south a basin surrounded by impressive granite walls and one-way canyons. A hill rises immediately to the west and a ridge runs parallel to the runway on the east side. During a south takeoff, where the winds tend to be westerly, best results could be achieved by turning with the wind when practicable and hugging the parallel ridge. Once past the end of the runway, it is necessary to reverse course in the basin and depart the area north-bound. High-performance aircraft sometimes barely made it past the end of the asphalt if they didn't use basic principles of ridge-soaring. There was a Beechcraft Bonanza lying in the trees off the end of runway 18, giving mute testimony of deadly wind shear and density altitude dangers. Weather conditions in this mountain paradise were changeable and tricky to beginner and expert alike. I once stopped my takeoff on runway 36 because a waterspout was crossing the southern section of the lake right in my path! Just how weird the wind shear could be was amply demonstrated when Larry Sheeley took his first lesson. We took off to the south in the Cessna 150 and with breathtaking speed gained a thousand feet. About the middle of the 8,500-foot-long runway, the bottom dropped out, and we were free falling. I aborted the takeoff and managed to stop while still on the runway.

As a pit boss for a stateline casino, Hal made good money, maybe a little too much at gambling, sometimes. Bridgeford provided a Cessna 150 for basic training. After soloing Hal in the 150 and flying with him on a few short cross-countries, he bought himself a 65 horsepowered Luscombe and had me check him out. He next announced that he was going to tour the United States in his plane. Instructors had no legal control over where their students flew in their own airplanes. Although I pleaded with him to get more training first, he went anyway. About a week later, Hal came limping across the ramp, one leg in a cast. He explained that he left his Luscombe in an Arizona farmer's field after running out of gas. He eventually had to leave town in a hurry due to some "funny business" he was implicated in at the club.

Joe was a mechanic for National Cash Register, and a very proper "up tight" easterner type; you know, let's get the job done *right now,* no funny business. After I soloed him, he bought his own 115 horsepowered Cessna 140, and I continued training him in that. When Joe had a few drinks his personality changed and became very improper, like Dr. Jekyll and Mr. Hyde. One night he got drunk and did aerial antics and buzz jobs over the city of South Shore for several hours. When he landed back at Tahoe Valley, the cops came at him, red lights flashing and sirens blaring. Of course, he took off into the night and escaped. He ended up sleeping it off in his plane at the Placerville airport.

Fortunately, it was summertime when son Jack was born. I was driving Judy through Carson City at a high rate of speed late at night. We were on the way to the hospital in Reno when the red lights from two State Trooper cars glared in the rear view mirror. I stopped and asked the officers if they would like to deliver a baby. Suddenly it was, "Follow me!" We received a high-speed escort through town, and Jack got to be born in a hospital.

I miscalculated how much coffee you should drink before flying on this charter. I flew the Skylane to SFO often with no problems after a cup or two. I had crossed the outer marker and was traveling down the glideslope and pegging the localizer when an interesting phenomenon occurred. The jet in front of me had created a tunnel that was twisted and turned by the air flow. It was tempting to follow the tunnel. A less interesting and more painful phenomenon was also occurring, my bladder was about to burst. In spite of a full load of passengers I had to let it go or crash! Fortunately the rug on the floor was absorbent. After parking, I let the passengers out and supposedly attended to paperwork so I wouldn't have to stand up and reveal my wet pants!

Judy and I had developed a nice circle of friends. We had a party one snowy night in our little cabin located just off the road to Emerald Bay. There were two fireplaces that needed tending constantly since you could see daylight through the missing chinks between the logs. All of us in the party group were in our early twenties and had kids. Frenchy, one of my students, and his spouse, Babs, brought their seven-year-old son who soon went to bed. Frenchy also brought his Colt .45 to show off. Babs had instigated an innocent spin-the-bottle game between drinks. When it was time to kiss, the lights were supposed to go off with only firelight for illumination. When it turned out that Babs and I were "It," I was a little surprised at the intensity of the kiss. Frenchy wanted me to go outside with him and try shooting his huge pistol, but I declined. It had been a very long day, and a long day loomed tomorrow. I was exhausted. I excused myself and crawled into Judy's and my bed where Frenchy and Bab's son was sound asleep. A weariness crept over me and I barely heard the roar of the .45 discharging in the freezing darkness outside. Suddenly a hot body slipped in next to mine and I was being smothered in kisses. Babs whispered, "You really turned me on out there!" My male mind and body came awake and for a moment they said, "Yes!" The gun roared again outside and my pilot's mind quickly surveyed the survivability odds of such a proposition. That, in turn, helped the faithful husband in me come to a decision. I kicked her out!

The Drum family had a successful plumbing business run mostly by papa Ed and son Eric. They both worked very hard themselves, but they also possessed excellent organizational abilities. Eric came to me for flight training and seemed at first to have "personality minus." He was so quiet and so round-faced; like a peach with fuzzy blond hair. Shows you how wrong first impressions can be. Eric soon became a Private Pilot and the stories began. He and a buddy were flying a friend's Comanche in the eleven-thousand-foot-high Freel Peak area one winter day when the updrafts became great fun. Eric throttled back and soared from eight to ten thousand feet on the windward side of the slope. This being fun, Eric decided to practice soaring and he leaned the mixture, pulled up into a stall and stopped the propeller. The fun continued as they soared from ten to twelve thousand feet. "This was fantastic," they thought, "Let's go to Reno" Eric said, and he pointed the aircraft north. Of course, the minute they crossed to the lee side of the ridges the bottom fell out. "No sweat," Eric figured, "we'll just start the engine." At that altitude in the winter the temperature rivaled the minus temperatures of the Arctic Coast. Hurricane-force winds howling through the cowling as well made a re-start impossible. Fortunately the Minden Airport was within gliding distance and the landing gear extended normally.

Adjacent to Bridgeford's office was a jolly little bar and grille where one could eat, drink, and tell flying stories. Free red wine accompanied all food (the chef was Italian). The sign over the door said, "Through This Door Walk The Best Pilots In The World!" The bartenders could tell you all about "boundary layer control," and were authorities on any aeronautical subject (or any other subject for that matter). I was in the bar when the shocking news blared out of the TV that President Kennedy had been shot. Even the most cynical pilot's eyes blinked with tears.

A practice I instituted was to wood burn the name of the student who had achieved his first solo in a large breadboard, along with the date of the great achievement. It was proudly displayed in the bar. I had always disliked ripping someone's shirt up and scrawling the information on the remnant. The bar's owner was a character by the name of Jack Beamis. One day he chartered me to fly him to the Washoe Valley home of Harvy

Grossman, owner of Harvy's Wagon Wheel Hotel/Casino at Stateline. He really hadn't been invited. Jack was already three sheets to the wind and requested that I land on the road next to Harvy's driveway. I refused (after all it was night), so we arrived by taxi with a little less flourish. Everyone was yucking it up in the front room while I hung around the kitchen, since I was in work clothes. Someone had left a guitar over in a corner and I strummed it a little. Before I knew it I was the center of attention and the pickin' and grinnin' just went on and on. Took me back to my old rock n' roll days!

Wes Stetson was another of Tahoe's dynamic characters. Retired from a full career with the military and Pan American Airlines, Wes filled his days selling scenic flights on Lake Tahoe in a Seabee. Wes pulled lots of stunts with that amphibian. One day he removed the landing gear and managed to land in, and more surprisingly, fly out of eight-thousand-foot-high Star Lake. That was quite a feat considering the meager performance capability of that aircraft. Another stunning stunt occurred when he landed in Emerald Bay with the gear extended and flipped the plane over. Apparently even former airline captains need checklists. One stormy day, Wes showed up in a North American T-28. He rumbled up to the bar, ran it up and shut the big radial engine off. After ordering fuel, he strolled in, downed a straight shot of whisky and started to leave. Outside, in the storm, I asked him what he was doing with that old military aircraft. He confided, "I'm delivering this hunk of crap for a friend. I picked it up on the East Coast. It's been missing and running lousy for the last couple of hours." I wanted to know what he planned to do if the engine failed—say over the Rubicon River Wilderness Basin—in this storm? He roared over the wind, "I'll bail out!" Wes donned his parachute and swung his lanky frame into the cockpit. The big T-28 looked and sounded impressive as it made a high-speed pass by the bar and pulled straight up into the storm.

Ken Burrough, one of my students, showed up with a ferry pilot in a Navy SNJ. It was a big, heavy and demanding military tail-dragging trainer with a 600 horsepower radial engine up front. On the runway in just a moments inattention, the low wing would "ground loop." Ground loop means to spin around in tight little circles on the ground, quite possibly causing great damage to the landing gear and airframe. A tail wheel-equipped airplane is inherently unstable directionally on the ground. The center of gravity is behind the main wheels, and once you get sideways it would rather roll tail wheel first than nose first. It takes skill to keep the tail *behind* the rest of the airplane! Just what a beginner needs, whose only training has been in an inherently stable nose wheel-equipped Cessna 150, right? Well, the airplane only cost him 800 bucks, but it was possible to burn thirty or forty gallons-per-hour when flying. Breathtaking, compared to the five gallons consumed by the little 150. For a little gas money, I got Wes to check me out in it. Other than almost losing it on roll out while trying to figure out how to read the old military tachometer, the checkout went fine and only took twenty-five minutes. Burroughs spent many hours just learning to taxi the military trainer. As an aside, Uncle David (Mom's brother), a military flight instructor, invented the procedure whereby you rolled the Texan (AT-6, the Army Air Core version of the Navy SN-J) inverted before bailing out. Previously, pilots had been killed by hitting the tail surfaces when they stepped out. Dave had to prove it one day and the maneuver became standard with the Army Air Corps.

Kelmont Corporation was a development company who was struggling financially. They had an oil-streaked Cessna 310, and a 210. One stormy late afternoon the Unicom picked up a garbled and faint message, but the Kelmont official and the 210 trying to get home from the Bay Area never showed up. The search was on. In the bar, news flashed rapidly that a large amount of Kelmont cash had been transported that day. After a while, with no trace of the airplane and its occupant or the cash, suspicious minds were active. They pictured the company official basking in the warm Mexican sun, sipping a martini purchased with the money the company needed so desperately. "What kind of bastard would pull something like that?" everyone around the bar wondered. The suspicious voices were silenced when they found the aircraft, the body, and the money the following spring under the cold waters of Emerald Bay!

Some of the tragedies that haunted Lake Tahoe involved more than one victim at a time. Many times the Paradise Airlines Super Connie materialized out of the blowing snow like a spirit. I wondered each time, "How do they do it?" I learned that they used the Biju standard broadcast station for ADF guidance. If, at a certain point, they hadn't seen the shoreline, they pulled up in a left turn and head to Reno. They almost never pulled up because the shoe string operation couldn't afford to bus the passengers back up to their Stateline destination after diverting. I fueled one of their DC-3s with ten gallons a side. I wondered at the time if it was some kind of joke. No joke; and with backs against the wall financially, Paradise Airlines was using every trick in the book to avoid crashing financially. Every flight was a desperate gamble. Luck ran out one wild and wintry day for Paradise Airlines and its Super Connie, crew, and passengers. The station manager strode into Bridgeford's office with a worried look. "Heard anything from my Connie on the Unicom?" he asked.

"Not a thing," was the reply.

"Sure glad I'm in this warm shack today," I said. You could hear the gusts of wind slamming into the building. The snow was blinding and wouldn't stop. As usual the station manager's official weather observation report read, "Thin obscuration." According to Federal Air Regulations, if the obscuration to a view of the sky is only thin, then the approach into the treacherous airport could be allowed to continue.

The four-engined Constellation vanished, and it was days before a search could actually begin. I tried but had to dive at the runway when the treacherous weather suddenly closed in again. What could have happened? Beamis' bar was full all day and half the night, buzzing with opinions. Some pilots speculated that the aircraft could have broken up in the air when it passed Emerald Bay, where dangerous wind shear always lurked during a strong west wind. The answer finally came; the captain had pulled up at the predetermined point on the inadvisable instrument approach and had begun his left turn as planned. What he didn't reckon for was the high winds out of the west causing him to drift. The Super Connie's tail smashed into a ridge, while the rest of the aircraft sailed across a canyon to smash into Genoa Peak. The passengers flew clear of the aircraft in midair and slammed into the ground, stacking up on one another while still strapped into their seats! This was supposed to have been a fun gambling outing and the passengers were loaded with money. Greenbacks were drifting around with the wind. Guards had to be posted to keep the scavengers out. There were many requests for scenic flights over the gory scene. To the dismay of my ghoulish passengers, I insisted on keeping the required 2,000 feet of altitude over the disaster area.

The crowd was treated to an air show at Tahoe Valley, but this day there was a gloomy overcast, maybe eighteen-hundred feet above the airport, and it threatened to screw up the show. Bob Hoover didn't let it bother him as he made his entrance; his yellow F-51 screamed down the runway, pitched up, and then executed perfect vertical rolls into the overcast. A short time later he came popping out at precisely the same spot diving for the ground and still rotating. He ended his show by touching down on the runway, gear and flaps extended, and then pulling up and landing out of a loop!

I was teaching spins in a Cessna 150 and had asked the student to recover. We were rotating straight down toward the impossibly-clear Tahoe water near the east shore. I barked the order more sharply and looked at him. He looked back; his hands off the yoke, fingers spread and palms facing my direction, "It's stuck!" I touched the yoke and, indeed, it was stuck. I whacked the yoke with the heel of my hand and it broke loose. I recovered from the spin without a lot of air to spare. Back at the airport, I crawled under the panel and found nothing that would make the yoke freeze in the full aft position. I sent the aircraft down to Bridgeford's maintenance facility in Stockton, but they couldn't find anything either. Gremlins?

If there are Gremlins, there must be Guardian Angels, too. Frank Sinatra Jr. was performing at South Shore. I met him a couple of times when he flew in with some buddies. The news broke big when he was kidnapped. It was my job that night to fly the KRCR news to Sacramento. It looked like a nice night for a ride, so Judy, young Teri, and baby Jack rode along. There were clouds and stars, but mostly clouds. I figured I could get through the layer and top them easily enough and make the trip over the overcast in the starlight. It would be beautiful. Bridgeford's king of the fleet was a trusty Cessna 182, and I knew it could do the job just fine. Up we climbed through Kingsbury Pass heading east toward lower ground in Nevada. The pitot heat was on. I checked for carburetor ice by pulling on the heat every so often. Hate to leave the carb heat on very long, though, because at this altitude the engine runs badly, and we were losing manifold

pressure anyway because of the thinner air. The climb to VFR-
On-Top was taking a lot longer than I had expected. Finally, at
sixteen-thousand feet we broke out and I turned west and aimed
at Sacramento. It was black and cold out there and the cloud tops
looked ghostly in the star light. Suddenly, somewhere west of the
Tahoe basin, probably near Pyramid Peak, the engine began to
shudder and shake. I richened the mixture and it got worse. Judy,
who was holding Jack on her lap, calmly asked me if she should
strap him in the back. My head bobbed in the affirmative as I
leaned out the mixture. By now we were engulfed by that gray
hell that hid all the granite topography lurking below. I shut off
the distracting strobe light on the tail and went to work.

Breathing heavily, I thought, "Now let's see, we need fire
(magnetos producing spark)—that's okay, we require fuel flow to
the carburetor, switching the fuel selector around didn't help, we
need air." I had checked the carburetor heat climbing out, but I
suspected that I might have melted some ice that ran back farther
inside the venturi. I could picture the inside of that carburetor
coated with hard, clear ice with only a tiny hole to let the thin
atmosphere in. I applied as much heat as I dared, plying with the
mixture control for best power. The manual says to apply full
carburetor heat, but I could imagine a chunk of ice breaking off
and plugging that little hole that was straining to suck the thin,
combustion-supporting oxygen through it. If that hole were to
become plugged, combustion would cease and the engine would
cool instantly. All hope of a restart would be lost. Carb heat on
and off, a little more heat each time, keep heading for lower
ground. An occasional look outside with the flashlight revealed
light structural ice. Finally the potentially killer ice was melted
and the lights of Placerville popped into view. I had rolled
twelve's on that pass! That guardian angel was probably tugging
my hand toward that carburetor heat control. Frank Sinatra Jr.

must have one of those Angels, too, because he came out of his kidnapping experience with only cramps from being locked in the trunk of a car!

Sometimes the day's work never seems to end. I had been flying all day and now the company wanted me to make a quick trip to Burbank. How quick could it be since the round-trip was about 800 miles over forbidding terrain in the winter night? Fortunately, a Private Pilot agreed to go with me if I would give him some 182 instruction time. He said he knew the route like the back of his hand and that I could sleep on the way home. On the late night return flight, the big moon overhead was flooding the backbone of the Sierras with its ghostly light. Snow banks and granite showed up in high relief to the black shadows. My pilot friend had been navigating quite well. Hell, all he had to do was follow the highway. The warm heater and drone of the engine knocked me out about Bishop. Suddenly I woke up with an inexplicable feeling of dread. I looked around to see granite and snow hiding the stars. A sharp glance at the altimeter showed us to be at over ten-thousand feet, and yet it wasn't nearly high enough. A granite wall partially hidden by shadow was coming at us fast. I grabbed the yoke and reversed course in a wingover. We flew out of that death trap, and I was shaken at the thought of what almost happened. My pilot helper missed the sign on the road clearly marked, "Dead end."

In the spring I trusted another pilot and learned yet another lesson. In late March of 1964, the coastal community of Crescent City suffered from a disastrous tidal wave. I flew an insurance adjuster and pilot to his damaged hometown of Crescent City to see if his parents were all right. When we arrived, it was still fogged in except for a few small holes. He insisted that he knew exactly where he was, and if I would dive through that hole where we could see a patch of ground, we'd get under it, "no sweat." I slowed my Cessna 180 to minimum speed with full flaps and pointed straight down. As I reached maximum flap speed, I dumped them and we hurtled toward that patch of ground. I rolled hard to the left and missed the giant redwood snag that stuck up well into the base of the fog. I looked at Dave with narrowed eyes and he said, "Gee, I don't remember that thing being there!"

It was December 21st and very cold at 18,500 feet. I had the door and right seat removed in my Cessna 180. There was a strong wind out of the west. The skydivers were dressed in bulky Santa Claus outfits which hindered them. One diver scrambled out on the step while holding onto the strut, and the other was poised to dive out the open door. The strut Santa kept gesturing toward the west and I applied more throttle, but the wind kept us suspended directly above the Tahoe Valley Airport. Finally, he gave up and let go and his co-Santa plunged into space right behind him. I was gasping due to lack of oxygen and the cold. I extended the flaps and began a spiral so I could watch the action. They were both extended into their maximum forward speed configuration. They said they could track speed of seventy mph over the ground in calm air. Well, there they were tracking at max, but still remaining directly over the airport. After a while, they both disappeared and I breathed through chattering teeth, "Oh my God, they froze to death and hammered in!" I imagined the two frozen stiff Santa's crashing through the roof of the bar, still in the maximum forward track position. The FAA would surely come for my license. The chutes popping open squashed my runaway imagination. But wait, they were drifting. That strong wind blew them miles away from the point where they had hoped to make a grand entrance. It was a long struggle back to civilization for them in waist deep snow.

One day that winter I taxied out in my '54 Cessna 180

behind electrical contractor George Stalls in his '53 Cessna 180. I had cleaned the snow off my aircraft, but he hadn't. I guess he figured the foot of snow on his wings and tail surfaces would just slide off. Down the runway he went, and incredibly the aircraft became airborne with the snow still hanging on! Suddenly, the right wing unloaded and gained lift. The 180 rolled hard to the left, only about twenty feet off the ground. Fortunately, the left wing shed its snow and George didn't crash. I watched in amazement as the red and white Cessna climbed out toward Lake Tahoe, still shedding snow from its elevators.

After an overnight visit to the grandparents, I made my first instrument departure from the valley, a feat hitherto only attempted by Herb. The base of the fog was about 400 feet above the ground. I took off in my Cessna 180 toward the west, then turned around in the small valley. Roaring back over the numbers at the end of runway six, I pulled up into the fog, climbing at the 180's Vy (Best Rate of Climb Speed). A few minutes later, I emerged into the brilliant sunshine. Lorraine Wardman thought that was pretty. It seemed that I could do no wrong in her eyes!

Jack was a popular barber at Harrah's Club. He could tell stories about all the stars he had tended to. I was teaching him and his teenaged daughter to fly. Jack decided to buy himself a Stinson sight unseen. We flew down to San Jose's Reid Hillview airport after work on a winter evening. In the darkness, I peered into the guts of this strange engine compartment with a flash-light to satisfy myself that nothing obvious was wrong. Jack flew the Bridgeford airplane while I ferried the strange Stinson back over the high Sierras through the dark and cold night. The next few weeks revealed so many things wrong with that plane that I felt fortunate to be alive. Never let someone push you into ferrying an unknown airplane anywhere after dark.

I was commissioned to ferry a pressurized Mooney Mustang

from Quincy to Tahoe. "No problem," I thought, "even though I've never flown one of the critters, they said the manual was in the airplane." Yeah, it was there, sorta. More accurately, it was all over the cockpit! The loose-leaf binder had come apart when someone had tossed it into the back seat and it had scattered everywhere! "Oh well," I sighed after poring over the pages, "I think I've covered everything." The run up was smooth and I had found the flap and gear controls, what more did I need? Rolling down the runway, the controls began to feel active and I rotated just before we started to dance. I knew the Mustang was ready to fly. Gear up, flaps up, first power reduction accomplished; turn left—urg! The controls felt frozen! There was a mountain in front of me; I *had* to turn left! "Let's see," I was thinking fast. "It's a goddamn Mooney, right, right?" Mooney's trademark was something called "PC," or Positive Control. It was a full time "wing leveler" autopilot that could be interrupted by a button on the yoke. I pressed the button and rolled into a graceful left bank.

A pilot from Hayward who was unfamiliar with some of the inner workings of the Twin Beech he was flying was unable to lower the landing gear. He was also almost out of gas and elected to belly the twin on the dirt edge of the runway before he ran out of fuel and lost power. (The emergency gear down procedure required pulling a circuit breaker.) The county dragged the Beech out of the way, but not far enough. I was going to deliver my Cessna 180 to Oakland for some avionics work and my student, Joe, was to chase me in my Luscombe and bring me back. Joe was running the engine up and I had my back to the runway. I was talking to Larry Sheeley about his second lesson. Suddenly Larry's eyes opened wide and he said, "I just saw an airplane kite off the runway." I spun around just in time to see my beautiful red and white Luscombe cartwheel across the Upper Truckee River and stop in a cloud of dust on the other side. Joe had caught a vicious crosswind gust and was spooked by the twin wrecked on the side of the runway. He'd tried to go around it on its downwind side, instead of into the wind, and had lost control. A few hours later, after we attended to his cuts and bruises, I suggested that he take a ride with me in the 180 so that he wouldn't be afraid to fly in the future. You know, like getting back on the horse. No problem; and away we went. The problem was I had no insurance on the Luscombe. Someone talked me into suing the county for negligence but I lost the money for that case, too. To add salt to the wounds, one night shortly after filing the suit, I flew a charter customer to Hayward and had to listen to the guy go on and on about the son-of-a-bitch that sued him because his Twin Beech had crashed next to the runway. He didn't know that the SOB was me. You would have thought that Larry Sheeley would have thought twice about continuing his flying lessons, but he went on.

It was winter and I had the itch to advance again. Sheeley and I flew my 180 to Fort Worth for another go around with Acme School of Aeronautics. Larry passed his Private, Commercial and Instrument writtens, while I passed my Advanced Ground Instructor, Instrument Ground Instructor and Airline Transport Rating written exams. On the first visit to the FAA to take the ATR written, they pointed out that I was a little short in the instrument flight category. I suddenly remembered that most of the trip to the Midwest was under the hood and I hadn't logged it yet.

It was spring of '64 and I developed my perennial itchy feet. I had gone to work for Capitol Motors in Carson City as the Company Pilot, expecting more pay and less work in the corporate environment. During this transition time, I sequestered myself at Oakland in pursuit of the prestigious Airline Transport Rating. My first ride with A. M. Thompson, ex-C-46 Captain for Alaska's Cordova Airlines, was not good. We sat in the airplane parked on the ramp and the 180's engine was making cool down sounds. Thompson sat silently for a moment. He then said, "*You* want an ATR?" It was humiliating. I had not flown instruments lately and had done an abysmal job and I was nervous. I just said, "Yes, and I'm not quitting."

One of the ATR flight test maneuvers the feds eventually threw out was the "canyon approach." This is an engine-destroying procedure that went like this: power off, full flaps. Hold your heading and maintain a maximum descent for a thousand feet, then level off at minimum controllable airspeed for one minute. Next, apply maximum continuous power, retract the flaps and execute a 180-degree double standard rate turn while climbing at Vx (maximum angle of climb airspeed). Level off and hold a heading after a thousand-foot climb. This procedure cost me a major overhaul with broken rings from the rapid heating and cooling, but Thompson and I went over and over it until I got it right. I was having trouble with the ILS (Instrument Landing System). The 180 had a light wing loading and reacted to every stray puff of wind. The localizer and glide slope needles were all over the place. The localizer needle tells you when you are right or left of the center line of the course created by the VHF beam transmitted from near the end of the runway. The glide slope needle indicates whether you are high or low in the glide path. The ILS also includes marker beacons at certain sites along the course that light up blue, amber, or white lights on the panel indicating your position. My tension continued to mount, and I was getting concerned about my native ability to do this thing at the ATR level. Thompson said, "Let's park this thing and go have a drink." I was only too happy to quit for the day. He sipped on some sort of drink while I downed several stiff ones. We had a very pleasant chat about everything but what we'd just been doing. After a while, he stood up, and I asked, "Same time tomorrow?" He replied, "No, now!" This is a terrible message to pass on, but I went up and nailed that ILS.

My instructors had trained me to depart Oakland, fly to Stockton and execute all the instrument approaches around that area. I could do it in my sleep. When it came time to take the ATR flight test out of Hayward, Pilot Examiner Virgil Simmons had me do a complicated ADF departure and fly places I'd never been. The only way I survived was to carefully sketch the route out before takeoff, and struggle mightily to maintain an awareness of where I was and where I was going. My 180 had the closed style of compass where the gyro remains rigid in space and the airplane turns around it. All you could see is what direction you were pointing, as opposed to an open faced compass. It made it especially difficult to visualize the unfamiliar ADF procedures. Somehow, I passed the check ride and went back to work.

Drum Plumbing bought an aircraft that I was familiar with, Herb Wardman's Cessna 180. Herb even gave me a commission for its sale. Herb now owned a six-place Cessna 205. The Drums had also purchased Capitol Motors, a Rambler dealer in Carson City. I flew as their company pilot, as well as selling and leasing cars. A lot of business was transacted via citizen's band radio. Naturally the 180 had to have one, even though illegal. Eric knew people *everywhere* and chattered with them constantly while enroute. When I wasn't flying, they put me out on the lot to sell cars. They showed me how to juggle interest rates to fit the customer's payment requirements, and I learned about kickbacks from the bank. I was assigned a brand new Rambler station wagon. For a while, I traveled with Roy, who showed me the ropes of selling and leasing. He said, "Use your imagination; we will provide anything you can lease or sell." In reality, he could *not* produce everything that I had sold as he had promised. I decided that being a car salesman was not my cup of tea, and I quit.

I saw Eric again after leaving Capitol Motors. After his company had gone bankrupt, he had hooked up with a salesman named Booker and was selling Champion Twin Lancers. The Lancer is a fabric-covered, twin engine, low-powered, non-feathering, cheap, flying trainer. "Yuck," I thought, "what are you into now, Eric?" Eventually, I learned where their association led. Eric and Booker had bought themselves a DC-3 and a DC-4 and started an airline in Cambodia. Eric checked himself out as captain. They got shot at, but managed to survive all dangers. After a couple of years they sold out just prior to the Cambodian currency devaluation. Eric came back with an Asian wife and bought a ranch in Idaho. Now that's landing on your feet!

The next job was driving a water wagon for a "gypo" logging outfit. I kind of enjoyed the job. It was pleasant and didn't require taking on any great responsibility. There were a few anxious moments though, when loaded logging trucks came "barrel assing" around blind curves, and I had to head for the ditch!

Later in the summer, I flew the Fire Season in Frank Nervino's "crosswind geared" Cessna 180. One day we flew for an exhausting eleven hours, 'round and 'round a huge fire, complete with air tankers and lead planes. In my idle time between fires, I had full access to his shop. Under Frank's supervision, I completely revamped my Cessna 180 and increased its value considerably, painting the airframe and overhauling the engine. I also learned about how *not* to break in a newly-overhauled engine. In those days the accepted method was to baby the new rebuild for a few hours. When you don't apply enough power, however, the rings won't seat properly with the cylinder walls and the engine will never stop burning oil; and it never did.

While flying for Frank, I met Don Beck who came over from

the Tahoe-Truckee airport to perform maintenance on his aircraft. Don had retired from the Air Force. He had flown P-51s and Spitfires in England and had retired, at his wife's insistence, after having done test pilot work in jets. He was now in real estate and was becoming a powerful figure on the Board of Directors of the Tahoe-Truckee Airport. One day, after hearing one of his exciting stories about Air Force flying, I lamented that by the time I had been set to go after military flight training I had too many children. They wouldn't take me. I had even tried to volunteer for Army Aviation. He replied haughtily, "Well, you made your choice."

On another day, Don was crying the blues because he missed the glories of Air Force flying. He said, "I could have been an astronaut."

He knew he'd been had when I replied, "Well, you made your choice!"

For years I found myself doodling on napkins, papers or some other medium. The subject was often an A-frame cabin facing south with lots of windows, a roof of sod, and a deck. The setting was Alaska, as I fantasized it. At the shore of the beautiful lake, my single-engine seaplane rocked gently, docked, catching the last rays of the setting sun. Arctic Char broke the surface of the water in search of insects. I was home after a glorious day of bush flying. Thinking that this scene might become a reality someday, I traveled down to the bay area and contracted with Commodore Aviation in Sausalito for my Single-engine Sea rating. The trainer was an 85 hp Piper Cub. I was run through my paces with cross wind, float-and-jump takeoffs, glassy water landings, and docking. Since the Cub had no starter, I learned to stand on the float and prop it from behind, and how to sneak up to the dock by turning the magnetos on and off. There was much to learn about wind, tendency to weathervane, and how to approach the dock upwind. For the flight test I had to fly across the bay, over the Bay Bridge, and then drop down low over the estuary leading to the Oakland Airport. It was thrilling and eerie to see the giant oceangoing ships so close from a slow-flying puddle jumper. FAA Inspector Leeney met me at the dock and the test went well. I was now ready for Alaska, or so I thought!

Chapter 6
Alaska

The family and I were back in Quincy. We were living in the house that I spent my first four years in with my dad and mom. It had been rented out until recently. It was winter and I was out of work, and bored. After the seaplane check ride, I dinged around here and there, working odd flight instructing jobs. I even went to Willows and got checked out in a Navy N-3-N by Lee Sherwood in anticipation of possibly going to work for him as a duster pilot for the spring rice season. I would have even taken a sawmill job if they had been hiring. "Anything," I wailed in desperation to Judy, "give me anything!" I'd sent resumes everywhere. Ring! Neil Bergt, Vice President of Interior Airways calling. "Copilot job, C-46, $700 a month, pay my own way up there? Damn right, I'll be there by the middle of January!" As I hung up, I wondered, what's a C-46 anyway?

The Pan American DC-8 was nearly empty except for a few servicemen plying cards way in the back. It was pitch black outside, but I could guess what was down there, mountains and cold. Upon arriving at Fairbanks, my watch said it was day, but a look out the window confirmed darkness with the town's lights shining fuzzily through the gloomy ice fog. I stepped out of the airliner wrapped in Grandpa's heavy sheepskin and leather coat and leather boots. The very air grabbed you, stinging any exposed skin, numbing your feet. At fifty below zero, each breath taken would hang in the air as ice fog until spring. My lungs ached as I inhaled, and my nose ran. "What am I doing in Fairbanks in February?" I wondered. "Even most birds head south." It was difficult to picture that idyllic scene of the Far North that I had been sketching in my doodling. People gathered in small groups on the street corners laughing and talking, their parkas casually hanging open at times. I was practically freezing to death and was grateful for the cheap hotel room with its steam heat. I learned quickly that leather was useless in these extreme temperatures. At a surplus store I bought a down jacket, a parka, and a pair of canvas mukluks with wool booties and inner soles. You needed mittens instead of gloves for outside work.

Morning came but the cab ride to Fairbanks International Airport was in the dark. The only one at the combination office, shop, and hangar was a friendly black guy named Louie who gestured toward the coffee. Powerful Herman Nelson heaters were chugging away in the background ducting warm air into the engines and cockpit of the biggest twin reciprocating-engined, tail dragger ever made. The exciting aircraft I would soon be flying. This relic may have flown "The Hump" over the Himalayas from India to Burma in WWII.

It wasn't long before I started meeting Interior Airways people and received first impressions: President Jim Magoffin in his native-made parka with Beechcraft Bonanzas sewn in. I wanted one! He was in his late forties. Dottie Magoffin had a bubbly personality and was good looking. She laughed about Jim's hunting dogs, one day saying with a slightly southern accent, "I think he loves those darn dogs more than me!" She flew a Cessna 180 on floats. Vice President Neil Bergt was stern, quick-witted, and fast talking. For him, new copilots were a pain in the ass until they learned a few things.

I was in proud possession of an Airline Transport Rating and no higher pilot rating was to be had. I couldn't be more self assured that I would be among the best with a little training. The personnel of Interior Airways soon blasted that idea all to hell. After a month or so with people who really knew what they were doing, I was humbled. There was no funny business. No dashing young men with their scarves flying in the breeze (it was too cold for that anyhow). Profit and survival were their motives. As an introduction to the company, Jim Magoffin said to me, "I love to fly and I don't ask anyone to do anything I wouldn't do." It wasn't until later I found out what *that* meant!

With no car to drive, getting to work was an adventure in itself. To catch a ride, I walked a half mile through the sub zero darkness of morning on the southern edge of Fairbanks next to a wilderness of muskeg. There were packs of wild dogs roaming the city that reportedly had attacked children. You would see them occasionally slinking around a corner. Wolves howled in the distance. It was so cold I had a sore throat from dryness. You could toss a glass of water up and it would freeze before it hit the ground. All automobiles had to have circulating heaters and be plugged in if you had the slightest hope of starting them. The Company Instructor and first Captain, Buz Dyer picked me up every morning. My first flight was with Buz to Prudhoe Bay, on the Arctic Ocean a little south of the Eskimo village of Barrow. We were supplying geophysical crews who were searching for oil. They needed equipment and sundries. The cargo was unloaded via a metal slide. I was busy down on the ice runway stacking boxes of dynamite. The wind-chill was minus fifty degrees Fahrenheit. My nose ran and froze. Buz yelled at me to get back in the airplane and I wondered why. I thought I was pretty toughened up after enduring the cold Sierra Nevada winters. As my nose, forehead, and fingers thawed out painfully I didn't wonder anymore why he called me in. I wore scars on my forehead for a lot of years from that frostbite.

I ran into Bob Shacht, who had been an air tanker pilot. I remember the first advice he gave me when I was staying at Charlie Jenson's strip in Sacramento, "Stay out of aviation!" He had married a native woman and settled in. I also met a copilot who had flown with Bob and who was quite a character himself. He worked when he damn well felt like it. One day he and Bob were landing a C-82 at Ton, an uphill gravel strip on the North Slope. The C-82 is a twin-engined, twin-boomed transport aircraft with the same two-thousand horsepower on each wing as the C-46. They got "behind the power curve" on final approach and crashed short of the strip. (Behind the power curve means that the aircraft will sink in a nose high attitude in spite of the application of full power and altitude must be lost to gain speed.) The left propeller struck the ground, twisted off the engine, and cart wheeled over the cockpit, chopping and whacking as it went. The copilot said that the only injury was when he released his seat belt, turned to run toward the rear of the aircraft, and clobbered his face on a bulkhead. It was said that Bob Schact was the only transport pilot in Alaska who didn't have an Instrument Rating. I asked Jim Magoffin if he didn't think that was strange and wouldn't the feds get him? He replied with his usual contempt for government regulation, "He seems to get around pretty good anyway." Unfortunately, Bob finally used up all the lives he had been granted, crashing for good in a small twin-engined Piper.

Don't you know that, while hanging around the coffee pot, the Alaska stories grow and grow. Like the "true" one where they were transporting a bunch of cattle in the back of a C-82. A herder was required to keep the cattle away from the open loading area. (For some unknown reason they had to fly with the clam shell doors off.) There was a chain across the back for "safety." The pilot had to pull up to slow the plane when he encountered a thunderstorm, and out the open back end slid cattle, herder and all! (Maybe this is where the joke about "I'm glad cows don't fly" originated.) It turned out that this story really was true, but it occurred in South America. A brief note of the incident was entered into the aircraft's log book. Another "true" tale unfolded with the pilot climbing out of the Arctic Coast enroute to Fairbanks. One engine had to be feathered right in the middle of the mountains, in bad weather, and there was no turning back. The Brooks Range consists of pointed peaks around the eight-thousand-foot level, connected by razor sharp ridges. The ridges are divided by deep canyons, usually shrouded in weather. This C-82 was capable of maintaining an altitude of only five-hundred feet below the level of most of the peaks. When the pilot was asked what his survival strategy had been he replied, "I flew straight ahead until I couldn't stand it anymore and then I changed course!"

Training time, jeez, I already had an ATR and twenty-five years of living on this planet. What more could they want? Buz Dyer made sure I found out that there was plenty more. He had been run out of Korea, escaping with his life. He had owned and operated a small airline consisting of a couple of C-46s until the government decided to "nationalize" it.

Another new copilot, Dick Magnisun from Florida, and I crawled around the innards of the big ex-military Curtiss. These were modified to meet "T Category" standards. The drag-producing cowl flaps were replaced by more efficient residual heat doors. When the gear lever was placed in the up position (assuming you were airborne and the squat switches weren't activated), the hydraulic pressure was isolated to the gear system to speed up the retracting process. During preflight inspections, you always checked the right outboard elevator hinge because it was the focal point of tonal resonance; that's where all the vibration ended up. Also, the submerged fuel pump vents must be checked for dripping fuel. If they dripped more than six drops a minute, they had to be replaced. Buz said they would blow up.

The engines were Pratt and Whitney R-2800s, capable of producing 2,000 horsepower. The superchargers had been locked in low blower because the altitudes we flew were not of Himalayan heights, and the density altitudes were low. For an example of heavy, cold air effects on the engines, according to the power charts, a takeoff from sea level at standard temperature requires a manifold pressure of fifty-two inches. At minus fifty degrees Fahrenheit, forty-eight inches produces the same result, and anymore would result in an over boost with disastrous consequences for the engine. Also, when high blower was to be used, it must be periodically exercised and results in a more complex and expensive maintenance procedure.

One copilot was much more experienced than we, and a native of Alaska. He was Joe Felder, an Eskimo-Indian, originally from Kotzebue. He had been captain of his own fishing boat at the age of twelve. Although at the time he was being trained as a copilot, he often rode along on Interior's Arctic Coast flights because he had the uncanny ability to tell frozen land from ice flows. We would sometimes fly for long distances at altitudes of only 100 feet above sea level, as indicated by the altimeter, while in the clouds or a whiteout. We would break out just for a few moments and he could tell you approximately where you were!

The link trainer was a nightmare. All I was required to do was make a ninety degree ADF intercept and proceed to the station. I had done this maneuver many times before, but I now had a mental block. I really thought I would washout because of this stupid thing. I remember Neil giving me my first takeoff at Sagwon, and being surprised when I had no trouble keeping the aircraft straight down the gravel runway. Referring to the link trainer thing, he said, "We thought you'd have trouble flying the airplane, not with navigation!" The first time Dick Magnisun got his chance to taxi the big transport aircraft, he ended up spinning around on Fairbanks International and taking out a couple of runway lights. The difference in our pilot skills was that I had accumulated a lot of tail wheel experience while he had mostly flown Cessna 150s. One night I sat up in bed, and the ADF intercept procedure became clear in my mind. The next morning I marched into the link trainer room and did that maneuver and more with no problem; funny how the mind works.

There came more flying and on-the-job training, especially in the area of loading and unloading. The copilots worked shoulder-to-shoulder with the loaders. The 48,000 pound aircraft can take about 12,000 pounds of cargo. We usually made two trips to the North Slope a day. That meant that 48,000 pounds passed through my hands personally. I was getting into shape. The forklift would roll a fifty-five gallon drum of oil into the cargo bay. Sometimes, I would roll it uphill all the way to the front of the cargo hold and stand it up all by my 160-pound self. Once the barrels were in place they were roped off with a trucker's hitch. When we loaded our twenty-four cases of dynamite, the Airport Authority required us to complete that activity out at the end of the runway. At least there they didn't see us sneaking propane bottles and blasting caps into the belly cargo hold.

We had to learn about load manifests, weight and balance, customer billing. There were two sets of documents with respect to loading, one for the FAA, and one for the customers, and they didn't often match. FAA Inspector Walser would ramp check us, and occasionally forced us to unload the Gooney Bird (DC-3/C-47) which could haul 8,000 pounds of cargo, and put it into the bigger C-46. There was usually fuel in the aircraft's auxiliary tanks that didn't show up on any documents. At the Sagwon bush camp, it would be sucked out and stored in underground tanks for use in the smaller company bush planes. This bush operation was a "can do" operation that "did do," in spite of constant government interference. They knew exactly what they could get away with in the physical universe. Interior Airways had a great record when it came to deliveries v. fatalities; deliveries, 100 percent; fatalities, zero.

Actually, luck played a part, like the time when Buz Dyer and Ed Brenner tried to land a C-46 at night on a North Slope ice runway built for small aircraft. They thought they were somewhere else. The Curtiss slid off the end of the ice and up onto land, ripping the landing gear off. Spring and summer passed and the water thawed and froze again. Mechanics were flown in with supplies to sustain them at the lonely spot. Finally, in the brief light of an early spring day the transport flew again with its landing gear bolted down and replacement propellers whirling. It was a cold, dark trip for mechanic Roger Burns and Jim Magoffin over the razor-sharp ridges of the Brooks Range and beyond to the Fairbanks repair shop.

I was with Captain Dyer, and our destination lay just ahead in the whiteness, with the sky blending into the ground. There they were, the barrels marking the ice runway were just barely visible through the blowing snow. The Captain banked the big plane over the strip to get a better look. "Before landing check list," he growled. "Watch it," I was thinking, "I don't like the looks of this; it's a dangerous whiteout." I knew that the minute those barrels disappeared behind us, we would be on instruments only a hundred feet off the ground. The loaded C-46 was in a slow turn to the left. "Gear down and locked, indicator lights OK, hydraulic pressure up," I called out. I could feel the satisfying bump as the landing gear locked into place. The barrels came back into sight on the left; the captain squinted through his thick bifocals. "Flaps one quarter," I repeated his command as the gauge moved to the desired setting. As we turned onto base leg, only one barrel was visible off the left wing. "Tough to judge altitude," I was thinking. "Look at that altimeter, too damned low!" I wanted to yell. I repeated my feelings aloud.

"Shaddup and read the airspeed!" Dyer barked back. We were on final now. The wind was picking up; sheets of blowing snow momentarily obscured the runway.

"One hundred knots, ninety knots, eighty." In my mind I screamed, "God damn it, can't you see we're too low?" I just barely quelled the impulse to grab the controls, an action tantamount to mutiny. "Pull up," I shouted. Thud! The wheels struck a snow drift in front of the runway. Throttles opened, engines roared, and we lurched forward, staggering, as the R-2800 engines strained to drag us forward. The bluish tint of the ice and a couple of marking barrels flashed into view as we materialized out of the blinding, swirling snow. At the very beginning of the runway, we fell three points onto the ice strip, the prop blades chopping the sub-zero air at the speed of sound. The heavy aircraft hit the eighteen-foot thick ice and veered one way, then the other. Buz desperately worked rudders and throttles to straighten out. I retracted the flaps and hung on, eyes wide as we rushed first for one snow bank, then the other. We shuddered to a stop, the abused engines idling. Fortunately, the braking action at these frigid temperatures was good. In the spring the ice melts from the top down, and controlling the big tail dragger can get really hairy. Except for the shaking of the engines, there was silence. The Captain was staring straight ahead, his grizzled countenance showing no emotion. I unstrapped my seat belt, thinking dark thoughts, and stepped through the cockpit door into the cargo area. While climbing back through the cargo ropes, I tripped as Captain Buz came awake and turned the aircraft around, swinging the tail into the unloading position. One engine rumbled, then the other, for directional control. I opened the cargo doors and worked the slide into position for the unloading of our cargo, some thirty-five, fifty-five-gallon drums of aviation gasoline. The engines wheezed to a stop leaving the sound of my heavy breathing and the shriek of the Arctic wind. I thought unhappily, "This is the second time this has happened."

Captain Ed Brenner lost his ATR one night, but retained his life. He took off from Fort Yukon in an Interior C-82 that was experiencing electrical problems. He reasoned that Fairbanks and the shop were only a stone's throw away. Just over the hill turned out to be longer than he had anticipated. An important factor was that the C-82 is largely dependent upon electrical power to operate its systems. The twin-boomed cargo carrier plunged into the storm raging in the darkness. The lights of Fort Yukon vanished as the aircraft pitched and rolled in the turbulence. The usual commands were issued to the copilot, "Gear up, OOPS!" Everything went black. Desperate hands flew around the cockpit to locate the flashlight. Without light, the crew had no horizon, no instrument panel, and no control. Finally, the flashlight came on and illuminated the important flight instruments. A quick aim of light out the window revealed that the landing gear was still ready for landing, not flying. Not only that, the radios were useless without electrical power. They could not navigate to Fairbanks or return to Fort Yukon. At least the vacuum driven gyro instruments indicated that the aircraft was still right-side up. After troubleshooting, there was apparently no way to fix the massive electrical failure. Brenner elected to circle and hoped to remain within the Yukon Valley that was flat and frozen. Meanwhile, ice was forming on everything. The shape of the wing was altered by the ice and vital lift was being lost. More and more power was required to remain airborne. An engine heated up and finally had to be feathered. ("Feathered" means that the propeller blades are turned knife edged into the wind to reduce drag, and the engine stops.) While covered with heavy ice, landing gear locked down creating drag, and with only one engine running, the inevitable landing occurred. The transport contacted the surface and slid through snow and small trees, and finally came to rest in a surprisingly undamaged condition. Captain Brenner opened the window and heard a popping sound in the darkness. It was the generator located in the nearby village of Beaver!

Once during a combined maintenance and training flight Jim Magoffin and a mechanic were crawling around in the belly of the C-46 checking the hydraulics. Jim suggested that I practice stalls or something. My idea of stalls was different from theirs. The airplane bucked and pitched and I lowered the nose thinking that I had done well when Jim came crawling out of the belly shouting, "My God, man, I didn't mean FULL stalls!"

Buz must have forgotten that he hadn't taught me how to accomplish a "manual aural null" orientation. As a result, I flunked the first check ride with FAA Check Pilot, Walser. It didn't make for warm relations between student and instructor. Our aircraft was equipped with dual ADF's (Automatic Direction Finders automatically point to low/medium frequency broadcast stations). Pilots were supposed to be able to operate them the old-fashioned way by manually moving the loop, finding the minimum reception, and then solving the 180-degree ambiguity; that is, determining whether the station is to your right or left. That's why the automatic feature in ADF makes a pilot's work load easier. The dual needles were mounted on top of each other in a huge round glass-faced instrument.

FEATHER RIVER BULLETIN
April, 1965
I wrote a letter back home to Grandpa and Grandma which they allowed to be published in the newspaper; *"In the average day the ground I cover is equivalent to two trips to Los Angeles. (Most of the length of California.) Cargo hauling is mostly supplies to geophysical camps which are searching for oil north of the Brooks Range. I help load and unload cargo, which is 12,000 pounds of dynamite, gasoline, food, oil-drilling equipment, and instruments. Sometimes even dog teams. I fly the transport category aircraft to main camps where the smaller bush planes distribute the goods to the smaller camps.*

My day begins at 6:00 a.m. with the checking of the weather at Point Barrow, Olicktok, Barter Island, Flaxman Island, Fort Yukon, Bettles, and so on. The C-46 is preflighted, the load tied down and the pre-heaters removed. We then taxi out for takeoff. Many days, the entire flight is made under instrument conditions (in the clouds). On clear days, you can see a lot of snow as we pass over low-lying hills, populated by moose and aspen trees, but very few people. Next, the Yukon Valley with more trees, lakes, rivers, and streams than I ever dreamed existed. About there, you cross the Arctic Circle. As we continue flying north, you can see the Brooks Range with millions of razorback white spires on which bighorn sheep and countless caribou eke out a meager living from frozen grass buried under powder snow. In every valley there are countless streams and small lakes, trees too, on the southern slopes. Emerging from the Brooks Range onto the flat tundra, I breathe a little easier. Many of the large rivers out here freeze to the bottom and the water flows over the top of the ice and appears as a dainty turquoise. The tundra also presents difficulties. When I first saw the landscape, I didn't see how it was possible to navigate with no apparent landmarks, especially when with an overcast the sky blends with the ground in a whiteout requiring the use of instruments to know which way is up. As I become more experienced each day, I find that the Arctic has more subtle landmarks than in other areas; frozen rivers showing up as a slightly different texture of snow broken by low-lying bluffs. Another difficulty is telling the ocean from land. We land on the frozen ocean all the time.

There is an epidemic of rabies on the tundra now and there have been several instances of foxes attacking human beings lately. There are also moose, wolves, wolverine, and polar bear out here.

Fairbanks is kind of a wild and woolly, dirty frontier town. We haul the roughnecks to town from the North Slope about once a month. Out there are no trees, no women and no booze. Worse yet, there is no water for bathing. They arrive in town in waves; wild eyed with fists full of money they couldn't spend up north. A few days later we fly them back, worn out and broke. A person willing to rough it and take a chance has an opportunity to make a lot of money. A family man must work a little harder, as the cost of living is high. As for my part, I couldn't have found anything closer to Paradise in reference to the flying machines that will be available to me in time, such as a C-46 right now. Later, Cessna 180s, Twin Beeches, Twin Bonanzas, Widgeons, C82s and Beavers on wheels, skis and floats."

One time, during a flight, I was serving sandwiches to passengers which included an engineer for one of the big oil companies. I asked him if they were finding any oil. He replied in a Houston drawl, "That's more or less a secret—mostly more." I learned another secret from Jim Magoffin on that flight, too. When you are serving passengers their lunch, wait until they are practically starving and they will think that catered lunch was better than Thanksgiving dinner with all the trimmings!

The Fairbanks of 1965 was an interesting place. The bars were connected back-to-back. You could enter one type of bar from the street, exit the back door and emerge into a totally different bar with different decor. One establishment might feature loud western music, while the next one would have a quiet piano bar. Whether it was the Western Club or the Wonder Bar, it was wild and woolly. At 3:00 a.m. the town's blue laws shut down the drinking and dancing, so the bands would simply fold up and move just outside of the city limits and party on!

I hadn't had a day off in months, so I felt like blowing off a little steam. After foolishly following the bands around all one night, I barely managed to get to work in time to start loading the first of our two flights to the North Slope. My body was dragging with exhaustion and I was probably still under the influence, so "Buz, the cruel" required me to fly hands on the whole damn day. This day, as was often the case, the ground vanished and wasn't seen again for hours until we descended into the North Slope with the Brooks Range behind us. The ADF needle twitched and an attempt was made to contact a DEW (Distant Early Warning) line station for weather. Sometimes we were successful and sometimes we relied solely on that twitching needle. The station at Sagwon was weak, but you could use that to your advantage since it helped to determine your distance from it.

Buz said to descend, so I did, trying carefully not to exceed 180 mph. The airplane was old and there were DEW line rules and speed limits. Briefly, we emerged out of the clouds into a kind of horizontal, tunnel-like hole that revealed a small mountainous area in the Brooks Range. You couldn't see the top or the bottom of the sloping mountain, and suddenly it felt like we were in a steep bank. I quickly confirmed our wings' level attitude with the ship's artificial horizon and turn/bank indicator instruments. Extreme fatigue wasn't helping my perceptual powers. I decided not to party that hard anymore.

Early one morning, I found out that it was possible to close the huge loading doors without removing the heavy stairs. When we arrived at our destination, the stairs were missing. I hoped that the heavy metal things crashed in a vacant lot rather than on someone's house. The copilot always got the blame, but the Pilot-In-Command shouldered the ultimate responsibility. At any rate, there are quite a few air stairs out there somewhere between Fairbanks and the Arctic Coast.

The creation of the ice runways for Interior Airways was contracted to Frontier Sand and Gravel whose owner had a distinct gravely voice. I was in the room when the discussion turned to the problem of a lack of cat skinners. I piped up and said that my friend, Tom Shannon, would love to come to the North Slope and skin cat for him. Gravel voice growled, "He'll pay his own way up from the lower forty-eight, and he better be a skinner!" I happened to know that Tom was desperately trying to break into the heavy equipment game, so I gave him a call and asked him to drive my Rambler station wagon up from California.

Tom had been working for the Frontier outfit for several weeks when one day he stepped on to the Arctic ice from his still-running Cat to move a barrel several yards away. When he looked up, a giant white wolf stood nearby looking him over with interest. Tom stepped back and the wolf stepped forward. Tom backed up into his Caterpillar and revved up the engine. The wolf bounded away.

Tom was indeed a skinner and stayed on the job plowing ice strips for a month before returning to Fairbanks, looking forward to his first bath. On the North Slope in the winter, liquid water is a precious commodity. The snow is so dry that it is necessary to melt many fifty-five-gallon barrels full of it to get any drinking water. On the way to my house to get that precious shower we had a quick drink and Tom threw down some money on the last chance for the famous Tanana River breakup drawing. Luck o' the Irish, and damned if he didn't win!

Some of the airstrips we used were especially interesting, such as "Liz A," located north of Cape Lisborne and in sight of Russia when visibility was good. A loaded C-46 relied on a twenty-knot head wind to land on the runway that was otherwise too short with cliffs at each end. The wind was so reliable that Interior Airways never had to divert to another strip due to lack of it. Although this region was infamous for its awful weather, this particular day it was beautiful with the blue-green water contrasting against the brilliant white ice flows. The yellow-geen of the tundra stood out against remaining areas of snow. We landed and unloaded the cargo without incident. It seemed that you always unexpectedly learned something. I learned that tundra was easier to walk on in the winter. With the snow gone the grass grows up in tall clumps; and if you're not careful you could break a leg stepping between them.

Larry McNutt became known as the "Arctic Fox!" He was another classmate from Quincy looking for a job. I got him hired as a loader. Larry was a powerful twenty-five-year-old, and was an excellent loader. We took Larry on his first ride to the Arctic to help with the unloading. By this time, my body had toughened to the rigors of extreme cold. No more freezing, but I was still impressed when I saw a guy at Sagwon unload propane bottles with his bare hands at thirty degrees below zero. Unloading cargo, I was dressed casually, my parka hanging open, just as I had seen the Fairbanks residents do the first day off the plane. Larry was crying like a baby, complaining of freezing hands and feet. Larry was nobody's wimp and had decided that the North Slope wasn't going to get the best of him. He signed on as the company cook at Sagwon, claiming that he'd been a cook in the Army. The job paid better, too, but I doubt that Larry had ever been a cook. However, he was very imaginative and did come up with more-or-less edible grub. Larry was also blind as a bat. Without his glasses he couldn't see diddly, but he could hear just fine. One dark Arctic morning he heard something crashing around in his kitchen. He sprang through the kitchen door, clad only in skivvies and wielding a pistol. His glasses were still in the bedroom. Crash, bash, smash! A huge form was just barely discernible in the darkness and "Mr. Magoo" pulled the trigger. It turned out to be a very large grizzly bear, and one lucky shot from the small caliber weapon killed the dangerous critter instantly. Larry proudly showed me a photo of him in his underpants standing with one foot on the vanquished animal, the frozen wilderness in the background. The photo was entitled, "The Arctic Fox."

Allegedly to become a sourdough you were required to make love to an indigenous female, piss in the Yukon River, and wrestle a grizzly bear. Thinking of Larry beginning to fulfill the so-called sourdough requirements in the grizzly bear incident conjured up the hilarious memory of my trying to pee in the relief tube in the tail of the C-46 while it was bucking up and down. I was alternately floating or being jammed to the floor. The relief tube simply exits out of the belly of the airplane, and we just happened to be over the Yukon River and only two more requirements to go. I wondered if it was OK to skip the bear part?

There were reasons other than peeing for the copilot to be in the cargo section. Barrels of gasoline being transported almost always leaked, and it was often necessary to remove the window designed as an escape hatch to let the fumes out. The copilot used a shepherd's hook to make sure the tail wheel gear was locked over-center when retracted or extended (especially extended).

Sagwon was located near the Sagavanirktok River, and in the shade of the Franklin Bluffs. The gravel runway ran at an angle toward them. The company had installed a low-powered, non-directional beacon to allow instrument approaches into the area. Buz and I were circling the bluffs and watching the clouds move in. Only the bluff end of the runway was visible. Orders were, "Gear and flaps down full." As I complied with the instructions, Buz pulled the power off and down we went. "Wow!" What a ride! We made it in just as the strip became engulfed in clouds.

There was certainly no doubt about Buz's experience. One time about twenty minutes out of Fairbanks, in solid clouds and still climbing, he suddenly did a one-eighty and told me to get clearance back into Fairbanks International. I asked why and he replied, "Didn't you see that left engine lose an inch of manifold pressure?" I replied in the negative, and he continued ever the instructor, "We just lost a jug!"

Returning to the Sagwon story, Magoffin (sometimes called Diamond Jim, but not to his face) was circling overhead in the C-47. The visibility on the ground was almost nil, possibly fifty yards. Everyone assumed that Jim would have to go elsewhere. Not so! I was standing by the cook shack near the bluff end of the runway when the loaded transport materialized out of the fog, tail still in the air. I could see Magoffin intently peering forward. He was going way too fast and would surely smash up at the end of the strip. No sounds were heard after the Gooney Bird vanished into the fog. The men were silent while the Arctic wind continued its endless shriek in the background. A couple of minutes went by and, to everyone's amazement, the seemingly-doomed airplane taxied up no worse for wear. I asked the copilot how Jim managed to stop that airplane without wrecking it. His shaky reply was, "I don't know."

Jim gave Neil good advice to take the inland route when he flew a bunch of partying Rotarians to a bash in Juneau. He ignored Magoffin and took the more scenic coastal route. The C-47 and Neil managed a hair-raising flight down the inland passage with the aircraft icing heavily. Rotarians were flying around in the back and throwing up all over each other because of the severe turbulence. No one gave a damn about the scenery!

Everyone makes mistakes. One of the Widgeon pilots was wandering around on the Arctic Coast lost in a storm. He called into Sagwon in a panic. "I've lost my ADF, what shall I do?" He had forgotten that it was a simple matter to call the DEW line station and get a radar vector to somewhere. Getting lost was easy, however. In this part of the world, the compass variation is over 100 degrees. In the winter it is mostly dark, and sudden weather changes are common.

We were equipped with a huge rack containing a single sideband HF radio capable of contacting our headquarters at Fairbanks International from the North slope. You could even do a phone patch to Anchorage. Every once in a while those radios would threaten to burn up and would have to be shut off. One time I was in the office and Jim asked me to make a phone patch to Anchorage. I said that I didn't know that I was supposed to know how to do that. "Listen," Jim said with flashing eyes, "pilots are people who know things." That was a lesson I never forgot!

I was riding third seat observing a training session with Joe Felder in the left seat and Buz Dyer in the right. Right after takeoff, the right engine quit and I noticed the low fuel warning light on. The boost pump was nearby. The other guys were fooling around with the fuel selectors, but I knew that boost pump needed to be on so I reached forward to snap it up, but my shoulder harness held me back. I released the straps and tried again, but collided with Buz's hand. He flipped the switch on and the engine surged into life. After things settled down, Buz turned and glowered at me saying, "Don't ever do that again!"

Just trying to help doesn't always get it for a copilot. In training, Buz would always put his hand on mine to indicate that the position of the throttles were advanced to takeoff power. This allowed me to look outside instead of watching the gauges. (Remember, it's a tail dragger.) When I tried the same procedure with Neil, he flung my hand aside and said sharply, "Just tap my hand." Logically enough, he didn't want any restrictions in case he had to do some fancy throttle jockeying.

I learned that just riding on Interior Airways flights could be a scary experience. I was sitting in the back with a bunch of drill rig equipment. Neil was training another copilot. On takeoff from Olicktok (on the Arctic Coast east of Barrow), the heavy bits suddenly slid back, drastically changing the ship's balance. To avoid getting my legs crushed, I lifted my feet out of the way of the sliding cargo. The cockpit door flew open to reveal Neil desperately spinning the trim wheel to maintain pitch control since so much weight had slid backward. Another time, I was riding in the Interior C-47, and on its takeoff roll from Fairbanks an engine went blam! The takeoff was aborted and the big tail dragger swerved back and forth. After regaining control, the pilot taxied back to the shop. The problem turned out to be a magneto.

In springtime, while unloading cargo on the North Slope and at Fort Yukon, one can expect to be attacked by mosquitoes. You must drown yourself in repellent and keep the engines running to produce a breeze. In wintertime, at fifty below zero, you often keep the engines running to ensure that you won't be stuck there permanently with solid chunks of frozen oil for lubrication. There were the hot problems and the cold problems, and sometimes one followed another. Every so often the C-46's two 50,000 BTU heaters would overheat and have to be shut down. Within minutes, it would be fifty degrees below zero in the cockpit. Can't you picture the transport crashing, its pilots frozen to the controls? You didn't get too far from your parka and mukluks.

Spring weather was miserable in Fairbanks, windy and wet. Enroute to the Arctic Coast, the clouds became more well-defined and full of ice. In the extreme cold temperatures, the world gradually disappeared as you flew into the milky white. The spring clouds made the world vanish instantly.

I got up extra early and rode as copilot on the scheduled flight to Clear Air Force Base. The scheduled flights were conducted only during the river ice breakup, on all other occasions people traveled over the ice or on the water to their destination. I was hoping to check out in the aircraft being used for the flights. The Twin Beech was extremely difficult to taxi from the copilot position, because from the right seat you could use just rudders and differential engine power for directional control. Brakes were a must, and none were installed on that side. We hit some of the worst turbulence I have ever experienced near Clear AFB; the sturdy Twin Beech pitched around, it's experienced captain barely able to control it.

The Twin Beech aircraft were in use extensively in Alaska. One day, after landing on Barter Island, Neil pointed out to me the wreckage of one whose pilot had logged more "Twin Bitch" time than any pilot in Alaska. He had been an expert at zero-zero landings. (The zeroes refer to no forward visibility, and that the base of the clouds is right on the ground.) His skill wasn't enough that time, and he died in the crash. From Barter Island we flew south a way to Lake Schrader. It was a gorgeous spring day, so we did a little low-level sightseeing on the way, spotting migrating caribou, moose, and sheep. Neil banked the C-46 over Lake Schrader, nestled in the higher and most spectacular areas of the Brooks Range. The nearly-vertical dark rocks contrasted with the brilliant white snow. The scenery flashed by at close range as we circled. Some of the lake had melted and was a brilliant blue. I wondered about landing a heavy transport on a melting lake, but it turned out to be fine as long as you didn't get too close to the edge of the ice. When I opened the cargo doors, I was treated to a fabulous sight, the ice, the snow, the mountains and lake creating a picture. It was warm and not a hint of wind. The hard part was unloading. We had to struggle off the ice and onto land with our cache of "case gas" for the Bureau of Land Management. Case gas consists of two five-gallon cans of avgas in a crate. It is awkward to handle. We struggled on as the incredibly bright sun moved across the sky and the Arctic char hit the lake's mirror surface near the edges.

Jim and I were taking off from Fairbanks with lumber destined for Fort Yukon. We loaded it from front to back and top to bottom. We were way over weight. Just as the wheels were retracting up into their wells, a tremendous vibration commenced. One engine was surging, alternately producing thrust, then drag. It was impossible to tell by rudder pressures or instruments which engine was malfunctioning because of the vibration and asymmetrical drag. I picked up the microphone and Jim knocked it out of my hand. I asked what was wrong and he yelled back over the noise, "Don't declare an emergency!" Evidently he didn't want to attract federal attention. I yelled back, "I was going to request clearance to return for landing." He signaled OK to that.

The mighty Yukon River began to move. Millions of lakes in the Yukon Valley had thawed and had taken on every conceivable shape and every color in the rainbow. Everything moved except Captain Brenner's C-82 which sat quietly at the end of its skid marks.

Summer in the Arctic produces clouds of insects driving

every mammal crazy. The geophysical crews couldn't get around on the tundra and the ice runways were now water. I was thrilled to be chosen to fly a Beaver on floats in the Arctic for the summer. That was a measure of how much confidence the company had in me to navigate and to fly safely on my own. I was doubly disappointed when Interior failed to get the contract. Business for the bush charter outfit was lean. Ground personnel and pilots were laid off all around me. One day, when I was removing paint from a Super Widgeon instead of flying, I decided to take a leave of absence and work in California for the summer. Neil said, "Too bad you're leaving, just when I was getting to like you!" Before I left, and just in case Interior Airways folded, I took a check ride in a Cessna 185 with Richard Wien, of the comparative giant Wien Alaska Airlines next door. Richard was perfectly happy with my flying in spite of my mistaking a waterway for a road on a simulated forced landing. He said he'd be pleased to put me on their bush routes next fall, if I wished. Some time after I left, the history was surprising; it was Interior Airways, not Wien Alaska Airlines, that persevered! Joe Felder also left Interior Airways and started his own company with small aircraft. I was saddened by the news that his Beechcraft Bonanza was found in the northern base of the Brooks Range, the body of the pilot scattered by animals. Within two years after I left the company, under the direction of Jim Magoffin, Interior Airways became the largest C-130 operator in the world. They hauled people and cargo for the Alaskan pipeline and, later, cargo all over the world. I could have kicked myself for leaving!

Chapter 7
Chico

Tom Shannon, the family and I, left Fairbanks at the end of June of '65, my cat skinner buddy and I taking turns driving down the endless Alcan Highway. We found ourselves slipping and sliding over the slimy Steam Boat Pass muck, stopping occasionally to stretch, but no motel stops. We once took a break to soak in a hot spring in the Yukon. All of us, including the two malamute husky pups, Mukluk and Tok, managed the trip mostly without complaint. Tom took Tok and we kept Mukluk.

We landed in Chico during a heat wave. A real body slam! My blood still thick from extreme cold, I could hardly endure the blazing heat of the Sacramento Valley, but "ya gotta make a living." To prove that I was good enough to work for Chico Aviation Services, Junior Stuart required me to do a slow roll in the company's Cherokee 180. When we returned with oil all over the airplane, he was satisfied. Ed Stuart Senior had recently had his nonscheduled airline certificate jerked by the FAA because of maintenance violations. He had been operating DC-4s and DC-6s that were now parked idly on the ramp. The experience left him a bitter person. I once politely agreed with an FAA

Inspector's viewpoint on an innocent enough subject. Ed Senior pulled me aside saying, "Don't ever let me catch you agreeing with those bastards again—or you can go find another job!" We had other disagreements. I was preparing a veterinarian for his Private Pilot flight test and found him unwilling to listen to anything I had to say. In my opinion, his attitude stunk, and I told Ed Senior so. He said that if I didn't recommend him for a flight test, I could find another job! I was hungry, so I complied, and the headstrong vet passed his test. Within a year or so, he flew his family into a Midwest predawn thunderstorm in his Comanche. They were all killed.

I had occasion to meet Dave Miller, the crook! Dave (not Steve's brother) was an aircraft broker out of Bakersfield who wanted my Cessna 180, and I needed money. Ever since the overhaul at Nervino's where I had babied the engine during its break-in period, it had never stopped burning oil. I was anxious to unload it. He said he'd give me eight thousand for the fancy chronometer installed in the panel and fifty dollars for the airplane. "Ho, ho, what a card," I thought, and I fell for his likable con man's pitch. I flew the 180 to Bakersfield on Friday and he wrote me a check about 4:30 in the afternoon. Of course I called the bank to see if the check was good, but by Monday it wasn't good. Dave claimed that he had sold the 180 to a third party who had already wrecked it (supposedly). Meanwhile, the money was sent south to a company that subsequently had gone bankrupt. Dave promised to pay me back, and asked me to take a Stinson 108 and a Luscombe T-8F Observer as partial payment. I took the Stinson but otherwise wanted money. This was foolish, of course, because I never saw a dime and that T-8F would have been worth a lot today.

While I was doing business with Dave Miller, we flew from Bakersfield to Los Angeles with him giving me dual instruction in a Cessna 310. We dropped that aircraft off and picked up a Skylane and returned to the San Joaquin Valley. Descending in a northerly direction from the Grapevine, we noticed that a solid overcast had formed with flat-tops at around five thousand feet. It looked innocent enough, so we asked for an ILS into Meadows Field. The sun was just going down and it got really dark in the clouds. Ice began forming rapidly and I began to hear a high whining sound. The back seat passenger looked out the rear window and shouted back that the VOR rabbit ears antenna was carrying heavy ice and was vibrating. I came down final approach to BFL carrying about three quarters throttle and hit the runway solidly. As we taxied up to the ramp ice was shedding; I looked at the forward facing surfaces and saw that it was clear ice. I'm sure glad we were descending instead of climbing. I learned *a couple* of good lessons while dealing with Mr. Dave Miller.

Al Sos was the monarch of Chico Ranchero Airport, and had been in business there as a mechanic and instructor for years. I was instructing a student in Stuart's Cherokee 140 and practicing landings at Ranchero. At the end of the runway, Al had a fence about three feet high with the crossbars just barely tacked on. We were too low on final approach, and I asked the student to add power. The carburetor heat was on. The student just stared straight ahead, apparently frozen at the controls. So at the last moment, I pushed the throttle in. Nothing happened; and I flared out with the bottom of the tires grazing the crossbar that splintered. I pulled up to a parking spot and was going to apologize to Al for busting his fence. He was viewing the splinters and stroking his chin saying, "That was a pretty expensive fence, Johnny." My heart sunk and I said, "Al, all I've got is $8.42 in my pocket. Here, take it." He took it. God knows how many times that Chicken Little fence had been clobbered, but it's probably been a constant source of revenue. I also learned why the 140 manual doesn't call for carburetor heat on a normal landing.

In April of '71 I took a non-air taxi flight to Sac Metro for Dr. Hewitt in a Cherokee Six, N4060R. The mission this afternoon was to fly a plane load of nurses to a meeting. We arrived at Sacramento Metro at dusk. Just before I was cleared to land, the primary and backup electrical power for the entire airport failed— the tower communications were operating on battery power only. I requested clearance to land, but the request was denied and the tower suggested that I divert to Sacramento Executive Airport. I replied, "Negative, my passengers are being met here, and besides, I can see just fine." The tower, somewhat taken aback, insisted, "You *can't* land here, the power is out, there are no lights, it is officially dark!" Feeling stubborn despite the rapidly failing twilight, I persisted, "The reg's require lights on the aircraft only, not on the ground facility." Silence, then the tower responded, "We'll check the regulations." After a while, they came back and admitted, "I guess we can't stop you from landing." I replied smugly, "Thank you." By this time it was pitch black and there was a stiff crosswind on runway three-four, but I had the strip in my landing light and landed. The hard part was yet to come— finding the terminal. After much slow taxiing and cautious, sweeping turns to illuminate areas from side-to-side, I finally made it to the General Aviation Terminal, guided mostly by memory. The tower was letting me stew in my own juices.

All of us in my party had to hold hands inside the terminal because it, too, was pitch black. I don't really remember how they found their ride, but it was interesting waiting in that busy terminal with only a few emergency battery operated lights to provide the vaguest illumination. It was a pickpocket's paradise! Fortunately, the power was restored before time to leave. I never did find out why the emergency backup power failed, too. I'm glad I wasn't on an instrument approach in a storm!

I was cooling my heels in Ranchero one day and was watching a gang of pilots attempting to start an Aeronca. They were going through all sorts of fancy procedures, you know, turning the prop backwards, switch off, switch on, throttle closed, throttle open. It was obvious to me the little Aeronca was flooded. They were going to give up in disgust, and I asked them if I might try. They looked at me as if I was stupid, but "Sure, go ahead." I instructed the pilot, "Mags hot, full throttle, brakes on," and proceeded to pull the prop through smartly about four times before it roared into life. Of course, I was the hero of the hour. Heck, you need a little ego-booster once in a while!

By August of 1965 I had recommended my pal, Larry Sheeley from Lake Tahoe, for his Commercial flight test. As you recall, he had passed his Private, Commercial and Instrument written examinations when he and I visited Acme School of Aeronautics. He had already managed to finish up the Private Pilot Certificate and Instrument Rating. I had been talking to Alma Hinds at H & H Flying Service, who was a Designated Pilot Examiner, and decided to send him to her for the flight test. Ego-boosters are often followed by ego-busters. She wouldn't fly with him because the gas boy or some other person at his various cross-country destinations, had not signed off his log book. There was not, nor has there ever been, a rule requiring such a thing. I had to send him elsewhere for the test!

I felt that I had been in Chico long enough. Although I had gained many friends, it was time to move on. In spite of my little clash with Alma, she wanted me to come and fly for her. What the hell, it was sixty miles closer to Alaska, should I decide to go back!

Chapter 8
H & H

Benton Airpark was located on the west side of Redding. Like Meta Pool, Alma Hinds ruled her 2,400-foot-long roost with an iron hand. Before I arrived, I had already heard stories of how she had served as a Ferry Command pilot in the war, and how she got burned in a Cessna 180 accident in Idaho. She had tried, unsuccessfully, to pull a passenger out of the burning aircraft. She'd been there and done it all.

Benton was an interesting place for Alma to stay in business. It was like landing on the deck of a ship; short, with a cliff at each end. The worst enemies weren't always the crosswinds and crashes though, sometimes it was the City of Redding who owned the airport. Due to a squabble with the City, Alma had to run her business out of a hotel downtown. By the time I arrived from Chico, however, the situation was in hand. I stepped into my job with enthusiasm, flying from early till late. Although I worked hard, Dave Hinds considered me a brash young man. He later told Al, the shop foreman, that I was the kind of guy that if I were to get my hands on a few thousand dollars, I would go into competition with them. In a way he was very prophetic!

For the students, I introduced the breadboard concept. After their first solo, I immortalized them by wood burning their names on a breadboard and indicating the date of solo. The board hung on the wall in the office like an honor roll. A similar honor roll had adorned the wall at the Airport Bar at Tahoe.

I developed the knack of sleeping for a half hour and waking refreshed and recharged, able to continue on. When I wasn't flying I was helping with maintenance. It was in the shop where I met Al Ewald, and we struck up a great friendship. Al was Alma's Shop Foreman. He was impressed with me, because, unlike the other pilots, I would help out in the shop when not otherwise busy. I didn't get any extra money added onto my salary for it either. I mentioned that I had taken my Private and Commercial flight tests from Mary Barr in Susanville. Al remarked how impressed he was with her. He told of how one day she flew in with her Cessna 180. She noticed that it wasn't positioned just right in its parking spot and she simply lifted the tail up and dropped it over where she wanted it. That was a feat of strength that a lot of men couldn't handle.

Al told me of the time when he was a new A & P mechanic at Palm Springs in the early 60s. He had lured his future bride, Jerry Ann, into a Cessna 182 for their first date. He really didn't know how to fly the critter so Jerry held the manual while Al flew. Al and I both had Triumph motorcycles and we enjoyed riding together on summer evenings. Sometimes our rides would take us to the Blue Boar Bar, where we would play shuffleboard and arm wrestle the locals for drinks. Fights were common. On one occasion, a big Indian guy whipped another fellow senseless, but was soon begging for mercy as the victim's girlfriend wailed the tough guy to his knees with her spiked-heeled shoe! There were a lot of fun places to party in Redding. We would take our wives dancing at Ricardo's, where the Chessmen would play regularly. The lead singer was gifted with a fabulous voice, and when he belted out the words to the song, "ABC, 1,2,3," all the minors scurried for the exits. That was the secret warning that Alcoholic Beverage Control agents were in the building!

H & H Flying Service contracted to fly other companies' airplanes for them. The Clair Hill Corporation did survey work and owned a Cessna 205 (which is just like a 206 but with less horsepower). Their field workers often worked in isolated places like Orleans, located on the Klamath River in the California Coast Range. The tiny community of Orleans had an air strip, sorta', which didn't show up on any aeronautical chart. It ran right up a hill into woods that rapidly changed into a steep mountainside. Headed the other way for takeoff, it ran straight down toward the Klamath river. In the summer, the air gets downright hot and rough in that deep canyon. The whole area has an aura of violence. In winter and spring floods, the river high-water mark is a hundred feet above the summer level, and the steep slopes slide down and constantly wipe out the winding little highway. The mountainsides are heavily wooded and brushy, and burn furiously in the summer. Sworn statements by local folk indicate that "Bigfoot" lurks here and was sighted. Bigfoot, they thought, could be related to the extinct man-like Gigantipithicus. I asked a couple of local Indians about this and one said, "If I can make you believe that, I can make you believe anything!" In this area, the Indians fight the Whites, the Fish and Gamer's fight the local poachers, and the dope-growers fight everybody. We just try to fly in and out, and mind our own business.

The CLM field personnel (they were affectionately known as the Clair Hill Mob by some of the personnel at H & H) didn't know the meaning of weight and balance control. Seconds after I plopped that 205 into the nine-hundred-foot-long strip and had turned around at the upper end in position for takeoff, the hot, dirty and thirsty crew had the doors open. They were throwing their packs and equipment in. None of them wanted to be on the **second** flight to Redding. They didn't seem to realize the consequences of overloading. If you didn't physically block them, they would keep on throwing things in the airplane. I usually had to pull a few thirty-pound packs out before attempting a takeoff. I ran the IO-470 Continental engine up until the two-hundred-and-sixty horses were straining before I lifted my toes off the rudder tops to release the brakes. As we hurdled down the bumpy hill, I knew we'd make it; but if the engine faltered in the least, we would crash in the river or into the tall trees. After liftoff, a hard right turn was required to avoid the canyon wall on the opposite side of the river. Next, it was necessary to stagger downstream four or five winding miles before enough altitude could be gained to begin edging eastward toward our destination. The Clair Hill Company got bigger and became CH2M Hill, and soon had a fleet of aircraft ranging from a Cessna 185 to a twin-engined Aztec. Their chief pilot, John Shackford, could tell many harrowing tales of aviation adventure, and yet he eventually retired from his corporate career with a squeaky clean accident record. One of his earliest feats was to land and take off a leased DC-3 on the 2,400-foot-long Benton Airpark on a regular basis. After retirement, however, he did a clown act for the Redding Air Show in a Piper Cub and spun the thing into the ground. Miraculously, he walked away from the crash. His spouse said, "No more air shows, John," but soon he was back at it again!

A man with a broken neck had to be rushed to the hospital in Medford and there was a decision to be made. Do I sneak under the weather, through the Cascade canyons and severe turbulence? I could see the poor guy's head banging around, even with a nurse to hold him secure. Do I file IFR through the thunderstorms? Never! The Cessna 206 is hardy, but stronger airplanes than that have been torn apart in the air. Could we go on top? According to weather and pilot reports, we could. I should have known better. The instability of the air increased, and by the time I was abeam the fourteen-thousand-foot Mt. Shasta, the clouds were topping twenty-thousand feet, and then some. Only a little way to go, so I filed IFR. It was a smooth flight for a while in the clouds with only minimal wing ice building. Interestingly, the heated pitot tube had no switch on the panel to turn it on, so I soon lost my airspeed indication with ice blocking its intake.

I heard airline captains asking air traffic control for permission to deviate from their assigned routes. They were detecting heavy thunderstorm cells on their airborne radar. So far I was not experiencing anything traumatic. The patient was resting comfortably, the nurse holding his head still. ATC called and asked me if I was all right. At that moment, it cleared for a split second and I saw the angry face of nature on the rampage directly ahead. We were instantly engulfed by the raging cumulonimbus cloud. Initially, it was like running into a big snow ball. I asked center to stand by. Suddenly we were all hanging from our belts in severe turbulence with jolts so hard you couldn't read the instruments. Outside, it suddenly turned dark with a greenish hue and I struggled to get my panel lights on. The 206 was quickly becoming a cake of ice, heavy stuff that was building at a breathtaking rate. We were virtually falling out of twelve-thousand feet. I called center and told them as much as we slammed our way through ten thousand. I had difficulty hanging onto the microphone. Lightning flashed, and I exercised the propeller to loosen up the ice that flew off, crashing into the wings. (I pulled the prop control all the way out to a "big bite" position and then back into climb rpm, thereby flexing the blades.) The leading edges of the wings were protected by five inches of ice, so chunks of ice flying off the prop weren't going to dent them, besides, who gives a damn right now!

I asked the controller to say our radar position and was told twenty-five miles south of Medford. Despite having every control pushed to maximum available power, we continued up and down, mostly down, and onward toward the lower terrain that I knew lay ahead. Suddenly we burst out of a clearly-defined cumulonimbus cloud into clear blue air flooded with sunshine. The ice flew off rapidly and the 206 began to fly like it was supposed to again! The airport was straight ahead. Had we been many more miles south when all this happened, no doubt we would have hit the ground.

Sometimes, for one reason or another, one has done some stupid things. One time a patient needs to get to the hospital, or the next time your boss says, "If you can't do it I'll get someone who can, and will." In the mid '60s era of air taxi you could do anything you were big enough or stupid enough, or hungry enough to do. Unlimited single-engine IFR was perfectly legal.

Here I go off again in the 206 for a routine instrument flight. Redding, to Hayfork, to Medford, drop off the passenger, and get back for a heavy schedule tomorrow. Damn! There goes the airspeed again. I thought that switch-thing got fixed. No problem, just light ice and I have an artificial horizon. Easy instrument approach into Medford, I dropped off my passenger and was directed to take off from the opposite direction than I had landed. It was turning dark as I penetrated the low overcast. "Let's see," I tried to think fast, "I thought the VOR was to my left, but no, I'm turned around because I took off in the opposite direction." Turning right instead of left had to be the hardest thing I had done in my life to date. "I think the clearance was a shuttle climb on the VOR to nine, though, no—eleven thousand," I thought I was sure, but I really wasn't. Shoulda written it down, but I was in a hurry. It was snowing now and pitch dark as approach control pierced my thoughts, "What is your altitude now?" (Altitude encoders were not in vogue for light aircraft.) I replied very professionally, "Holding at eleven-thousand, sir." He shouted back, "Get outta there *now*, get down to your assigned altitude of nine-thousand. You are occupying the same airspace as an F-27!" (An F-27 is a Folkker twin-engine turboprop used by West Coast Airlines.) I dove out of that deadly situation and held at my proper altitude, cursing my stupidity, and vowing not to hurry so much. After a while, he cleared me back up to a higher altitude and allowed me to join the V495 Airway to Fort Jones VOR and then V23 to Redding.

There was a powerful wind out of the southeast. I was holding a ninety-degree heading in order to make good a one-hundred-and-fifty-seven degree course along Victor Airway 495. This heading pointed me right at the 14,162-foot-high Mt. Shasta, a sleeping volcano. Who knows, with my luck it'll blow tonight! Well, the wind was blowing all right. It was blowing right across that rugged terrain and beating the hell out of me. I looked outside with my flashlight and quickly turned it off as the blizzard conditions coming at me gave me vertigo. I thought, "At least it's not sticking." I looked at that one measly little VOR receiver and decided that I didn't want to trust my life to it. I asked the center for a higher altitude. A little while later I asked for a still higher altitude and the center replied, "Son, you can climb as high as you want, there's nobody else flying tonight!" The first things I saw after launching from Medford were the lights of Shasta Dam. I descended, trying to keep them in sight. Finally plopping down on the 2,400 foot-long Benton Airpark runway, I heaved a sigh of relief and thought, "Cheated death, again!" I shouldn't have been so smug; it rained and blew so hard on the way home I was nearly washed off the road.

I got a call from Leo Purington, who operated the Redding Sky Ranch, one of the three working airports in the Redding area. He said, "Johnny, I've got a Mooney owner who would like to get home to Cottage Grove up in Oregon." He paused and continued, "How would you like to take the job?" I told Leo that yes, I did have some time off today, "But let me check the weather and I'll call you back." Somehow, I didn't trust Leo in this matter. If it had been a good deal, he would have taken the flight himself. The weather report was as dangerous as I had ever heard. It included conditions of heavy ice, precipitation, and turbulence. I'm certain that if I had attempted such a feat in a little Mooney, that I would have been converted to a statistic. I called back and said, "Leo, why don't you take this little flight?"

He replied, "Hell man, do you think I'm crazy!" I attributed his phone call to sick FBO humor.

Alma asked me one day if I was interested in taking a charter to Minnesota in the Cessna 310, a gorgeous twin-engined airplane I had been wanting to fly. I enthusiastically nodded yes saying, "That would be great. Would you mind riding around the pattern with me once—it's been a couple of years since I've flown a 310." (I thought that was a reasonable thing to do.) She replied, "That's okay, Bud will take it." I was disappointed. No, crushed! Another day Alma asked me if I wanted to take a charter to Oregon in Television Channel 7R's company 336 (a Twin Cessna Skymaster with fixed landing gear). I said, "Sure," and that was all. I had never flown an in-line, center-thrust twin in my life. I was getting paid by the hour and I wasn't going to lose this one. I sneaked over to the twin-boomed thing and looked over the operating manual before we took off. I forgot to extend the flaps for takeoff, as the manual required, and almost dragged the booms on the runway. Fortunately, no one noticed. Wouldn't you know it, all of Oregon was socked in and my first landing was down to minimums at

Medford. It was a long day with many IFR takeoffs and landings. I stayed in the airplane diligently studying the manual, while the executives were off doing business.

Channel 7R Television had two fixed-gear Skymasters. My assignment was to fly company people to Monterey. I was IFR when the wheels lifted off Benton's tarmac. Shortly thereafter, the left fuel gauge started to sink slowly toward the empty mark, and there was moisture streaming over the top of the cowling. "Probably from the humid air in the clouds," I thought, "but who knows for sure?" As a precautionary measure, I shot an instrument approach into Oakland and had the fuel tanks topped off. Sure enough, it was a flaky fuel gauge, but it could have been fuel pouring out somewhere. I didn't relish staggering around IFR with a heavy load on one engine because of fuel starvation, or an engine fire because of a fuel leak.

Off to Monterey, in solid IFR, but the approach was a piece of cake. I waited most of the day for the folks to get their work done, and about dusk we were off again into the clouds. My assignment was to track outbound on an ADF bearing from the Locator Middle Marker to join V87 and proceed northwest. After I crossed the Middle Marker, I turned northerly on course. Suddenly, the ADF needle started going around in circles. I informed departure control of the problem. As per further instructions, I just held my heading and intercepted the Victor airway.

While enroute, the weather in Redding and Red Bluff had dropped to below IFR minimums, and one of the VHF navcoms had joined the ADF on vacation. Intersections were more work to determine with only one VOR. (It is necessary to determine a line of position from two different stations, which is easier to do with two VOR receivers.) The front, with its evil weather, had arrived. I elected to put down in Marysville and wait. A couple of hours later Redding Municipal Airport was above minimums and off we went again. My passengers and I were all tired of this long day. A few miles north of Red Bluff, the storm shook us like a big dog shakin' a little dog and I gritted my teeth and hung on, crashing through the storm. I was maintaining nine-thousand feet in a holding pattern over Redding VOR, located in the center of the Redding Muni. It was raining like hell. Finally the clearance came to descend. I throttled back a little but the thrust warning lights in the throttle handles began to flicker. This was distracting because it was supposed to mean that the engines were losing power. Everything else looked okay, engine sounds, manifold and oil pressures, cylinder head temperatures, so I ignored the lights and concentrated on the descent. We were directly over the airport anyway; if I had to dead stick the son-of-a-bitch, then I would! We emerged from the clouds in a driving rainstorm and rough air. I was exhausted, but at least I knew that we would not have landing gear problems (since the gear was bolted down). We flew on over to Benton and landed uneventfully. The very next flight that airplane took, the rear prop flew off and nicked a boom on the way by! Apparently, **everything** didn't go wrong while I was flying the junker!

Bud had a couple of drinks too many the night before and was battling an awful hangover. He was taking off from Wichepec, a hairy, one-way strip that plunges off into the Klamath River, not far from Orleans. He couldn't understand why the center line thrust Skymaster wasn't accelerating normally. Just before they took the plunge off the cliff and into the river, he figured it out. He had simply forgotten to start the hidden rear engine. With a few expert manipulations by the desperate pilot, the rear engine roared into life just as they reached the deadly end of the strip, saving them from certain disaster.

Al yawned mightily when a call came through shortly after midnight, which was shortly after he got to bed, and shortly after the last cocktail. Chet Derby needed a copilot to fly the company Skylane on an IFR ambulance mission to the foggy coastal town of Eureka. The two pilots launched into the night in the single-engine aircraft and managed the instrument approach into Eureka without incident. Waiting for them in the dark were two very appreciative black guys, one obviously injured. They said they had someone waiting for them in Redding. As it turned out, the check bounced and the two guys that Chet and Al picked up had just robbed a convenience store, and one of them was suffering from a gun shot. Alma was not happy about the bad check when she returned.

I was Al's instructor throughout his attainment of the Commercial Certificate and Instrument Rating. He put the certificates to work right away. As Alma's shop superintendent, Al was also the mechanic-in-charge for U. S. Plywood Corporation's aircraft. They liked him to go along on some flights as copilot/mechanic. Al and Charlie Holcolm were good friends. Charlie had worked for Alma until he sold himself, as a pilot and Alma's Cessna 195 to U. S. Plywood. Soon Plywood became the larger Champion Paper, which required bigger and faster airplanes. The company moved up through a Cessna 310, an Aero Commander 680, a Grand Commander, a Beech King Air turboprop and finally the turboprop-powered Merlin. Al rotated around as copilot/mechanic and gained excellent flying experiences. Charlie insisted on operating the big airplanes out of the tiny Benton Airpark instead of the large, better-equipped Redding Municipal Airport because Charlie and Alma were buddies. He wanted to purchase his maintenance and fuel from her even though each landing in the bigger aircraft must be accomplished with great care. A famous local saying was coined one day when the Merlin lifted off, the wheels were retracting into their flying slots and the nose was pointed toward Ketchikan. Charlie looked over at his copilot, Al, and asked, "Did you check the weather?"

Al replied, "No, I thought you did."

Charlie laughed and uttered the timeless corporate pilot saying, "What the hell, we've gotta' go anyway!"

One night Al and I extended Hank's life. He had been drinking all day and that evening it was time to fly his Cessna 205 home to Sacramento. He couldn't get it started and Al and I were called upon to help him. We helped all right, we made certain that the damn thing wouldn't start so that he was forced to stay the night. Miraculously, it started just fine the next day. Unfortunately, Hank scattered himself near Sacramento a few years later; yep, he'd been drinking.

One afternoon at Benton I heard the Comanche 400 call in for a landing advisory. It was an aircraft that we recognized as from the area and had been recently purchased. I noticed that he was landing too fast. He began to porpoise and started a go around, but pulled the gear up too soon, and the three-bladed propeller began chopping into the asphalt. Suddenly, the 400 horsepower let out a terrible roar as the propeller tips bent forward, thereby reducing the overall diameter of the prop blades. He kept going toward the north, the engine winding up to an incredible rpm because of the damaged propeller. After staggering over the cliff at the end of the runway, he came around for another attempt, throttle wide open. There was no attempt to lower the gear. He bellied it in and skidded to a stop. One mad spouse stepped out on the wing and shouted, "I'll never fly with you again, you son-of-a-bitch!" The word was out that this pilot's ego wouldn't let him take the time to get a proper checkout. I am reminded of another belly-in at Benton, where the Unicom operator was trying to warn the pilot of a twin Piper that his gear wasn't extended. He replied, "I can't hear you with all this noise in the cockpit." The offending noise was the landing gear warning horn blowing, loudly proclaiming that the wheels were still tucked inside the wing even though the throttles were retarded in preparation for landing!

One day, after a visit with Grandpa and Grandma, Judy and I took off in our Stinson from Quincy with the kids in the back and a heavy load of baggage. (The Stinson had been acquired from the crook, Dave Miller, from Bakersfield.) We were on the downhill runway with a quartering tail wind. Judy was at the controls. As the tail struggled to come up, we suddenly headed for the left side of the runway. Judy struggled with the heavy controls. I yelled, "Right rudder!" She yelled back, "It's to the floor!" I stomped my foot down, and indeed, it was to the floor. I grabbed the control yoke, and with the aileron, I lowered the right wing to within an inch of the runway, ready to drag it if necessary. We skated along like that until the rudder finally became effective enough to control direction, and the heavy aircraft finally struggled into the air. Upon arriving at Benton Field, I investigated and, as I suspected, the problem had been that we were very tail-heavy. I punched a hole in the fabric and water from a heavy rain the night before ran out for an hour!

Instructors tend to have strong feelings about what kind of airplane you should or shouldn't start a student out in. It depends a lot on their own background. Claude McAlexander was a person pushing sixty when he decided to buy a Cessna 180, and begin his flight training from scratch. He lived in the tiny town of Hayfork nestled deep in the rugged coast range. I ferried the airplane back and forth to give him lessons. Claude did fine in spite of the naysayers who considered the 180 way too much airplane for a beginner. Less determined people would be over-whelmed by some of the 180's cantankerous characteristics, such as poor forward visibility and the need for aggressive tail dragger directional steering. Also, there were complications like constant speed propeller control, cowl flaps and a powerful horizontal stabilizer trim mechanism. Claude eventually parked the aircraft on his ranch and flew out of a 600-foot-long dirt strip. One day I was ferrying Claude's 180 to Hayfork for a lesson. Downwind for landing, the propeller failed and ran away, turning up to 3,500 rpm's. (The propeller had gone into a flat pitch where no amount of rpm's would provide thrust.) Had this occurred farther out I would have surely crashed in rough terrain.

I had been with H & H Flying Service for less than a year and I was already getting itchy feet. Just for speculation, I wrote to Air Asia requesting information about pilot jobs, and received a reply from Air America! They gave me a toll free number to call, which I did at once. It was H. H. Dawson, in Washington D. C., who said that I would make a lot of tax-free money, but that I would be flying behind enemy lines most of the time. He went on to mention and that some pilots had been found beheaded. "Furthermore," he rasped, "if you go down, we'll disavow any knowledge of your existence." He went on to explain that the family could live in Bangkok.

I replied, "Yeah, but what kind of aircraft do I get to fly!" The next week the contract arrived; I signed and was on my way out to drop it in the mail box, when I hesitated. "Wait a minute," I thought, "here I have this fine young family, and I'm about to take them to a war zone." I tore up the contract and headed up the hill, back to work at Benton Field, dreaming about the things that could have been.

I was getting interested in college again, and began taking night courses. Much to my surprise, I was pulling straight A's. One course that didn't go too well was the Instrument Ground School taught at Shasta Junior College by J. C. Hamaker. J. C.

was a long time friend of Al's and ran the Airframe and Powerplant School at Shasta JC. We thought we'd take the course for a lark, and an easy "A." It was pretty boring since I was up there doing what he was talking about. I even missed a class and lost marks while out in the night navigating around in a wild storm. Al and I usually had a pitcher of beer or two before attending class in order to work up our enthusiasm. I ended up with an F because I missed the final exam due to work requirements. I pleaded with J.C. to let me take a make-up test, because I really did want to go on and get my Associate of Arts Degree. He finally relented, and I learned not to take things for granted.

J.C. flew for Alma and others during the summer; one day he found himself transporting Mary Barr to Burbank in a twin. They were flying into IMC (Instrument Meteorological Conditions). Awhile back Mary Barr had accepted a position with the U. S. Forest Service and had moved away from her flying business in Susanville. She had moved up fast and was now the chief check pilot for the organization. She made her authority clear when she told J.C. that she would act as a check airman on this flight. They plunged into the watery mist over the Tehapachi transverse range, and down into the complicated airspace of the L. A. Basin. Soon after that harrowing experience, J. C. decided to retire from commercial flying and concentrate on navigating his boat around Whiskeytown Lake.

In the spring of '66, Herb Wardman's Cessna 205 entered my life again. The mission was to fly the six-seater back to Wichita to pick up a new Cessna for Alma. The factory had also promised to replace the radio gear Herb had been having trouble with. I was in the right seat giving Bill Boyer dual instruction. Earl Weaver, another commercial pilot, rode in the back. Near Reno, the IO-470 Continental engine began to run rough and we landed. All the spark plugs were fouled and the mechanic replaced them. I called and reported to Herb, who was thoroughly disgusted. He assumed that I must be running the damned engine too rich. (Too much fuel flow leaves lead and carbon on the spark plugs.) I assured him that was not the case. We made good time heading east with the wind howling at our tail. At Austin, we smelled smoke and landed. At six-thousand feet the powerful wind was also cold, but we uncowled the engine anyway and found nothing visibly wrong in there. Up and away again until, while passing over a deep canyon just east of Austin, the engine began popping and snorting. I went through the familiar routine: boost pump-ON, switch fuel tanks, mixture as required for best power. We were sucked down into a rocky abyss by the strong west wind just after passing over the lee side of the drop off. I headed for the east side hoping for an updraft. There was only death waiting down in those rocks at the bottom of the canyon. The ridge-soaring technique paid off. I was barely able to slip over the east edge of the canyon and stagger over to, and follow, the highway heading straight downwind for Eureka. We were still hanging in the air with the highway right under us so why not go for it? I instructed the other pilots to keep close track of our location on the chart to be sure no mountains had to be climbed between here and there. The airport was a welcome sight, except for one little thing: the powerful wind was howling across the north-south strip; and if I was to miss, it would be curtains for sure! There was simply not enough power available to manage a go around. Just down the road I spotted a pasture oriented directly into the wind. A large metal boiler once used in the mines lay discarded at the east end. The other side of the pasture connected with the highway that ran from Eureka to Elko. I dove over the boiler and onto the grass, ending with a successful off-airport arrival. The engine ran fine at an idle, so I taxied the 205 down the road and back to the airport. Bill and Earl struggled to lift the wings over the snow stakes that lined each side of the road. We tied the bird down securely and hitched a ride to town. Eventually, the factory report revealed that a cam follower had disintegrated and had been digested by the engine. The factory ended up replacing the engine as well as the radios! It happened to be St. Patrick's day and the mining town of Eureka was going wild. I ended up banging on an old guitar in a bar all night and the drinks were on the house.

The Ewalds and the Moores went on a motorcycle ride. We decided to take a mountain back road to Trinity Lake. Al waved a map in front of my face, proudly proclaiming, "I've got a map!" The implication was that we wouldn't get lost. We didn't get lost; but it turned out to be a little early in the spring to be riding our motorcycles on the north side of that mountain. We should have brought skis instead. It was almost dark when the four of us staggered out of the snowy road on to dry pavement. We were soaking wet and exhausted after pushing the two heavy bikes downhill in the deep snow. Once committed to the slope it was impossible to turn around! After that, everybody booed when Al announced, "I've got a map!"

The H & H Flying Service employees often relaxed at the local pizza parlor with a couple of cold beers after work. Bill Holland, a high school classmate, was working there as an apprentice mechanic, and was usually short of money. This evening he won everyone's affection by showing up at the table with a large pitcher of beer instead of an empty wallet. Picture him standing at a table where thirsty pilots and mechanics sat. He's holding a frosty pitcher of beer and asking, "May I sit down?"

In May, Alma sold my services as a pilot to my old friend, Denny Mansell, a physician and student pilot from Quincy who wanted to take a tour in his 200 horsepower Beechcraft Musketeer III. Our wives were to go along, and he was covering all expenses. Such a deal! We all piled in and took off. Eight hours in the air brought us to El Paso, where you had to join a club to get a drink. Membership was supposed to be of lifetime duration. Join we did, and enjoyed a scrumptious steak dinner as well.

At the end of another long day of flying, we arrived in New Orleans for more expensive drinking and dining. Denny and his wife never ordered less than a quart of the expensive Lancer's wine. My string tie didn't pass inspection at "The Court of the Two Sisters," and the maitre d' sent me trotting back to our Bourbon Street hotel room for a real tie. After some real Roquefort dressing and a huge gourmet dinner, it was out on the town for round after round of drinks. We finally ended up at our hotel where all-female bands played on and on. In fact, the bands would change personnel right in the middle of a song without missing a note or a beat. We had an exceptionally beautiful and scantily clad Cajun dancing on our table. Judy didn't want me to look, but I took an upwardly pointing flash picture!

Off to Memphis. Why Memphis? I think because Johnny Rivers' song about Memphis was popular at the time. We had to pull up short because a tornado was in the process of destroying twenty-six homes, and the clouds were turning green at our present location. We spotted a strip that didn't appear on the chart and noticed that there was an airplane on the end of it. I made an approach but pulled up when I could see that the strip was too short for the heavy Musketeer and the airplane on the ground was not parked, it was wrecked. We circled back and landed at a duster strip I had spotted earlier near Coldwater, Mississippi. This dirt strip was also short, but useable. The folks invited us to join them in their trailer as the wind and rain hit. As the trailer rocked and the lightning flashed, I hoped that the hail would find something else to ruin besides the Musketeer. I was grateful for these folks' Mississippi hospitality. The storm passed quickly and due to the shortness of the strip I had to ferry the Mansells and Judy to Memphis in two loads. There were still puddles of water left by the intense storm, but now the sky was bright and sunny. There was one thing Denny didn't count on in Memphis—the town was dry. No booze, period! Always inventive, he requested extra brandy on his cherries jubilee. That night it poured and flashed lightning all night. We were happy to have a hotel room. We could have easily been stuck in that trailer, or worse.

We were off again to Kansas City, and then to Denny's hometown of Omaha. We visited the racetrack and were wined and dined. Frankly, Judy and I were sick of food and drink and wanted to just take a walk, have a hamburger and watch TV, but no. Denny's Italian childhood friend, who looked like the mobster stereotype in his black pinstripe suit, insisted that we try his restaurant. We were forced to endure more fine wine and endless huge trays heaped with gourmet Italian food.

Heading west to Cheyenne and Ogdon was slow going into the wind. Denny was anxious to get home, so I believed the weather reporter at Ogdon that the thunderstorms had dissipated along our route tonight. I filed IFR to Reno. Dissipating would have been a better word. There were mostly downdrafts and rain. Picture the little Musketeer loaded to the eyeballs and just barely able to maintain altitude, constantly on the edge of a stall in the downdrafts. Frightening, when you thought of those cruel, rocky ridges that would rise into our path if we were unable to hang on to our altitude.

I enjoyed following the careers of my friends. Steve "Stevie Wonder" Miller was a gas boy at H & H Flying Service, and an entrepreneur. With his meager wages he managed to buy apartments, with almost nothing down, and get tenants to pay the payments. Meanwhile, the property was gaining in value by leaps and bounds. Not only that, Stevie put on great parties. His was *the* place to go. When you bellied up to his bar, you had to use a doily for your drink. That was being polite so that the almost-naked girl lying on the bar posing as the counter wouldn't get cold shocked when you rested your drink. Steve had a couple of brothers: Paul, who was very artistic and considered a genius by some, a hippie and a low achiever by others. I liked him a lot. Equally as interesting was Dave (no relation to Dave Miller, the crook), a purchasing agent whose main job was to purchase pro-phylactics (rubbers) for use in checking internal eye pressure for glaucoma. The company owned a Skylane and Dave got to fly it on business.

For my own career, I was beginning to feel trapped in time. Forever destined to take orders, helping to build someone else's business.

Chapter 9
Sky Park

The gravel strip called Manzanita lay quietly out in the country east of Redding

Mount Shasta was a stunning sight at the north end. The access to the area was a dirt road full of chassis-jarring chuckholes. Drainage was bad and every rain produced small lakes and mud holes. The land was owned by millionaire George Farley, a long-time pilot. He allowed Bob Lockwood to talk him into keeping it as an airport, and Bob renamed it Enterprise Sky Park. He also let him convert a house into an aeronautical operations office. Bob had recently returned from a seven-year venture in Australia and was interested in all kinds of business—tires, airplanes and bars. He thought he'd try his hand at airplanes first. He ran a projection on the area that included the probability of future freeways, business, and population growth trends; and presented a proposition to George. Thus, Bob became the manager/owner of a yet-to-be-created Fixed Based Operation. The Lockwood/Farley deal included three airplanes: a two-control, two-seater Ercoupe; a four-seat Cessna 172 in bad condition; and a '60-model, four-seat, retractable-gear Cessna 210, in terrible condition.

I was still flying for H & H Flying Service. I was getting bored when I received a telephone call from Lockwood, who requested that Al and I stop by and pay him a visit at the Manzanita strip. Al and I sat there on one miserable, rainy day looking around with disbelief at the chaos. The house was in the process of being converted to a bar and office by carpenters and near-carpenters, most of them volunteers. Lockwood gave his pitch with hypnotic enthusiasm. You could almost see them as he pointed out the features of the future capitol of aviation in Northern California. This trash-littered room was a plush office. That section of the building beyond the fireplace (not yet in existence) was a bar and restaurant. The adjacent upstairs building was perfect for a ground school room. In the summer we'd have ground school outside on the patio roof (yet to be constructed). The avionics shop would be downstairs. Land adjacent to the strip (yet to be purchased) would be ideal for a fly-in motel. Adjacent to the phantom bar, one could almost see the pool, its iridescent lights reflecting on the nearby oak trees that were also bathing in subtle, but colorful, indirect lighting. Children were plying in the grass while their parents and friends were lounging in the bar discussing aviation. This was to be a social experiment and the vehicle that was going to make us all wealthy! Its name was the Enterprise Flying Club. Bob pointed out the spot where the fifty-foot metal tower would stand. Bob's uncle had a farm with a metal tower that he would donate for the rotating beacon, non-directional beacon, and Unicom antenna. The tower stood just inside the parking lot that had yet to be bulldozed and paved. Of course all this, according to Bob's projection, would easily be paid for, especially since he could use Farley's name for credit references. He offered me the scintillating title of chief pilot. Moved by the audacity of the whole situation, I said to Al, "I haven't done anything really stupid in a long time," and I accepted. I was to receive a percentage of the gross. Bob offered Al the position of chief of maintenance. He visibly shuddered and turned it down, thinking of the pitiful excuse for a shop, a filthy building nearby with a leaky roof, and the no guarantee percentage deal.

The entire project was crazy. Redding was already supporting three other well-established, working airports, with all of their operators scratching for a living. These groups laughed loudly when they got wind of our plans. It was evident that Bob had experience in some types of businesses, but he was woefully ignorant of the in's and out's of general aviation, especially the narrow profit margins offered by charter, flight instruction, and aircraft rentals. He didn't know how labor intensive the aircraft business was. Bob was either the luckiest, or the shrewdest, guy around with his strong optimistic approach. Before long, he had many people donating their time and labor. They would pound nails, wield a paint brush, borrow equipment, and donate materials. Holes got dug for tiedowns while graders and sweepers worked on the taxiway. Wives picked up litter and washed windows. It was like an Amish barn-raising except the workers got paid in beer and bullshit. Bob even talked Texaco into installing fuel pumps and paving around them at no charge. The paving alone would have cost thousands of dollars. True to the projection, a freeway was being constructed that flowed directly from the center of town eastward, right by the south end of the runway. One of the club members worked as a construction worker, and he managed to talk the paving crew into bringing in their leftover paving, for use on the club parking lot. They became heroes for a day and collected plenty of ice cold beer as their reward. The bar construction was more-or-less completed and became the focal point for all activities such as pre-flight and post-flight discussions and business transactions. The regulars always showed up certain mornings to read the paper and drink coffee. It became their second home.

Lockwood was operating dirt cheap, and maintenance was a do it yourself thing. Non-mechanic students and club members were expected to pitch in and help with the dirty work; and, hopefully, some qualified person would handle the more complicated stuff. This was the oldest trick in aviation, and so far it was working. The airplanes were flown at low rates commensurate with their shabby appearance and poor mechanical condition. The flight line and facilities were totally inadequate. Wouldn't you wonder why anyone would hang around a place that looked like a heavy equipment yard? The answer was in the social structure. The customers liked a place where they could have fun and forget their financial difficulties. They channeled money that was going to be spent on entertainment anyway, to flight training instead. They invariably met other people in this social setting, all of whom were enthusiastic about airplanes. The desire to spend money to help the club was weird; it became almost cult-like.

I was assigned to pick up the Ercoupe at Napa where it had been sitting all winter. It was full of water, so I drained and drained until it appeared likely that all the water was gone. It was windy and I had never flown a two-control Ercoupe before. My stray thought that the takeoff should be a piece of cake vanished as the nose wheel came off and the craft started skittering across the runway in the crosswind. In desperation I yanked it into the air just before running off the side of the wide runway. I figured it out as I turned north toward Redding. In a cross wind, one must leave the nose wheel on the ground so that it can be steered with the wheel (yoke). Then, yank it into the air when you're sure you have plenty of airspeed. The Sacramento Valley was covered with its winter zero visibility tule fog. Above was beautiful sunshine that made me feel warm and sleepy, that is until the engine began spitting and coughing! Slugs of water were ingested into the carburetor, but it hung in there, burping and coughing all the way to Enterprise. Next time I would know that the carburetor bowl must also be drained, and that the last drop of water does not run out of the fuel tanks until the last drop of fuel is out. "Hmm," I thought, "what about landing, now that you're up here?" I reasoned that when landing crosswind in a crab (on touchdown with the nose wheel off the ground, the nose will try to turn in the direction that you are traveling). When the airplane swivels in the direction of travel, you then lower the nose wheel to the ground and steer it like a car. I tried it and it worked like a charm!

I was determined to convince Bob that good maintenance was necessary, even though it cost more to hire real mechanics. I had argued with Bob that the main strainer drain on the Ercoupe was rusting out and requested that he replace it, but he would not. One day while I was giving him instruction in the Coupe on a business trip, we were over the rugged Trinity Alps. I described what it would be like if the drain were to spring a leak, and if raw fuel sprayed over the hot exhaust. His face drained of blood as I foretold how the engine would catch fire and quit. We would cook on the way down to our rocky destination. The airplane would crash and burn, probably explode. After that, the mainte-nance improved dramatically. ESP, as it was nicknamed, experienced a bewildering array of A & P mechanics, mechanic's helpers, college trainees, and sometimes even Al would sneak into help. I would often be elbow deep in a greasy engine to help keep the gross up and protect my percentage.

I enlarged on the "solo board" concept. At previous locations, I had wood-burned the names of the first solo students on a breadboard to make a permanent public record. I believed that for an operation such as the Enterprise Flying Club would become, establishing tradition was important. I used 4' by 8' heavy plywood panels and engraved the solo names on them. I also included a photograph of the students at the proud moment they stepped out of the aircraft after flying by themselves for the first time. They say that is one of the moments in your life you'll never forget. A new tradition was born, or at least an elaboration of an old one.

We began to show signs of respectability. I conducted regular tours and lectures to the preschool and grade school children, a fact that set well with the mothers. We also became a base for the Civil Air Patrol when they were training and when they searched for downed aircraft. I appreciated their mission, but didn't think much of the teenaged "little Hitler" drill sergeant ordering his younger charges around military style. At any rate, their activities produced excitement and profit, especially when the gas guzzling AT-6s pulled up to the pump. Some CAP members were also club members and used our aircraft on searches. Of course the beer parlor boomed at night when the search was on.

Bob lured another club to the Sky Park, the Shasta Enterprise Soaring Club. They agreed to send me off to obtain my glider certificates so that I could teach the rest of the group to fly. I trained for the Commercial Glider at Auburn, and the Glider Instructor at Freemont. Soaring was great fun and I got comfortable with the Club's Schweizer SGU 2-22C. I felt good enough to do demonstrations of the craft's agility by demonstrating lazy-8s down Enterprise's wired-in 3,300-foot strip. I had the expectation of stopping in front of the bar *every time*. (Ya don't want to miss on that one.)

Our association was necessarily symbiotic although, in principle, the glider folks carefully separated themselves from power plane drivers. They needed our 172 to tow the glider and they needed pilots to fly it. They also needed me to instruct the glider pilots and tow pilots. This was all to the club's advantage monetarily; and, of course, the glider gang joined everyone else at the bar when the day's flying was over.

I trained a lot of tow pilots. It was a tricky job in the 1957 model square tail 172. You towed the Schweizer at fifty-five mph while using ten degrees of flaps. No other combination would do. One very large "Bill" showed up in a very proper suit and tie looking for flight instruction and tow pilot work, so I broke him in. He turned out to be a good pilot, but the Sky Park social atmosphere had a bad influence on him. Soon his spouse divorced him and he became heavily involved with drugs and partying. Some mornings would find him out cold on the club's pool table. The Enterprise Flying Club was a dangerous place for some people.

A maneuver I used to demonstrate our new Bellanca Super Viking was done with flair. When the north wind was blowing, I would fly the Super Viking down the centerline on the deck at redline airspeed (two hundred and twenty something). Next, it was straight up right in front of the bar, up over the power lines while rolling ninety degrees to the left. I would flip the electric gear and flaps to the down position and roll back to the right, completing a turnaround into the wind. One hundred and twenty was the speed necessary to allow a safe power-off, flare-out, and touchdown. The speed would quickly dissipate on the flare with those 47 degrees of flaps, and I could make the first turnoff that was only about a quarter of the way down the strip. At the Red Bluff air show, the FAA officially sanctioned me to perform slow rolls at 1,500 feet above the ground. They asked me if the maneuver was prohibited anywhere in the manual. "Of course not," I replied but thinking secretly, "The manual doesn't mention slow rolls." The inspectors laughed saying, "This I gotta see!" The rolls were going fine until about the end of the runway when the engine quit while inverted. I rolled out; the power plant roared back into life, and the propeller surged. As far as I was concerned, the show was over. I quickly dropped gear and flaps and touched down safely not daring to mention what happened. Everyone thought the maneuver was done on purpose. I was low on fuel so as to be light. While flying inverted all the liquid was on top of the tanks and could not get to the engine since the fuel lines on the bottom of the tank were sucking only air.

The Flying Club held special parties every month or so. They were joyous affairs lasting into the wee hours. Couples swaying to the melodic pulse of a band, and families, including kids and dogs, feasting on a luau pig that had been buried the day before with much fanfare. Occasionally, I would fly up to Quincy and pick up Larry Crayton, my former band singer and troubadour companion, and bring him down to perform. Everyone loved Larry and Larry loved to perform; so did I, especially when you had a partner like Larry.

The chef and party organizer was a character with a handlebar mustache named Gerry Sluder. He looked for all the world like the circus strongman with his bald head and big shoulders. Besides being the consummate chef and host, Gerry became a flight instructor. On these special occasions, airplanes from all over filled every available parking area, and sleeping bags covered the grass in the morning. Everyone either brought something pot-luck style or paid something into the kitty. The Sky Park never lost money on these occasions. In the morning volunteers always showed up to help clean up the litter created by the sumptuous luau.

Ike Yeager had himself a pretty blue and yellow Swift. The only trouble with it was its wimpy little engine. That wasn't trouble until you stacked the deck against yourself. Gerry Sluder and Red McCormick did just that one day when they wiped it out. It was a hot summer day at Enterprise and the two men loaded their heavy asses into Ike's airplane and took off to the north. With Gerry in command the little Swift managed to get into the air but wouldn't climb. Gerry selected the gear up position (the gear comes up slowly due to a small hydraulic pump) and lowered the nose to try to gain speed. Under normal circumstances, this would have been the right thing to do, but the two speed aeromatic propeller sensed the airspeed change and changed into high pitch automatically. This was like shifting into high gear, and any possibility of climbing over the trees at the end was lost. They crashed and miraculously walked away from it!

Interesting aviation personalities haunted the bar, such as Bud Pedigo, Reno Air Races contestant and owner of a gorgeous Cessna 195. There was Stu Burnham, sea captain, bar owner, and candidate for a Commercial Pilot Certificate. C.D. Sleight, the iron worker who erected the tower. Gene "Ole Dad" Robbins, from whom I bought my rag-wing Luscombe. Joe Redmond, Superior Court Judge and glider pilot. Jerry Flint, who flew a DC-6 (a four-engine airliner) for both sides in an African civil war, and Grace, his pretty spouse who had been his flight attendant. Buzz Blazedale, a mountain of a person, ran a construction company. It was common in the evenings to hear someone playing the piano, me strumming the guitar and Buzz's powerful operatic voice belting out a popular tune. The dice would roll and the beer would flow. Rivals in construction work, Buzz and just-as-big Charlie, would continue to be rivals while throwing dice. There were roars of laughter when one or the other lost a round. Charlie and Buzz both helped a lot around the place, running a grader on the strip to get it into shape. They even taught me how to run it.

Gene bought himself a Cessna UC-78 Bamboo Bomber (also known as the AT-50), which was barely in condition to ferry. It had old non-feathering propellers. He parked the old military twin at ESP. Soon it was sold to student pilot, Harry Miller, who was going to fix it up. Harry had recently retired from the railroad and had no aviation experience as a mechanic, and only a few hours as a student pilot in a little trainer. No one believed that the thing would ever fly again, but Harry tinkered away and continued to take flying lessons in the Aeronca. To everyone's amazement, the project gradually came together as he methodically went through each of the ancient aircraft's systems. Finally, Al pronounced the hulk airworthy again. I was called upon to give Harry lessons in the fabric-covered taildragger. Quite a thrill, since I'd never flown one before, but I just started by taxiing faster and faster! Although Harry had little formal education, he possessed tremendous innate mechanical ability and, by golly, he fixed the old war bird. Not only that, he also learned to fly the twin, round-engined, non-feathering, tail-dragging thing. That's a feat that would have many hotshot pilots shaking in their boots.

The glider began making headlines. It was a good trainer, but not such a good glider. One time it landed in Dr. Nash's hay field half a mile short of the runway, so I landed in the field and towed it out with the 172. Later in that 1967 summer, the *Record Searchlight* newspaper got me in trouble with "Horrible Howard" of the FAA, who was doing his best to shut us down.

The reporter wrote, *"John Tahti had just released the cable that connected us to the tow plane, a Cessna 172 piloted by John Moore, and we were on our own in the sunlight, soaring just over the tops of some low-lying cumulus clouds. Except for the moan of the air rushing past the plastic canopy at forty miles an hour, it was silent."* So far, so good. But the reporter continued truthfully; *"Moore, the instructor who taught Tahti and the club's four other licensed pilots all they know about gliding, whipped the Cessna into a sharp left turn to get out of our path, then went into a spin, finally pulling out when he was about even with the base of the clouds. Moments later, he was landing at his, and the sail plane's homebase, Enterprise Sky Park."*

Horrible Howard waved the article in my face and threatened to ground me. I replied, "You know these reporters, always have to sell newspapers with something sensational!" The FAA man grumbled and set about to do his level best to make us abandon our Approved 141 Flight School. He finally succeeded making life so miserable it wasn't worth it. It didn't help our operation anyway. It seemed that the fewer FAA approvals you had, the better. Government surveillance and interference had never been helpful to us in any way. I didn't understand why they had to bother an organization that had, so far, a perfect safety record.

We always appreciated free newspaper advertisement and always hoped to get more. One day at an air show at Benton Field the glider failed to gain headlines. I was performing for the air show. I had just completed a series of loops, rolls, and a spin, and was ready for the grand finale. I buzzed the crowd at high speed and pulled up with the intention of executing a 270 degree turn to the right for landing. As I pulled up, a trainer paddled across the sky directly in my path. I was forced into maximum altitude saving maneuvers because it was obvious that he planned to land in front of me. In fact, he didn't even see me. We had no way to communicate. The trainer was at the far exit as I crossed the cliff at the end of the runway with just enough airspeed to roll the left wing tip roller wheel on the pavement. I soared in ground effect through the first turnoff, popped on the spoilers and skidded to a stop right in front of the crowd. I thought my performance was stellar, but the crowd wasn't watching me; the cheers were for the guy that was flying a radio controlled snoopy astride his dog house! He captured the newspaper's front page while the glider show wasn't even mentioned.

Speaking of radio-controlled aircraft, at one of our many play days, I had some fun with a large radio-controlled aircraft. I flew in a tight low circle over the runway in my Luscombe while the RC pilot flew in formation with me. This was really tricky because the RC pilot must not lose sight of his aircraft. It was easy enough to see my bogey as long as I remained close, since its wing span was at least six feet. One thing I noticed while trying to avoid hitting the thing, was that its movements, when seen at close range, were very jerky. We also dropped flour bombs at the bull's eye, a fifty-five gallon drum. I casually tossed a bomb out of the open canopy of a company Alon, but the judges couldn't find it. You guessed it, it was in the barrel and I won the trophy!

Some of the people living in the area were not friends of the airport. Tacks mysteriously turned up on the taxiway and signs were torn down that directed customers to us. Police were continually directed our way for disturbing the peace and for night flying operations. Due to a neighborhood protest, the Enterprise Flying Club's beer license was held up for several months. Bob just gave away beer and a kitty sat unobtrusively on the end of the bar. The beer license problem was solved when the matter came up before the City Planning Commission. The room was filled to capacity with Sky Park supporters, including several lawyers and a judge. Bob had bought plenty of good will with the beer he had pumped, supposedly without profit.

Drinking and then flying was never allowed. This applied to outside visitors as well. One morning two couples flew in and fell out of their 210 drunker than skunks. They could barely walk as they staggered into the bar looking for another drink. In the midst of their howls of protests, I chained their aircraft to the ground and secured it with a huge padlock, and then drove them to a motel to sleep it off. They thanked me the next day. All potential customers were greeted with enthusiasm and a free cup of coffee. This was in contrast to one's typical experience when inquiring about flight training. Often, when the perspective student is finally noticed, a self-impressed, overworked instructor would give a canned, unenthusiastic speech about learning to fly. In contrast, our enthusiastic approach and the social aspects of the club led to our cornering the market on the student instruction and aircraft rental business in the Redding area. All students were initially welcomed, no matter how nerdy, ignorant sounding, or strange looking, as long as they had money to spend to *support the club*! So much for the horse laughs from the other three working airports!

Bob loved the little Ercoupe, and after a while, so did I. It could fly circles around a more conventional Cessna 150 despite having fifteen fewer horsepower, and it could be landed in a hell of a strong crosswind. Its knuckle-type landing gear has been adopted by modern-day corporate jets. In the 1940s it was way ahead of its time. I delighted in demonstrating short-field landings to the nonbelievers. This fact set Bob up for the arrival of O. J. Miller, smooth talking and very likable aircraft sales representative. He was peddling the Alon A-2, a modern three-control version of the Ercoupe boasting of ninety horsepower. I opposed the decision to buy one of the damn things because I believed that they probably would not be accepted by the public. Miller convinced Bob that this airplane could spell success, all we had to do was educate the public. Since we were stuck with the Ercoupe look alike, I began to croon the Alon song. After getting acquainted, the tune became easier to sing. It was a sturdy little ship with good performance and low maintenance costs. The main drawback was in the torrid heat of the Redding summer. The canopy, when closed, was like a pressure cooker and the ventilation woefully inadequate. The visibility was great though, and often we'd fly with the canopy slid back to let fresh air in and observe the outside world directly. With it open, one could dramatically increase the rate of descent if the pilot and passenger held their hands out on the leading edge of the wing creating a spoiler effect.

One day I was taxiing in with a student in the Club 150 and, as usual, carefully avoiding ruts in the gravel taxiway. I happened to look up and see a Jet Commander whizzing by very close to our downwind leg for runway 15. It was smoky and I figured he was looking for Redding Municipal just a few miles to the south. Suddenly I was startled by a roar, and right next to us the Jet skidded by, its tires smoking. It powered up to full reverse thrust! The jet came to rest with its nose inches from the scrub oak trees at the end of the south ramp. It couldn't even turn around. We taxied closer, shut down and climbed out. To my amazement the door opened and Governor Ronald Reagan stepped out. He said, "I'm still looking for the Eel River" (referring to a campaign boo-boo he had made while running for office). We gathered up the Governor and his entourage, and drove them all over to Muni. The pilot said that he crossed Redding VOR, looked down and there was a runway. Even in the smoke I didn't see how he could confuse a 7,000-foot-long concrete runway with a 3,300-foot gravel strip. We helped him push the Commander around and position it on the very end of the runway. He then ran up to maximum power, creating a huge dust storm behind him, let go of the brakes and roared down the little gravel strip. We all held our breath as he rotated at the very end, almost scraping his belly on the trees. I heard later that one of the tires blew out in Sacramento. Bet he was looking for another job.

John Johnson (nicknamed J.J.) came to work at Enterprise Sky Park as a novice flight instructor. Before long he was a tow pilot and busy flying charters and instructing. One day while out giving dual in one of our two Alon's, his engine quit cold. John managed to guide the craft to some fairly smooth hills. They had quite a ride for a while, rolling up and down the grassy slopes, but no damage was done. We received more newspaper advertisement that said, "It isn't every day that Shasta County sheriff's deputies are asked to escort an airplane through Enterprise, nor is it a daily occurrence for motorists driving along Highway 44 to see an airplane rolling along with two sheriff's cars escorting it." (The cops provided traffic control.) On another occasion, one of the beer stories was about the time J.J. was parked at Trinity Center in a little Alon. He was locked in a passionate embrace with an unidentified female when the storyteller sneaked up behind and shook his elevator. J.J. didn't even look back. The Alon's engine roared into life and the craft roared across the little ramp to the runup area at high speed! Life at ESP was just one adventure after another!

Of course Bob almost had a heart attack during Johnson's engine-out incident, but the best was yet to come. Two days later I was giving a visiting student a demonstration in the other Alon in an attempt to lure him into the Club. Suddenly the engine quit cold and gasoline blew in around the rudder area inside the cockpit. I spotted a road on top of a mesa and at the same time grabbed the mic informing Enterprise Unicom that I was going down. The landing site was a jeep trail that bumped over rolling terrain strewn with volcanic boulders. I maneuvered into position, descended over a group of trees, and touched down lightly. Confidently, I stepped on the brakes. The confidence vanished when the brake pedal squashed to the floor with no result. "Damn," I remembered, "we've been having a hell of a time getting those brakes to bleed the air out properly!" The low-winged aircraft continued careening down the trail at close to takeoff speed. Suddenly two fence posts capable of ripping off the wings appeared on either side of the road. I saw that there was no fence associated with the posts, so I took us on a wild ride through the boulder-dotted countryside, and finally back to the road without any great damage. The Alon finally coasted to a stop. I reached under the panel where the fuel valve was hiding (I often wondered why the manufacturer would hide something like that) and stopped the fuel from pouring out the bottom of the cowling. It was later determined that the needle valve had stuck open in the carburetor. Almost before the dust cleared, the sky was buzzing with airplanes wondering via radio if we were all right. I radioed back in the affirmative and we began walking off the mesa to a ranch where I could telephone in. The student thanked me for an interesting lesson and never came back. The next day the carburetor was repaired and after a bumpy takeoff, I flew the Alon home to ESP.

We attracted our share of characters. One day I was flying with Tammy, a pretty blond school teacher who liked adventure, and had a pill to enhance every mood. I was giving her spin training in the Aeronca when the nose decided it wanted to rotate around on the horizon instead of pointing properly downward. I realized that her 110 pounds in the front and my 180 pounds in the back wasn't working, and the out-of-balance condition was getting worse as we burned fuel (thus losing weight) from the nose tank which was located forward of the center of gravity. I instructed her to return home. She was furious because I cut her fun short—even after I explained about flat spins. While pulling back on the stick (elevator) and increasing the angle of attack of the wing to the relative wind, the sudden break (full stall) is accomplished cleanly. Full rudder is then applied and the throttle retarded. The airplane will rotate with the wings in a stalled attitude while the stick is held firmly back. The nose appears low on the horizon, but the wing chord angle to the relative wind is actually high. The relative wind is coming almost straight up and the airspeed remains below the stall speed. I explained that when the aircraft is loaded too far rearward, it may be difficult, or impossible, for the elevator to have the authority to reduce the angle of attack enough to recover from the spin. Real bad news!

Al Ewald became a member of the Shasta College staff, teaching the airframe section of the Aircraft Mechanic Course. The job included medical insurance, retirement benefits and the works! While celebrating Al's good fortune, we drank a few beers at the Sky Park. All the girls there pestered us for a motorcycle ride, so we romped around on some nearby trails that wound through the woods. I happened to have Tammy on behind me when I hit a rut hidden in the red, powdery dust. The Triumph Bonneville flipped hard and threw Tammy about thirty feet. She was fine after a couple of bounces in the pine needles. As for me, the handlebars caught my arm and threw me into the unyielding ground like a judo move. When I opened my eyes I knew I was hurt, and the motorcycle was bent, but I was still able to right it and ride back to the bar.

Al and I ordered another pitcher of beer and I noted the collar bone sticking up and almost breaking through my skin. Finally Judy drove me to Mercy hospital to get it checked. The nurse said she'd have to call the Highway Patrol since my injury occurred on a motorcycle. I said, "See you later." She shouted, "You can't leave!" I replied, "Watch me!" I checked into Memorial Hospital for the operation that involved resetting the bone and inserting several steel pins. Dr. Hankin laughed and traded pinches with the nurses as he operated. That night I had a nightmare. (I was back in the Luscombe in that dark canyon where I couldn't reach the controls.) It resulted in my sitting up suddenly and reaching out which effectively rearranged the doctor's careful work. I screamed bloody murder with the pain.

Thank God for morphine!

Even during days off, I was working for the Sky Park. Several volunteers and I constructed a fishpond and a waterfall, complete with driftwood and a live bamboo backdrop. It was nestled among the oak trees next to the parking lot entrance. Volcanic and granite rocks were hauled in from great distances. Indirect colored lighting at night created quite a romantic effect. Everything wasn't perfect though; the waterfall pump shorted out and killed all the frogs and Tammy planted a small alligator there that murdered all the fish and hissed at you if you got close. The pond took its place in the overall scheme of things.

Tammy got in trouble one day when she brought the Aeronca back with the top of the wings ripped up. She had been flying low over the Sacramento River and had encountered tree branches overhanging the river. In other words she had been flying *under* the trees. Another time she bragged about her and her boy friend diving the Super Viking in excess of 300 miles-per-hour. As chief pilot I asked her to resign from the Club.

I met Ed Herzog when I checked him out in the Aeronca He had an unusual Beatles-type haircut and became another one of our characters. He bought himself a Luscombe and figured that if he could fly one tail dragger he could fly another. I warned him that the Luscombe was a horse of a different color from the Aeronca. Yep. He washed out the landing gear in a crosswind. Ed signed up for the airframe course at Shasta College, mainly to use Al's expertise and the college facilities to help him repair his Luscombe. Ed went on to get all of his flight ratings and went to Alaska and made big bucks in construction. He bought a Cessna 185 and used it travel to Wyoming where he and a partner disassembled oil rigs. Later, back in Alaska, he procured government contracts to fly supplies to remote villages.

Bob Lockwood felt it necessary to go on the road selling tires again. He thought the money injection was necessary. I thought it would be better for him to concentrate on the business that he already had, but I agreed to try and run things as best I could while he was away. Bob had a scheme worked out where he would write checks to pay bills in advance. That way he always knew what he had to work with in his check register. The Texaco representative was at the bar one evening griping about not getting paid. I said, "Those checks have already been written, I'll get them for you."

The rep was ecstatic and thanked me very much. When Bob returned he was livid! He said, "You have just run us out of money for the rest of the month!"

I thought privately, "I'm flying for you, not trying to run your business. You should stick around and run it yourself." Later Bob told me that if he hadn't sold some tires, ESP would be out of business. I was still skeptical.

Bob drove a lot selling tires. One day I was riding with him when the red light came on behind us. Bob's face turned white and he said to me, "One more speeding ticket and they'll pull my license. Quick, swap seats with me!" We accomplished the maneuver quickly.

The Highway Patrol Officer eyed me suspiciously and asked, "Are you sure you were driving." Fortunately I was issued a warning instead of a ticket. I told Bob that he owed me. That was beyond the call of duty!

There was some time in the winter when the weather was lousy and no money was coming in. Stu Burnham, the sea captain, owned a hard drinkers bar called The Elbo Room. He set me up with a job as a bartender. My shift was from 6:00 a.m. to 11:00 a.m. After that, I was free to go back to the Sky Park, if I could. I say "if I could," because while in training, the new bartender was required to drink his mistakes. I learned some things about bar society; as I was filling up the tubs with ice and getting things cleaned up, the first customers would be those who had spent the night in the car lot after closing down the place the night before. After a coffee royal, or something, they would stagger out the door, dodging the next onslaught of customers, the graveyard shift. This was their nighttime, and by 7:00 a.m. balls would be slamming around on the pool tables and the juke box was vibrating with country and rock music. About 9:30 the executives would arrive dressed in suits and ties. They would roll the dice for three or four shots of Johnny Walker Black Label, and march out the door back to work. Next to arrive were the regular "brandy and water alkies" who made the bar their home. They had shuffleboard tournaments and potluck dinners. On a rare occasion I would drop in late in the evening and the place would get wilder and wilder as the witching hour approached. About a month was enough for me!

I heard from Denny Mansell again. This time he wanted me to accompany him and his wife to the other side of Texas in his Turbo Aztec, in which he was not yet rated. The mission was to pick up a hunting dog puppy! The Aztec was in Redding. After a long day's work, I jumped in the twin, picked the couple up in Quincy, and we flew on to Las Vegas. The next evening found us in El Paso facing towering thunderstorms. Denny was irritated when I refused to go on. Imagine that! I didn't want to be flying a strange airplane at night in unfamiliar country, especially without IFR charts. I guess I was just gutless. We had the Aztec fueled and took a taxi to the club that we'd stopped in a couple of years before. Denny's membership card was still good, and we settled down for another great Texas steak dinner.

In the morning the thunderstorms were gone and we were off. Heading east on a bright, sunny day, Huntsville and the puppy awaited us on the other side of Texas. OOPS, why is that left engine cylinder head temperature gauge pointer moving toward the red line? It's running kinda rough, too. I immediately banked left and pointed us toward San Angelo. I feathered number one and Denny suggested that we should cross feed fuel. I said no because we didn't have that far to go. Denny insisted on messing with the fuel controls, and I finally told him to go ahead. I was too busy keeping track of our location. I definitely didn't want to miss San Angelo. Suddenly the right engine quit, too, and a shriek of terror came from the spouse in the back seat. I kept my eyes on a dirt road directly ahead of us that looked landable and said to Denny, "Whatever you did, undo it!" Shortly the right engine roared into life. Denny had set the cross feed controls properly, but had forgotten to turn on the boost pump to purge the long line of air and, of course, the engine won't run on air.

We arrived in San Angelo without further incident. I couldn't help imagining what it would have been like if we had continued the flight yesterday, winding our way between thunderstorms. Sometimes it pays to be gutless. "Bad gas," the mechanic said, waving the leaded-up spark plugs around. I thought that it was a good thing we were not successful with the cross feed, maybe all the bad gas was in the left tank. Nevertheless, we had him drain all fuel and we started over.

In Huntsville we took a little time off and went grouse hunting in the surrounding pine forests belonging to a wealthy black person who was a friend of the dog breeder. The next day we snagged the mutt and took off for Pheonix. There, Denny exchanged our Aztec for a loaner. The company that sold him the Aztec brand new wanted to do some further checking on the engine-out incident.

The tandem-seated Aeronca was great fun to fly, especially in a strong wind. Have you ever done a vertical pattern? "A vertical pattern?" they would ask. I explained with a mischievous grin,

"Well, you take off into a real strong wind and fly to the end of the runway, climbing to pattern altitude, then you slow down to minimum controllable airspeed. If the wind is strong enough, you can back down the center line and then land straight ahead." This maneuver drives the controllers at Muni crazy!

Student pilot, Jim, owned a side-by-side Aeronca Chief and dreamed up a unique way to buzz his sweetheart's house. He would whiz by the chimney on the bottom side of a continuous loop over and over again. He got so good at it he could even adjust for wind drift. Unfortunately, the neighbors weren't impressed, nor were the feds, and Jim had to sit it out awhile, his student certificate suspended.

A couple from the state of Washington hitched a ride to ESP after they ran low on fuel in their Cherokee 180 and had made a precautionary landing in a field next to Shasta College. I drove back with a five-gallon can of gas, fueled it, and flew the low-winged Piper out of the field and back to the Sky Park. There had been reporters at the scene taking pictures for the newspaper. Immediately after the incident, I took off from Enterprise with a student in the Aeronca to practice spins. We climbed out to the north in the general direction of Shasta College, and began a series of spins. It is a curious sensation seeing the earth spin around while your wooden prop, in contrast, was stopped. "Damn," I thought, "I knew that idle should have been set higher." I recovered from the spin and dove in an attempt to increase the airspeed for an air start, but the light wooden propeller wouldn't respond. Since this rag wing aircraft had no starter, I figured we'd better find a place to land. I lined up on the same field that I had just flown the Cherokee out of and tried to ignore my student's incessant questions. He obviously didn't have a clue as to how much danger he was in. Just moments after the reporters left, the little orange and white tail dragger touched down with its motionless propeller. I climbed out and propped it, and we flew home to adjust the idle rpm's.

One day I was checking out instructor Will Haley in the Club's '60 model Cessna 210, which is gentle in most flight regimes. I asked him to perform an accelerated stall to the right with climb power and see if he could recover with rudder only, while holding the elevator all the way back. As I expected, the bottom wing whipped over the top and we executed a horizontal spin faster that you could blink an eye. The next day, Will rode in the back while I checked out Montel Work. As I made the same request of Montel, I looked in the back seat and grinned. Will was positioned with both hands and feet outstretched in a rigid brace stance. His face was white as a sheet. He knew what was about to happen.

We were not satisfied with just netting the local fish, so we embarked on our missionary effort. Several days a week John Johnson and I flew to the remote communities of Hyampom, Hayfork and Trinity Center near the Trinity Alps, and to Fall River Mills in the Cascade mountains. None of these places had local instructors available. The missions went well. Often I would return after a long day with one or two new club members to add to the list and eight hours on the aircraft. Each member would pay an initiation fee and $10 per month for dues. That didn't sound like much a month until you multiplied it by 100 members. To put it another way, if the percentage of profit was twenty percent of the gross, you would have to gross $5,000 to net that much. That was equivalent to a hundred hours of aircraft flight time per month at the average rate, without turning a wheel! Plus, you could count on many of the members to spend money at the bar, and for items such as club shirts, hats and patches.

Jane Armstrong, barely five feet tall, was from Weaverville.

Her husband, Dick Armstrong, D.D.S., had long been an aviation enthusiast. I began flying with both of them. We became great friends, sometimes meeting with a whole crowd of flyers from the area for dinner, or maybe sailing on Trinity Lake. The influence of Enterprise Flying Club spread steadily. Jane decided to invest in a Cessna 150 and lease it back to ESP. She also went for her Commercial Pilot Certificate, but not all came up roses. One dangerously windy day full of whirlwinds and wind shear, she attempted a landing at the one-way uphill strip at Weaverville, but lost control in the powerful gusts and whacked a parked aircraft. Her 150 was demolished. The fact that she was not badly injured attested to her flying skill, but not to her judgment on that day.

Near the end of our stay at Enterprise Sky Park, we lived out of town on a hill we called "Chocktaw Ridge." Near us lived a large family who had emigrated from Guam after selling a large chunk of ancestral land. They engaged in cock fighting and other traditional activities. Their luau-like celebrations were something to see. I taught young George how to fly and he became a safe, polite, and competent pilot. I liked him a lot, but apparently there are more dangerous activities than flying. He was murdered. Some say it was drug-related.

Dixie Norton was a remarkable individual. She owned Paul's Club, a topless bar. Aviation was very much a part of Dixie's life. Her husband flew a STOL-equipped Seneca for Shasta Livestock Company. Dixie became Al Ewald's student at Shasta College and earned herself an A & P Mechanic Certificate. After five years working in the field, twisting wrenches, she earned her Inspection Authorization and went to work for the FAA.

Denny Mansell graduated up to the bigger and more expensive Piper Navajo so that he could comfortably fly more of his family around. He had not yet gotten his instrument rating, so he called me on occasions when it was necessary to fly in bad weather. Where his parents lived in Everett, Washington, the weather could get really bad. We were churning away through a veritable wall of water just south of Everett and the controller was giving us a vector to final approach for the ILS. Denny was at the controls. He wanted to try out his new Navajo's autopilot on the approach. The controller vectored us in with too large of an angle for the device to capture the beam and we flew right by the localizer center line. I said, "I've got it," and I disengaged the autopilot. I probably should have asked for another vector but there were aircraft in line to make the approach, so all things considered I rolled into a steep turn to the right and "bracketed the beam." A descending lazy-eight might be more accurate, but all was in control by the time minimums were reached. After an overnight stay, the time to leave had come and despite the fact that Denny had bought the finest money could buy, I once more refused to fly. The flight service specialist said that in the terrible weather covering the area, a Cessna 210 had disappeared from radar and was feared lost. In addition, a pressurized Navajo had repeatedly attempted a climb out only to be forced back with heavy icing. We waited and the next day was bright and sunny, and the flight home uneventful.

One night a student, with significant other troubles, stole an Alon and began buzzing the girlfriend's house. Sluder talked to him on the Unicom. The student said he was gonna commit suicide. Jerry jumped in another aircraft and flew around with him for a couple of hours valiantly trying to talk him out of it. Finally, the Alon's fuel was nearly exhausted, and so was the student. He was ready to quit and come home. Gerry guided him to a private strip nearby because he couldn't make the Sky Park with the fuel he had left. As the student made the approach, the engine starved for fuel and the Alon mushed into trees just short of the runway, and its pilot got his original wish.

After I left ESP I began hearing of various screw ups. Former student, Monte, was trying to check out in the club's Cessna Cardinal 177. The early model Cardinal was a terrible airplane to use in a Sky Park-type of operation. Later models modified their horizontal stabilator design, but even so they tended to drop you about the time the nose came through level on the power-off flare-out. It didn't hang on like its cousin, the 172. Monte usually had the capacity to party all night and work all day, but this day it all caught up with him. The new instructor became impatient with Monte's lousy hippity hoppity landings, so he climbed out and said, "Go do a decent one, I know you can do better."

The instructor missed the boat on two points: (1) Monte was too tired to be flying that day, and (2) he assumed that a 172 and a 177 were practically alike. He mistakenly believed that if you could fly one, you could fly the other. During the solo landing attempt, the hapless "checkoutee" tried to force the aircraft to stay on the ground, thereby creating the classic porpoise. He pushed and pulled the yoke, the pitching up and down got worse and worse until the firewall buckled and the nose strut failed. The heaving airplane crashed into a tree. The horrified spectators in the bar had a front row view.

I was also sick to hear of how ESP's students were being instructed to land at the one-way Weaverville airport. The technique being taught was to simply chop the power, apply full flaps and drift down to a landing in that configuration (sorta like a leaf falling off of a tree—same amount of control). It was a sure-fire way to get yourself killed if you encountered an unexpected updraft, tail wind, or turbulence. Once committed, there was no possibility of a go around since the airport rose rapidly uphill into a canyon. The proper approach, in this instance, would be to create a flatter glide path utilizing power, so that when you throttled back, the aircraft would land for sure, rather than floating down the runway.

I left Enterprise Sky Park broke, even after pouring my heart and soul into it. One person should never pack so much work and fun into a couple of years. One year I flew twelve-hundred hours of nothing but student instruction! I also had the feeling that ESP was doomed in its present location because of the land value and because of disgruntled neighbors. Early on I thought we should be trying to make a deal with the City of Redding to lease one of the revetments at the Municipal Airport away from the rest of the businesses. We could have built a neat little club house in among the native oak trees and had it all to ourselves. Bob even checked into it once, but said the city wanted too much money to lease the land.

Bob, sick at heart after all of his desperate efforts, decided to sell the business. The new corporation was made up mostly of "Lockwood hecklers." They kept the name of Enterprise Flying Club, but refinanced all the airplanes that were due to be paid off in two years. There was a fire, and the solo boards were damaged, along with the photo albums. The past wasn't important to the newcomers. The solo boards, along with their pictures and wood-burned names and dates, and the albums disappeared.

I accepted an offer from Flying Tiger Airlines to get flown down to Burbank to take a pre-employment test. Several other guys flew with me in the Tiger Canidar. We had an afternoon to hang around in the city, and some of us had way too many drinks. I didn't feel all that great in the morning. The Stanine test covered nine subjects, including general information, mechanical ability, psychological stability, reasoning ability, aeronautical knowledge, and so on. The test takes eight hours and is exhausting. I grappled with the light box, a hideous device that measures your ability to visualize and carry out orders. Apparently pilots were supposed to know that Beethoven's Third Symphony was "Eroica," or that a one sided figure is called a "mobis," my mind was a blank. I wasn't surprised when the letter came from Tigers' that I hadn't scored high enough to get hired. It was time to wise up. I found out that there are schools to prepare one for these tests. You had to wait two years to take the Stanine test again. When that time was up, Montel Work and I traveled to San Diego to study. We were told that it was all a matter of familiarization. Of course it was! I never saw a test I couldn't pass with flying colors, if only I could study the test. This was how these people were scoring such fantastic scores. You had to be smart enough to cheat in order to compete!

TWA sent me a ticket to fly to Kansas City for their special test. I had it memorized. I tried to look busy while the other pilots, all younger than I, sweated and cursed. I missed one on purpose so it wouldn't look phony. The young men with their thin little log books marched in one-by-one for an interview with the chief pilot. I also went in with my several thick logs and my coveted ATR certificate ready to whip out as necessary. I must have said something wrong in the interview while desperately trying to say the right thing. Most of the young boys were hired, but I was sent home.

Northwest Orient Airlines sent me a ticket to travel to Minneapolis, and I easily passed their little pre-employment test. It was reminiscent of the Pacific Airlines test that I had failed in San Francisco. Next, Northwest sent me to Palo Alto to take the Stanine test again. This time I was ready and I knew I had scored right up there with the geniuses. I received a letter informing me that I had passed. My bags were packed and I was ready to go, but the next letter said, "Sorry, we're full up."

Chapter 10
Firebomber

During five summer months I flew for Aero Union Corporation. The idea was to go to college in the fall and spring semesters, but I was always a month and a half late in the fall. Judy attended classes, kept notes and I struggled to keep up.

For a time I commuted from Redding to Chico in my sixty-five hp rag-wing (fabric-covered) Luscombe with a fellow college student paying for the fuel and receiving dual instruction. One day on a long final approach to Ranchero, a pair of wheels appeared almost *in* the windshield. I grabbed the stick away from my student and dove out of the way, completed a tight 360-degree turnaround and came up behind the Cessna 150. It turned out to be Al Sos' wife, Polly, who was shooting touch-and-goes. She was unaware of the close call. Maybe that's why people clamor about straight in approaches, especially with no radio.

Gary Hendrickson was familiarizing a friend with a stock "two holer" Navy N-3-N at the Ranchero airport. This morning the lesson was to hand prop the aircraft without assistance. The instructor was standing by the wing tips displaying supreme confidence in his student's training. His confidence vanished when the student got the sequence wrong. He left the throttle wide open, turned on the magnetos and then pulled the propeller through. When the right combination of air, fuel and fire occurred, the ancient biplane leaped forward with a mighty roar, nearly gobbling up the student. The berserk craft crashed from one parked airplane to another, finally burying itself in a fabric-covered Taylorcraft. Gary sadly confided to me that only the day before he'd turned down a full-coverage insurance policy. Incidentally, have you ever seen those pilot statues with the helmet, goggles, and beard whose label drolly states, "Why, yes, I fly." I'm certain that Gary posed for them!

During this intensive college time we moved back to Chico. I would spend eight hours at a time sequestered in our bedroom studying—first for the Bachelor of Arts, and then for the Master's Degree. Teri was a cute little Girl Scout and Jack proved to be a holy terror in grammar school. Both were very bright. My grandparents, as always, visited from Quincy, and helped provide a feeling of stability, purpose, and pride.

Gerry Sluder, now the chief pilot of the new Enterprise Flying Club corporation, was giving night instruction in a customer's Tripacer. They crashed, killing student and instructor. ESP had lost their great luau host. There was speculation that the windshield had separated in the air.

It was summer again and I was away in Redding flying "Airco" for Aero Union Corporation when the shocking news arrived. Grandpa and Grandma would not be attending any college graduation. Grandpa was driving down the Deer Creek highway to visit us in Chico. Their Oldsmobile left the road, struck a tree at the fifteen foot level and killed them both!

Judy's brother, Tom Rahn, was taking post graduate courses at Chico State in pursuit of his M.S. in Biology. We found time to fly the Luscombe together. He was a fast learner and possessed blazing intelligence. He soon soloed and took his Master's Degree, too. He then used his GI Bill to complete various advanced flight ratings. Soon after, he began work as a wildlife biologist with California State Fish and Game.

As a winter recreational thing I enrolled in a group that taught Kodenkan jujitsu, a unique combination of the soft arts of aikedo and the hard arts of karate. In between were the throwing-and-falling arts of Judo. It was a complete package. It opened up a whole new world to me, including their interesting philosophy that said, "If you operate from a position of power, you can afford to be generous." I learned the art of massage and bone manipulating, because after you hit the mat a hundred times in an evening, you would be sore without such treatment. I improved my technique to the point that I could do a high flat fall on concrete without damage to the thirty-something bod.

It's easy to misjudge someone from first impressions. For example, I liked Dave Miller right away. You know, the crook who cheated me out of my Cessna 180. On the other hand, when I began giving flight lessons to Vine Wheelock at Chico Ranchero, I imagined that he might have a different sexual orientation than I, from observing some of his mannerisms. I thought, "If he puts his hand on my leg, I'm gonna clobber him." I felt very secure since I was such a martial arts hotshot. Vine was a construction worker, currently working in Utah. I thought, "Oh great, he'll probably need lots of help with the written stuff, probably a drifter with no education." Somewhere in conversation I accidentally let a word slip that was used in the martial arts, specifically Kodenkon Jujitsu.

Vine said, "Oh, do you do Judo?" I admitted that I did. He allowed that he knew a little about it. I found out by asking my sensi (instructor) that Vine had been studying since he was a youngster. He held a prestigious third-degree black belt! I lost a lot of confidence in my ability to size somebody up at first glance. Awhile later I also found out that my drifter friend owned a lot of land around Chico and held a teaching credential requiring five years of University time! So much for having to help him with the written stuff!

For a little extra income and free drinks, I played and sang crossover country a couple of nights a week in a Chico hangout. Also, Larry Crayton, who was now working on a paving crew near Chico, and I, performed around the Chico town and college scene. Anthropology professor, Hal Nelson, who sometimes played an electrified Tahitian gut-bucket with me at the bar, almost convinced us to go to New Guinea on tour. I wisely decided to stay and finish my Anthro studies. instead. One night I was plying to a wild crowd of dancers when an Indian girl stepped up on the two-foot stage to help me sing. There was no denying her the microphone and her friends at a nearby table clapped and sang along. Suddenly the evening's libations took their toll and she toppled like a tree onto the hard concrete floor. Her friends dragged her back to her table, propped her up in a chair and ordered another round of drinks. I didn't miss a beat of "Your Cheating Heart!" Tom, his wife, Maggie, and Judy were also in the crowd when a young, drunk Ag student persisted in trying to get Maggie to dance. A fight broke out, and Tom whipped him soundly. Meanwhile, I didn't miss a beat of "Mountain of Love." The young fella got up and was preparing to blind-side Tom, who thought the fight was over. By then I was on a break. I slipped up next to the would-be attacker and applied a "Hadaka Jime C" art that was Kodenkan Jujitsu's carotid artery choke. I skipped the other part of the art where you throw both legs straight up in the air, rotate and plunge your opponent's head into the hard concrete floor, crushing his skull. He merely collapsed and the barmaid dragged him to the door and threw him onto the sidewalk!

Instead of driving to the archeological site, I preferred to fly to the Werlitzer dig and land on a nearby road. One day professor Keith Johnson wanted me to fly him out so that he could take aerial photographs of the site. He requested the left seat because the window on that side opened. The only trouble with that arrangement was that there were no brakes on the right side. I thought I could get away with it and showed him how to use the heel brakes, just in case. Of course, it got windy while we were out on the photo mission, and the landing required brakes while rolling out. The untrained professor couldn't respond well enough, and at the end of the short runway we went around in a little circle, surviving the ground loop without any damage.

The first three seasons with Aero Union Corporation I flew "Airco" for the California Division of Forestry (CDF) on contract. We used high-winged, single-engine aircraft. The Airco carried a California Division of Forestry observer to coordinate between the ground crew boss and the air tankers. The observer was the air boss who told the lead plane where to instruct the tankers to drop. In turn, the lead plane would develop the drop strategy and was charged with the responsibility to lead the air tankers on a safe path for their approach, drop, and exit.

With little to do between fires, pilots would reiterate stories with a point. A typical story was of a fatality that occurred in the Castle Crags. The pilot of the A-26 was descending over a ridge, his landing gear and flaps extended in order to descend steeply enough to get to the fire and complete the drop. The drop was accomplished and a transition to climb began when one of the powerful engines failed. No one knows what went on inside the cockpit, but the aircraft was observed to roll into the dead engine with gear and flaps still extended. The pilots discussed what should have occurred. With the mixtures, propeller controls, and throttles all up in the climb power positions, the landing gear should have already been up and the flaps in transit on the way up. The dead left engine should have been feathered. None of this happened and the aircraft rolled over into the cliffs. After the accident, flap settings for air drops on the A-26 were restricted to less than full flaps. On the other hand, there were sometimes good fortunes to discuss. Like the time Bill Harnden was dispatched from Redding to a fire in a TBM when an oil line blew. He released his load of slurry and dead sticked the big single-engine bomber on a dirt road without scratching a thing.

On both the Shasta and Butte ranger districts many of the observers were either pilots or pilot wanna be's. I would inevitably end up checking them out in the right seat, the left seat, or both. Their rationale was suppose I died, etc. I had lots of characters ride with me, none more colorful than Don O'Connell, a very large individual who once tried out for the Los Angeles Rams. Don ran his CDF tanker base with an iron hand. Behind his back he was called "Big Foot." O'Connell and I were taking movies for a fire training film in the Feather River Canyon. The B-17 and 206 crossed paths as the bombing run began. As the Fortress rolled out over its fiery target deep in the canyon, I tucked us under the wing in close formation. Don filmed the heavy red slurry falling out of the bombay doors, and as the bentonite came out, the war bird lurched upward while I held my position. With a lot of speed built up, I carefully pulled up into an immelman and rolled out the opposite direction, all the time keeping track of the steep canyon walls. We would pay special attention to the Bidwell Park area while on recon flights looking for smoke. Deep in the lava beds, Big Chico Creek flowed and the nude sunbathers lurked. Who knows, maybe one of them would start a fire? The aircraft we were flying had a powerful loud speaker installed in the back. One time we were flying over a high school where Don's son was plying a football game. From the heavens came the thundering voice. "This is God speaking. You better win this game or else." We slipped away before anyone could get our number.

It is a continuous learning process in the art and science of air tanker drops and fire fighting techniques. For example, I was amazed to see a B17, piloted by Mel Hoagland, ripping up large oak trees with low drops. The industry was just learning that low drops can be destructive, deadly to folks on the ground, and ineffective for fire control. Mel had grown up as a pilot with TBM's and the like, and captained a B17 competently, but one incident shook his confidence. In those primitive days of air tankering, there were no time limits imposed on the copilot, nor did that individual have to be trained. All that was required was possession of a Commercial Pilot Certificate. In most cases, the copilot worked seven days a week for the duration of the federal or state contract. Sometimes captains would change, but the copilot would labor on. Based in Fort Hauchuca, Arizona, that year, Aero Union needed to supply a warm body in the right seat of Mel's B17 for contract purposes. Up pops an enthusiastic military man looking for multiengine experience and willing to work for close to minimum wage. What pilot wouldn't want a chance at hands-on experience in the legendary Flying Fortress? Anyhow, this poor guy had worked all night at the military base and was expected to perform his job as copilot all the next day. Mel and his copilot had just completed a drop over rough terrain and were departing the scene when all four engines quit one after the other, commencing from left to right. Mel attempted a restart on number one when number two failed. Feather number one and attend to number two, and so on. It seemed that nothing would bring them back. Pilot and helper pushed and pulled levers and switches to no avail, and shortly there was no choice but to pick the best spot to crash. The copilot didn't have his seat belt on so just before impact Mel turned off the magnetos and grabbed the copilot in a great bear hug. The four-engined bomber slid and slued down an arroyo creating a boiling dust trail and finally came to rest, wings had scattered but the cockpit remained intact! Mel and his recently-hired hand escaped without any great injury. No satisfactory official explanation as to the cause of all four engines quitting nearly at once was available to the public. I can guess at a few possible causes, the mixture controls are backwards to conventional controls, forward is lean and aft is rich. Secondly, on the throttle console there are two magneto switches for each engine, and a kill switch that grounds all eight magnetos as a safety feature. There's another safety feature that isn't all that safe. Lined up in close proximity to the fuel boost pump switches are the firewall shutoff valve switches. In case of a fire in an engine you toggle the appropriate switch that cuts off all fluids to that engine; that would include fuel and oil. Aero Union made sure that those fluid line shutoff switches were protected by a special guard after that!

Sometimes well meaning pilots get their aircraft in the way of air tanker drops. Such was the case northeast of Willows in a grass fire. I was flying with "Two Beer" Chuck Kimball, (so named because two beers would get him roaring drunk.) Much to our amazement there was a green Super Cub flying in and out of the flames while the tankers were thundering around overhead waiting for us to issue drop instructions. Chuck was angry. "Get his number," he shouted. From the looks of the skill with which the Piper was being maneuvered, I doubted that the task would be easy. As I dove on him, he darted away, understanding what I was trying to do. After an incredible dog fight, where the 206 was badly out maneuvered by the nimble Super Cub, I finally got his "N" number. He sneaked away, slipping down shallow valleys in the rolling hills and we finally got our tankers into the action. We found out who the pilot of the Super Cub was, none other than the long-time crop duster Frank Michaud. He was one of the crazy biplane tanker pilots I had admired way back when I was first learning to fly. I asked him over the phone what he was doing down there and he said, "Taking care of my customers." "What do you mean?" I asked with puzzlement. He replied, "If you guys had just left me alone, I would have blown out those flames. And by the way, that was a hell of a good job flying that clumsy 206!"

As a member of the Aero Union flying team, I attended an annual meeting for air tanker pilots that was hosted by the U.S.F.S. whose key speaker was Lee Myers. I was shocked at the tirade of insults he spewed out at the pilots and their crews. You would have thought that he was the only one who knew how to fly an airplane or knew anything about safety and fire control. He called us all a bunch of assholes and worse! In spite of the mantle of power Myers carried, after the first shock subsided, the angry pilots returned his insults. Myers had apparently forgotten that these pilots were all one of a kind, and were not easily pushed around. They were definitely not timid souls. In the end, the discussion covering pilot mistakes during the previous season became more scientific and cordial.

Air tanker pilots were certainly a cross section of types. There was ultra-conservative Aero Union chief pilot, Ken Otten, who kept his collar buttoned right up. Conversely, there was the kid captain who flew for Roseberg Flying Service. He was in his twenties, and had wild blond hair draped over his shoulders. I was impressed at his audacity when he stepped out of the captain's seat of his Douglas DC-7 wearing nothing but cutoff Levis, thongs, and a pair of sun glasses.

It was late November of '72 and Harry Miller and I had

attended the first U. S. Forest Service-sponsored Air Tanker Pilot's School that was conducted in Marana, Arizona, courtesy of our employer Aero Union Corporation. The school was very interesting, but not as interesting as the long and tiring flight home to Chico in the company's Cherokee 180. It was one of those high pressure dominated times when the Sacramento and San Joaquin Valleys were socked in with heavy fog. Harry made a nice instrument approach into San Jose to drop off a pilot, and was in a rush to continue on to Chico since darkness was closing in. He thought we could make it without refueling. I said, "This aircraft leaves here full of fuel, or I don't go!"

I was well acquainted with the deadly nature of fog in the North State. Off we went over the gloomy tule fog and into the gathering darkness. No sweat, if we're unable get into Chico, there's always Paradise that is higher and only a few minutes away. Maybe—I was tense as the altimeter insisted that we should be rolling our wheels on the ground. I could see the lights of the ramp going by, but no runway. Harry made three or four useless ILS attempts and we headed for Paradise, still fairly fat on fuel. Paradise was about ten feet under the fog, and try as we might, there was no chance of landing. The Sierra Nevada mountain range loomed up to the east, its forbidding bulk only hinted at in the blackness tempered a little by meager starlight. I shuddered to think that we would have been *out of gas right now* if we had not refueled! There are no other suitable airports near the valley up and down the length of California. No sweat, we'll just climb up to my hometown of Quincy and have a beer before turning in. Harry poured the coal to the Piper and we began a gas-gobbling climb up over the chasm of the Feather River Canyon. Quincy lies in a bowl surrounded by mountains like a mini-Los Angeles. A temperature inversion occurs and favors the formation of fog during nights under high pressure. Quincy was fogged-in tight and so was the Chester airport area to the north. No sweat, we'll just continue on east to the Beckwourth Airport. It was actually a rather pleasant starlight flight without a bump, except that the fuel gauges were reading kinda low. Better not make any navigational errors. Guess what? Sierra Valley where the Beckwourth Airport was located was engulfed in a sea of fog! Next stop was the bright lights of Reno. It happened that slot machines clanging, whisky flowing, good food, and a warm bed beat the hell out of some of the rocky alternatives available out there that night!

My friend Harry and I had a fine time in Reno. Sadly for Harry, a terrible last moment in the near future would find him pitching straight up, then straight down through the swirling smoke and flames of a forest fire to his death. His final flight was in an Aero Union TBM air tanker. A Forest Service lead plane, a twin Cessna, struck and severed the Avenger's tail. The crippled 310 bellied into the grassy Humbug Valley, but the Forest Service pilot escaped unharmed. They dug a hole and buried the TBM.

On many occasions Everett Fox or Reid Steinbeck and I were called upon to chase fire bugs. These are individuals that get their jollies by starting fires. A standard joke going around the tanker bases suggested that most of those weirdoes were probably on the company's payroll. (This was never joked about in the presence of management personnel.) Executing circles on pylon, that is keeping your wing tip on a speeding car on a winding road, is a fun way to simulate wind during the maneuver. On some occasions we followed suspects in this manner at night, running without lights. While engaging in these operations, one must be careful not to run into power lines and towers. Everett Fox's colorful comment regarding the avoidance of mistakes was, "Don't shit in your messkit!"

For me, flying out of Redding was an opportunity to increase my multi-engine logbook time. Merl Blevens allowed me to fly first as an unpaid copilot, and later as co-captain, on Shasta Flight Services' nightly mail run in Piper Navajos. The route was from the homebase in Redding to Sacramento Metro, San Francisco International, a layover there, and a return flight over the same route. It made for a long night, but I catnapped on the SFO layover. I also helped load and unload the mail. Sometimes when the tankers were busy I had the opportunity to fly all day *and* all night except for catnaps. I wanted to be a pilot, so I needed experience, right? One night I occupied the left seat the paid captain, in the right seat. We were behind schedule and very much in a hurry. He impatiently rushed me through the checklist; we fired up and were soon hurtling through the moonless night sky. I leveled out at four-thousand feet above the valley, set the power for cruise and settled back for a routine flight. Suddenly the Navajo viciously pulled to the left! My hand and the Captain's collided in their efforts to turn on the overhead fuel pumps and switch the fuel selector. The left engine surged into life, but the right one sputtered and died, causing asymmetric drag and thrust, yanking the airplane back and forth. Same routine to get the right engine going; meanwhile I pointed the aircraft toward the nearest airport at Chico. The problem had been with the rushed checklist. The fuel selector positions for the auxiliary outboard tanks and the inboard main tanks are not obvious unless you really look at the levers closely. The fuel gauges indicate the quantities contained in the tanks selected. This should have been a clue since the gas person had left the fuel selectors on the auxiliary tanks while checking quantities and they probably indicated almost empty as we taxied out for takeoff. Neither of us noted the fuel gauge indications in the rush. We knew there was plenty of gas because the Navajo had just been fueled and the tanks visually inspected by me on the preflight. The captain blamed the gas boy. I blamed us. I always wondered how many B17s screwed up on fuel management during the war. The wartime configurations included many auxiliary fuel cells, called "Tokyo tanks." The trick was knowing where your fuel was, and keeping fuel rather than air in all those fuel lines. The night was not over!

At San Francisco International we were cleared to land on runway 19L and ordered to hold short of 28R. Still being in a hurry, the captain, now in the left seat, continued inbound at high speed. He then put on the brakes by shoving the propeller controls forward thus flattening out the pitches and creating drag. (Good trick, except that the effect was not powerful enough, and it is terrible for the engines.) We rolled right through 28R and 28L barely escaping with our lives as a heavy jet was forced to maneuver because of the incident. The captain somehow escaped with his Commercial ticket intact.

Most days were pretty boring and the pilots found ways to fill in the time. Some read girlie magazines and some took correspondence courses. Copilot Bill Waldman built a perfect radio-controlled replica of the Grumman AF. He spent $500 on the project. The time came to test his beauty.

As evening approached at the Redding base the mini-aircraft was launched. We watched in horror as it executed a figure "D" and hammered straight in, leaving almost no recognizable parts. We assumed he could fly real airplanes with more skill!

While flying Airco for the CDF, I watched Don Rogers' great skill. A master of the AF, he would sort of swish his tail over a spot fire and very rarely miss. Roy Reagan (the President's nephew) made his debut as an air tanker pilot. There was no doubt that he was skillful. Whether he was sane or not was another matter. One night after everyone left the Redding

Tanker Base, I stood on the ramp, mouth agape as Roy took off in the AF, its powerful radial engine roaring and ADI water injection fluid squirting. He reversed direction, back toward me, and gathered speed. The screaming AF headed right at the Forest Service headquarters and pulled straight up at the last moment. It continued in that attitude for a seemingly impossible time, almost stopped, and then reversed direction to a straight down attitude, the engine sounds changing. I honestly thought he was going to crash straight into those buildings. I didn't think he would be able to pull out, but the big single-engine machine missed disaster by a gasp! If any Forest Service personnel had seen that action he would never have flown a tanker again!

Reagan and Waldman clashed one day when Bill allowed fuel to overflow during the refueling of a C-119. The volatile stuff was spilling off the wing and onto the running engine of the fuel truck—a very dangerous situation indeed! Roy was outraged and called Bill every name in the book. I was surprised that Bill took it since he was a bodybuilder and quite able to take care of himself. It was probably just as well considering that he would have to answer to "Chief Pilot" Roy in the future. For non-military pilots, Aero Union had a policy of requiring a certain amount of agricultural aviation experience in order to move to the left seat. They felt that crop dusting required a continuous series of decisions that lent itself well to building the skill necessary for fire bombing missions. Waldman spent time spraying crops in Canada.

I finally talked myself into the right seat of a B-17G with Bob Walker as my captain. Bob tended to be cantankerous but took care of his copilots if he liked them. One time I complained about how much work it was to pull the propellers through by hand (to free any possible hydrostatic oil locks in the lower cylinders). Bob allowed me to run them through with the starters in defiance of company policy. One day Bob and I were launched out of Redding to a fire located some miles to the north. We leveled out for a while and set the power and mixture controls for cruise. Later, Bob asked me to reset the power for climb. I dutifully started by pushing the four mixture controls forward to the rich position. Suddenly there was silence as all four engines quit firing in unison. Bob's hands leaped off the wheel and flew around the cockpit, slapping mine away. The engines roared back to life as he pulled the mixture levers to the aft position. I just knew my copilot career was over. After things settled down Bob looked over at me and grinned, "Got awful quiet, didn't it?" (Increased fuel flow, or "rich mixture" in most aircraft is forward with the red-colored controls, but backwards in the Fortress. In the B-17 pushing the mixture controls forward cuts off the fuel to the engines, effectively killing combustion.) Bob was near retirement, and although he loved to fly, he didn't like to show it. For example, he would say, "When I retire I'm going to buy a little fishing camp in British Columbia. I'm gonna have an old wrecked airplane out back so I can go out every morning and piss on it!"

Dale Newton, the president of the company, had his share of challenges. Once, while I was circling above the action, Dale was dropping into an area where he had to turn his B17 in front of a parallel ridge. The obstruction was rising up from the Pit Arm of Shasta Lake. Sometimes the air gets to roiling around and won't let you do what you want to do, especially in an aircraft designed for high altitude bombing. The B17 was heading for the ridge and not turning. My gut tightened up. Was I about to observe a horrible crash? Nope! The lumbering tanker suddenly slewed to the left and avoided smashing into the ridge. Later, I asked Dale how he managed that. He said, "I had to chop the power to the two left engines." (That created an extreme amount of drag on the left wing like sticking a giant oar in the water to turn a canoe.)

It was fun to watch Dale's partner, Dick Foy, land a B-17. He flew the thing like a Piper Cub and would touchdown in a three-point attitude while most pilots preferred the safer wheel landing. I was pleased that Bob Walker let me do a lot of landings. It was necessary to wheel on the B-17 when landing loaded, but I rather enjoyed the three-point touchdown myself.

Roy, who had flown military fighter jets in Korea, did not qualify to fly multi-engined air tankers. To remedy, this he checked out on a C-141 Starlifter operated by his reserve company, took a trip or two to southeast Asia, and then promptly resigned his commission. He then progressed upwardly within the company to hold the title of chief pilot. I watched him take off on a ferry trip to Idaho in a four-engined DC-6 with several engines trying to quit and restart. It sounded ugly with those engines missing, quitting and restarting as the big bird's nose pointed toward Boise. Pretty gutsy on Roy's part, but then, he'd never been short on nerve. This aircraft had been sitting for a long time. Who could know what lurks in unused fuel lines and tanks.

Gary Hendrickson flew fighter jets for the Navy for only a minimum period of time. He disliked the regimentation of military life. After resigning, he returned to Willows to work with his colorful "old man," Harold, who was a crop dusting pioneer in the Willows area. He taught his son to take life with a grain of salt. Gary's natural inclinations drew him to Aero Union Corporation, who actually flew old war birds. Where else can you get paid to fly these wonderful and expensive relics of history? The company asked him to break into the large aircraft by copiloting a C-119. He was hesitant. He told me the airplane looked at him with an evil eye and said, "Come to me, I am going to kill you!" Going against his better judgment he copiloted the damn thing anyway. By hook or by crook Gary ended up in the left seat of a B-17, but he still had his own ideas about when to come to work and how to accomplish the day's mission. Several company tankers were on standby at the Siskiyou County Airport waiting for the smoke to clear so they could go earn some money. Gary and his copilot showed up a couple of hours late for standby after a night of revelry in the village. Being offended at an official reprimand, Gary made it clear that he knew they couldn't fly anyway because of the smoke. In every air tanker crew, the copilot is responsible for washing the corrosive bentonite slurry off the belly of the aircraft. Not Gary's! He hired someone to do that dirty job while he and his copilot watched from the relaxed comfort of their lawn chairs. Bill Harnden would say, "In order to be an air tanker pilot you must belong to the IWW union."

"What the hell does IWW stand for?" I asked.

He replied, "I Won't Work!"

Gary's B-17 was dispatched to Montana, but didn't arrive when expected and the brass began to worry. Not to worry, when the war bird finally showed up the explanation was that they had to stop off for lunch. Some days it seemed as though the whole world was burning up. Gary thundered out of Lewistown to a fire. All that thundering took a lot of fuel, a commodity that Lewistown was out of. When you ran out of fuel you couldn't go make money, so Gary asked permission to divert to Miles City where it was reported that fuel was available. It turned out that slurry was available, but no fuel. There was just enough avgas sloshing around in the B17 to make one more drop and still make it to a third point where more fuel might be had. Gary called into somebody, and thought he heard permission to divert to the new destination over the radio static and traffic. Unfortunately, the word didn't make it back to Aero Union, or the right fire boss, and for a couple of days nobody was sure where Gary went. Rumors were flying that he was barnstorming—not only selling rides in his B17 and conducting tours, but buzzing and sightseeing. Of course Gary denied all and insisted that he had been out flying on fires, and had been given permission to drop on targets of opportunity. With the Western United States burning up, who knows? A guy could get lost in all the activity.

After a few seasons with Aero Union, flying all sorts of aircraft, and even restoring an AF for them, Gary moved on to single-engine experimental biplane firebombers in Nevada and Utah. It was a ball except for the time he hit a mountain. He was flying a Grumman Agcat equipped with a standard 600-horsepower Pratt & Whitney R-1340 engine and had written the *Before Drop Checklist* himself; mixture-full rich, propeller-full increase, etc. Somewhere south of Wells at the 8,500-foot level *it* happened. Swooping in on a spot fire, Gary made the usual precise drop made possible only because it was an Ag Cat with an ag pilot at the controls. Pitch up, power on, bank downhill. All going well except for the power part—no power! Gary instantly assessed the situation; it was perhaps barely possible to glide to the valley below, except that such a pass would take him across the raging fire. Hitting the ground and blowing up didn't sound good. Right in front of him was a bare ridge with an uphill aspect. No time to do anymore assessing, he hit the ridge, rolled up the hill, and stubbed a wheel on a rock. With surprisingly little violence, he came to a stop with the tail pointing straight up. After helicoptering the Agcat off the ridge, the engine was run on a test stand to determine why the power didn't respond to Gary's request. Gary figured it out himself; at 8,500 feet above sea level, the checklist shouldn't read "full rich," but "rich as required." The combination of too rich a mixture and a rapid throttle demand resulted in—well, you know.

I finished up the Anthropology M.A. in 1972. I had become fascinated with what we believed about the development of the Homo sapiens brain. My Master's Thesis was entitled, "Belief System Components and their Interrelationships." Subjects such as perceptual screening and decision making were very germane to flying. It was all arranged for me to step into a teaching position at Butte College the moment I had the Master's Degree in hand, but I was sick to death of college life by then and went back to flying full time.

Chapter 11
Crop Duster

The duster pilot stood by the pearly gate
His face worn and old,
He merely asked the man of fate
Permission to the fold.

Saint Peter replied,
"And what did you do on earth to gain admission here?"
"Oh Saint Peter, I was in ag aviation
For many a weary year."

Then the gates swung sharply open
As Saint Peter touched a bell.
"Step in," he said, "and grab a harp,
You've had your share of Hell!"

Uncle "Dinty" was a senior captain for American Airlines. I had been begging him for years to put in a word for me somewhere—anywhere! One day I received a letter from Dinty saying, "It occurred to me that you might be airline pilot material. I have called a friend of mine at American Airlines and you will be hearing from him." Soon I received a letter from T.M. Meldon, vice president of flight. He wrote, "—we would love to have another Moore in the American Airlines family. We'll just put you in the next flight engineer school. Please fill out the enclosed application and send it back to me." I was shocked! No tests, no nothing, just report for work. I was higher than a kite. I went to work every day at Enterprise Sky Park with a new buoyant attitude. After all, I was a short-timer, wasn't I? I could just see me aboard one of American's shiny 727's working my way up to captain, wearing one of those nifty suits in the terminal. I could picture the adoring passengers taking note of my captain's stripes as I strode down the ramp to the cockpit. Meldon's next letter came as profuse apologies. At thirty-two I was too old. I would never make captain. "Sorry!"

That was disappointing, especially considering the fact that we were broke. Working for ESP and going to college had been expensive. I needed to find some way to save us from starvation and the streets. Just at that time, I ran into Gary Hendrickson and some of his crop duster friends, who convinced me that I could become one of them! Little did I know what *that* meant! Over a few beers I heard about the thrills, adventure and big money. I remember how I had thrilled at watching them work. I couldn't help stopping on the highway and observing their artistry. I had to become one of them!

Wardman Flying Service ended badly. Herb and Lorraine had been divorced for some time and Herb been skating on thin ice politically with county officials. He got drunk at the bar at Sacramento Executive Airport while on a charter. An FAA friend stopped him from taxiing out and got him a room at a nearby motel to sleep it off. Soon afterward, however, his Navajo was again rolling down the taxiway toward the runway. Airport officials blocked his path with a gas truck. This led to Herb's dismissal as airport manager by the Plumas County Board of Supervisors. He sold out and left town. The message was clear— flying and drinking do not mix!

Just before resorting to the crop dusting thing, I thought that maybe I would rather come home to Plumas County. I made a bid with the board to replace Herb who was all for it. Unfortunately, any help from him was to my detriment. I wrote letters and brought enough supporters from the Enterprise Flying Club to fill the Board of Supervisor's chambers. In the morning the Board of Supervisors said that I was their man. Satisfied as to the probable outcome, the Enterprise bunch flew home. Before the afternoon board session rumors were passed around about my wild childhood, and though the actual juvenile records were supposed to be sealed, the Supervisors reversed their earlier affirmation. Not only that, I was told that if I tried to go into business on the airport on my own, I would soon be run out of town! A pilot who had previously worked for Herb, but later schemed against him, took over. The first thing he did was remove all the first solo shirt tails generated by the Wardmans over the years that adorned the knotty pine walls (including mine). He tried to destroy any reminders of past successes.

I figured that I might as well check out the crop dusting scene. I soon found that nobody would trust me to fly their valuable airplanes. The first ag season was working for Hendrickson Air Service. I began by standing on the bug-infested ground, waving a flag instead of roaring across the fields with wild abandon, my white scarf whipping in the slip stream, and bank account swelling. Actually, I can see that was the best place to start to learn the business, from the ground up, as long as you didn't get stuck on the ground too long. Also, when your crew complains bitterly about the hard work and low pay you can smugly say, "I used to do it." When the flying season arrives and the ag operators get swamped with job orders, operators and pilots alike tend to panic. New pilots jockey for position for a seat in an airplane. The experienced pilots watch and are amused. There was rarely enough time to keep up with the work. In an area that depends on a single crop, such as planting and fertilizing rice in California, or spraying weevil infestations on alfalfa in Nevada, everything happens at once. It seemed that everyone, except for Harold Hendrickson, worked their pilots and crews at maximum capacity. They would insist on the heaviest possible loads aboard the aircraft and maximum hours on the pilots and crews. There were no safety margins left on takeoffs, or any other part of their operations. The old pros usually got away with it, but what about the new pilot? After taking a few light loads, the new pilot was expected to perform right along with the pros without making costly errors. When he struggles to keep up and can't, his already shaky confidence is further undermined. The pilot will then try harder and get into more trouble by rushing around on the ground and turning tighter in the air in an attempt to keep up. He would rather die than see the look of scorn in his flying partner's eyes when he misses a flagger and slows up the whole operation. The newcomer grits his teeth and thinks, "If they can get out of this lousy narrow, short strip with that heavy load then, by God, so can I." Well, maybe you can and maybe you can't. Could it be that the pro you are flying with told you that he only uses thirty-three inches of manifold pressure for takeoff when actually he uses thirty-six? Your partner may tell you that he never uses more than thirty inches in a turn when he really uses thirty-two and flaps. He might not have mentioned his use of flaps to decrease his turn radius. Not being wise to the lies and omissions, you chalk up his superior flying performance to superior ability and vast experience. You don't dream that this is sick crop duster humor. The plain fact is that many established ag pilots have won their reputations through incredible hardships and are not just a little jealous of their knowledge and their hard-earned positions. Some of these miserable bastards will make *certain* that you will not soon take *their* jobs.

Gary's dad was an old-time military pilot with flying experience most can only dream about. He was also a gambler and did not fit any mold. For example, he was passing through Elko one day, and thought he'd try and change his luck. Change it did when he hit a big one at Keno. He bought a Grumman Agcat with the proceeds which became known as "The Keno Kat!"

As I said, Harold ran his business like no other. First of all, he paid me well as a flagger and also paid for my motel room (very unusual in the crop-dusting business). He told me to think of my position as a ground school. I took his suggestion to heart and set out to learn all I could. I could see there was a lot more to the crop dusting industry than I realized, including the art of flagging.

The typical day would begin at dawn with a strategy meeting. Afterward, the loaders and flaggers would spread out and soon the pilots would begin the first sortie. Aircraft would come and go with great precision and the fields would receive their fertilizer and rice seed. About noon the airplanes would go silent, leaving the flaggers idle in their fields and the loaders cooling their heels at their trucks. The pilots and Harold would gather at the Blue Gum Inn for a huge lunch and (it was rumored) several rounds of martinis, all paid for by Harold. Work usually ended early, and when all hands arrived back at the hangar there would be a giant tub of beer on ice waiting for them. The events of the day would be rehashed followed by instructions for tomorrow. Then, the pilots and crew would go out to dinner and engage in lengthy bull sessions. After a hearty meal came the live band music and far too soon, closing time. The bands would play especially for rice season and people would gather from far and wide to join in the excitement. I even played a few solo guitar and singing sessions for extra money or a free dinner. Once in a while, though, you just had to go to bed early to catch up on your rest. It was a good thing that rice season only lasted about six weeks because a body could stand only so much.

I met a lot of new friends. The Hale brothers, Wayne and Don, who claimed part Cherokee ancestry and who were as different looking as day and night. Wayne was powerfully built and about six feet tall, dark complexion with bright blue eyes. He spoke softly with a West Coast accent. Don, on the other hand, was also powerfully built, stood six foot five, was very light complected and blond, had bright blue eyes. He talked with a deep Oklahoma drawl. They were both lady-killers! Don enjoyed plucking on the guitar, and one morning we were still plunkin' and drinkin' whisky when the sun came up. Don said that he guessed we'd better go to work. I went out in a field and waved a flag and Don waved back at me grinning like a fool as he flew by in an Agwagon. Later that day he ran out of gas and landed in a field!

Wayne and Don sprayed nights down south. I bribed them with many drinks to get ag pilot ground instruction. They told me that during night operations the flaggers use a flashlight that should be aimed at the airplane and moved in an up and down motion. The flashlight should be on when the airplane is about halfway through his turn around. The pilot may be looking back to estimate his required turn radius, enabling him to roll out efficiently and begin his application in the minimum amount of time. Surprisingly, a standard size flashlight with good batteries can be seen for miles. If the flagger goes to sleep (or passes out as the case may be), it's dangerous staggering around with a heavy

Mom

Dad

Uncle David

Johnny at Quincy Sky Harbor 1944

Mom's last flight

The borate crew at Beckwourth

Twenty years old—flying and actually getting paid to do it!

Sacramento Sky Ranch 1960

Bob Lockwood issues a unicom advisory at Enterprise Sky Park

Training glider pilots at Enterprise Sky Park

Red and Gerry at Enterprise Sky Park

Two tricky machines!

Orbiting a fire in an Aero Union Corporation C-119

Fall flying was cold in this 600HP Stearman

The eager crew services my N-3-N at Chico

Goodbye crop dusting—hello Sugarpine Aviators!

What is a crop duster pilot in his seventies doing on a Navy Seal ship?

load on a dark night with no guidance to the field. After ordering another round, I was instructed that, day or night, sometimes the pilot will elect to fly under the wires. Flaggers should be trained to hit the deck if it appears that the airplane is going to come unexpectedly close. Flaggers have been killed because they were not alert. Of course, the pilot must shoulder the prime responsibility. If he hits a flagger, it is his fault. If he snares a power line in order to avoid a flagger it is also his fault. The flagger should remain alert to things the airplane is doing. For example, if the airplane stops dispensing material part way across the field for some reason, the flagger should not move to the next position. Likewise, the pilot should watch the flagger for possible attempts at communication. Novice pilots have been known to make four or five passes before they realize they are out of material.

One day while flagging, I saw Bill Whitfield speeding by in his Ranchero pickup, and although he waved at me he wore a strange expression. One of his rookie pilots had the opportunity to fly the big Thrush Commander and earn some big money. As the day got hotter and the engine temperatures soared, the pilot insisted on taking big loads. The heavy aircraft plowed up dirt with its overheated engine when a jug (cylinder) finally blew. When I waved at Bill speeding by I didn't realize that he was going to the scene of the crash. No wonder he had heart trouble. *Something* happened on a pretty regular basis at Willows Flying Service.

The stories and safety tips went on and on, (especially if I kept buying), like the discussions about when power and telephone lines pass through the middle of the field you are spraying. According to journeymen pilots, it is often more comfortable to pass under them than to take a wild ride over the top. When pulling up over lines or obstructions and then jamming the nose down to quickly return to appropriate spray altitude, the negative gravity forces will cause your gravity-fed engine to run out of fuel. When you level out and resume positive G forces, it will *probably* start again. I was definitely all ears, trying to be ready when my chance to fly came.

The boys told me that the practice of approaching a set of wires heavily loaded in a nose high and slow configuration will get you someday. You are blind and susceptible to wind shear. You may find yourself behind the power curve and out of luck because you can't see, can't climb, and can't turn. When crossing over the lines while arriving at or departing a field, it is better to watch the poles rather than the lines that may be invisible in certain light conditions or backgrounds.

Les Waterman spent years trying to work his way up from a truck driving job to a duster cockpit. Finally Harold Hendrickson took pity on him and made an offer. If he bought the company's 300 hp N-3-N and fixed it up he would be allowed to fly for them during rice season at ground crew wages, plus expenses. The aircraft was in several thousand pieces. Hendrickson got rid of a basket case and Waterman got a chance at the brass ring! Les grabbed at the brass ring and tore into the mess of parts and pieces. Hundreds of man hours and many midnight candles later, there stood the N-3-N as good as new and ready for its mission. I doubt that Harold ever expected the basket case to fly again, especially by rice season. Nevertheless, there it was, and it was time for him to hold up his end of the bargain.

As I flagged for the new ag pilot, I saw his expression as he putted by in his low-horsepowered craft. He was grinning so widely I thought his face would tear in half. After the season the N-3-N was still in one piece, and Harold requested that Les sell his toy and join the flying team. So Les became a highly-paid professional ag pilot flying powerful built-for-ag Agcats.

Like Waterman, I wanted like hell to get into the cockpit. I was tired of learning the business from the ground up. Unfortunately, the rice season was drawing to a close and there was no light that I could see at the end of the tunnel. I happened to talk to Chuck Stangle, an ag operator flying in Willows for the rice season. Afterward, he was to return to his operation in Nevada for his own alfalfa spraying season. Chuck offered me an opportunity to learn more about the business by loading for him. He would even pay me minimum wages while I was gaining experience.

Chuck told about the time he was spraying a field down south in a Pawnee. He struck a vertical pipe that was virtually invisible sticking out of the crop. The strike caused him to hit the ground and flip the Pawnee. He was hurting but alive. His partner continued to spray out his load when Chuck signaled that he was OK. He staggered out to the edge of the field where he could be picked up when the crew got around to it. That took a while since there was one fewer aircraft to help finish the job. After a medical exam, the doctor informed him that he had broken his back!

Chuck's Mid Valley Dusters was a true pioneering operation. By pioneering, I mean that most operators in their right mind wouldn't consider stashing fuel caches in fifty-five gallon drums all over northern Nevada. There were quite a few acres to spray around Lovelock, but Chuck's out of town customers were *way out of town!* He was about the only guy that could figure out how to make a living serving the tiny ranches scattered from the Black Rock Desert to Austin. To try and fill every possible niche, the Stangles owned a pizza parlor, too.

Chuck frowned on using rubber gloves to load poison because, "If you get a pin hole in those gloves they'll poison you every time you use them. Just be careful and wash your hands regularly. He said, "You'll know when you are getting poisoned, because your shit turns black!" The loading procedure for bug spray was to pour the organophosphate poison into the hopper with a five-gallon bucket and then add water. At the home strip, high pressure water was available for quick loading and an electric pump for fueling, but out in the field you often relied on a garden hose for water and a hand pump for fuel. Fuel pumped out of barrels had to be filtered through a chamois because of rust and water contamination. Sometimes those barrels sat there for months, or maybe even years. Chuck would make the rounds before the season began and place the caches at strategic points. It took a lot of forethought and salesmanship to make the season work out, and Chuck was a master at the practicalities of it!

Don Hale and Cliff Anderson also went to Lovelock after the California season was over. While I was loading methyl parathion into their hoppers with my bare hands, they flew Chuck's Pawnee and an N-3-N. Chuck flew his Stearman. The year before Don's brother, Wayne, had flown the N-3-N for Mid Valley, but it had ended up in a ditch upside down due to a faulty brake. Don and Cliff stayed in a hotel downtown while I camped in my pop-top Volkswagen van at the airport. Cliff's spouse showed up later in their motor home. Quitting time always came late, and by the time I ate dinner, I was exhausted. It seemed like only moments after I crawled into bed that Chuck would bang on the VW yelling, "Daylight come!"

Sometimes work was one big party. Cliff 's wife whipped up a big jug of martinis near the end of the day, but not quite *at* the end, and began serving them to the pilots as they loaded for the last few runs.

Don was flying the 600 hp "N" one morning. I was at the loading pit talking to Chuck and Cliff, when suddenly there was silence in the direction where the N-3-N was working. What happened to the engine noise? We all jumped into a pickup and charged out a dusty road toward the area, fearing the worst. There was the wreckage. You could see where the heavy Navy trainer had contacted the ground with a good landing, but then it had ripped through a fence and crashed into a deep ditch. Barbed wire encircled the cockpit and blood stains were drying on the panel. Where was Don, laying ripped to pieces in the brush? Nope. Finally a farmer drove up and told us that someone had taken him to the hospital with a gashed face and cracked ribs. Lucky guy! That barbed wire could have torn his head off. The fuel gauge didn't quite read empty, but since I was loading and he was flying, one of us might have remembered to fuel up had our brains not been running on empty from staying up all night. The N-3-N had a small reserve fuel tank, but Don didn't have time to operate the selector. The engine lost power suddenly, just as he pulled up from his last pass. It always seemed to happen that way.

Don headed back to the San Joaquin Valley, and Cliff and his wife left, too. Suddenly, there was only Chuck and me, two airplanes and lots of work to do! Chuck looked tense, then sighed and shrugged his shoulders and said, "Go ahead, show me what you can do." He pointed at the Pawnee. Even though I had assured him over and over that I could handle the job, he'd heard it all before. The long-sloped nose of the Pawnee can be deceptive if you are not accustomed to ag planes. The airplane was easy to fly and I yanked it around the sky in a manner I hoped looked skillful. After making a couple of simulated spray passes down the runway, I rolled into a steep power-off descending turn. Rolling out in a landing attitude, I plopped down right on the end of the runway in a nice, full stall. Traveling only a short way, I smartly flipped around, outwardly displaying boredom at the obvious simplicity of the maneuver. Evidently he was impressed enough, because he let me start flying (at loader's wages, of course). The part that he didn't know and I didn't tell, was that I hadn't intended to land on the very end of the runway. I thought I had plenty of airspeed for a longer flare. It was fortunate that there was runway under me when I hit the ground so elegantly. The sloping nose gave me the impression that my nose attitude was lower than it was.

Later, Chuck even let me try out his Stearman. That must have taken courage! I thanked him for giving me a break and he wondered out loud if he was really doing me a favor!

I began by flying light loads out of the home strip and spraying a few easy fields south of Lovelock. The break-in time didn't last long, though. I had just barely mastered the approach to the loading area when we went to work in earnest. Incidentally, to look cool you must place your wing as close to the loader as possible without hitting someone or something, and without raising a bunch of dust by using power to jockey into position. You must also remember to release the tail wheel lock.

Chuck made sure I understood that I had to shut off the wind-driven spray pump after emptying the liquid load, otherwise the seal would burn out. He didn't tell me what would happen if a blade flew off though. When it did, I thought I had serious engine trouble and I almost landed in the nearest field. The shaking ceased abruptly when I pulled on the spray pump brake!

Soon, I was assigned to fields completely surrounded by huge popular trees on all sides. The only way to spray them was to force the nose down so fast that the gravity fed carburetor on the 235 horsepowered airplane starved for fuel and the engine would quit. Chuck assured me that it would start again soon after leveling off. Yep, it did after flaring out from the hundred-foot plunge, and after I had been spraying several seconds (just like my barroom instructors said it would). The ride up the other side was just as interesting. If you didn't get close to the base of the trees, that area wouldn't get treated. Whenever there was a little break in the trees, instead of taking the wild ride over the top, I would just roll into a bank and fly between them in a momentary knife edge maneuver (just to see if I could do it). Naturally, your timing had to be just right, and there better not be any wires hiding in there!

Just east of Lovelock a series of ridges rise almost ten-thousand feet high and run north and south. On the east side of those there's a valley where several alfalfa farms with their bright green fields contrast with the purple-gray sagebrush. My loading operation was set up right by the county highway. I had miles and miles of paved road to takeoff and land in, and the fields were close by. It was an ideal situation, and the Basque farmers were friendly. When it was time for lunch, I dragged out my paper bag with a dried up sandwich inside and prepared to eat while sitting in the cockpit. The farmer wouldn't hear of it, so I accompanied him back to eat with the family and crew in the dining room. I gorged myself on bacon, eggs and pancakes. There were huge pitchers of ice cold milk and juice. They stuffed me until I could hardly walk. These were great people!

Chuck and I had another memorable meal far to the north on the edge of the Black Rock Desert. We did a spray job for an old couple who had a little ranch house and a small patch of alfalfa. The couple's wooden walls were adorned with an amazing collection of surface finds, ancient Indian spearheads, and arrow points. The old woman prepared us a breakfast fit for kings. Earlier that day, before dawn, Chuck began driving the water tanker to the job site. Later, I took off in the Pawnee guided by a set of travel instructions in the form of crude drawings. The driving was the more difficult part of the operation. Chuck had decided to take a shortcut over the narrow road around the west side of the treacherous King Lear instead around the longer, but safer, east side. The tanker was a huge, beat up, ancient blue thing capable of carrying more water than any nurse rig I'd seen before. When Chuck arrived at the work site, his face was ashen. He relived the moment, "I lost my brakes on the steepest part of the road and almost got killed!"

I used a winding road for the Pawnee's airstrip. The road cut through a slope of rocky debris that displayed a complex geological history with all the colors and shapes. It was necessary to drag the wings through the brush on the takeoff and landing rolls. A single strand telephone line stood parallel to the road and I had to fly under it immediately after takeoff, while loaded. Once, I lost concentration and accidentally clipped the line, effectively cutting off the farmer's only contact with civilization. Chuck fixed it himself later and took it out of my pay.

A new learning experience was spraying a crop near a lonely railroad crossing known as Jungo. We flew off of a dry lake bed whose surface was so featureless that you could not tell when you were about to touch down. A "glassy water" landing technique had to be used. I flew during the day and tended to the smudge pots and the loading for Chuck while he flew at night.

Occasionally on big jobs, Chuck managed to hire a few helpers. One time, after working from dawn until dark in Paradise Valley, Chuck dropped me and the tired crew off at a brothel in Winnemucca and gave us each enough money for a quickie. He said he was too tired, but for us to have fun, and drove off to the hotel. We too were tired, so we kept the money and opted for an immediate shower instead!

My first crop dusting season was winding down when I received a call from Aero Union's chief pilot, Roy Reagan, who had a copilot's seat for me in a C-119. I accepted the seasonal job with the provision that Roy was to give me a type rating check ride at the end of the season. (He had procured Examining Authority from the FAA as a necessary part of Aero Union's business to be able to produce appropriately rated pilots for their heavy bombers.) It was June of 1972; I was thirty-two years old and still ready to try anything.

Bill Harnden had worked himself into the captain's position through his tool box, but he was one hell of a fine pilot. I had much to learn and he was willing to teach. From the tool box side of the picture I learned that this aircraft, like most, was designed for steady flight and steady engine temperatures. As copilot, I was supposed to handle power and flap settings and manipulate the electric cowl flaps so as to maintain stable cylinder head temperatures. Every time I got too busy to screw with the cowl flaps, the cylinder head temperatures would fluctuate. Metal would expand and contract, and I could count on getting greasy changing the inflexible broken intercylinder oil lines at the next breathing spell.

The C-119 was known in tanker circles as "the box." It had served the military as a troop carrier. After a while it became known as a killer. You don't belly-in a C-119. Past experience has been that the weak bottom of the aircraft grinds off first and then the rapidly-passing terrain starts on the crew, feet first. There is a chute (like a laundry chute) you are supposed to step into that exits you out the bottom of the airplane in case a bailout is necessary. The only one I knew who carried a parachute was Bill Waldman, who was also a skydiver. I wondered what the captain would be thinking as Bill disappeared down that chute in an emergency.

The "Box" had some other bad characteristics. Forget about a single-engine, go around with the flaps and gear extended, even when empty. The performance simply wasn't there in spite of its

6,200 available horsepower. Also, the wings tended to come off in turbulence. The wings thing brings to mind the memory of Denny Conners. Denny worked hard and played hard. He was gutsy enough to dabble financially in the air tanker business with his own money. One fateful and fiery day in the Los Angeles area, he piloted his C-119 into severe turbulence and lost a wing.

There were some up sides to the Boxcar in terms of maneuverability. It went downhill well. Bill Harnden and I were seeing the bottom of many deep canyons of Glacier Park in Montana and the Selway wilderness of Idaho. We circled a fire while a B-17 attempted to descend to a spot fire in a particularly difficult and dangerous place with steep canyon walls. The Fortress seemed to have too much wing area to allow a rapid enough descent without exceeding its operating limitations. Its control responses were too sluggish to be able to make the approach low enough and still maneuver in the winding canyon. The pilot wisely gave up, and Bill decided to give it a try in the Boxcar. Gear down, full flaps, power reduced and steep banks, along with stubby wings, put the Box right down there where we were looking up at almost everything. Gear up, flaps retracted to drop position, power coming up, roll out, drop and out of there! Looks like we cheated death one more time. Actually, that's not altogether B.S. If the gear and flaps failed to retract—if the retardant doors failed to open—if one of those tremendously complicated R-4360 engines chose that moment to fly apart—if a crew member made a false move with a power or fuel control—if the captain failed to see that extra tall snag sticking up—if the exit route was misread—if if—. Well, you get the idea.

While flying a Box out of Chester the year before, one of Bill's engines failed. Of course, among the first things you do, is to lighten the load. He released half of his retardant, and to his surprise, the aircraft pitched up violently and he thought he was going to lose control in a stall. After everything settled down, he followed the winding Deer Creek Canyon, it's treacherous canyon country, to Aero Union's Chico base carrying a half load and one engine feathered. This tale came back to me in vivid color one smoky day when Bill and I were attacking a difficult area of a fire on the Klamath River. We followed the Forest Service lead plane to the drop area and pushed the button. Shit! Nothing happened; the load didn't drop. So, up to maximum power, flaps up, and we staggered over the ridge and into the canyon beyond to a relatively safe position with respect to the steep terrain and smoke. You'd better *always* plan to carry that weight out of the drop area, or someday—well, you know. We settled back in our seats with thoughts of ferrying back to base to get this deadly glitch fixed. Bill returned the drop control to the "safe" position. Blam! One drop door flew open and the Box pitched up and down out of control. Both captain and copilot struggled to dampen out the wild vertical gyrations and avoid hitting a canyon wall. Bill eventually wound his way out of the smoke-filled canyon and we returned to base to get the damn thing fixed.

On takeoff the usual procedure in any air tanker is to be in a state of readiness to get rid of its disposable load. Anytime you take off with a load, you should have your selector positioned to drop the load. When the critical segment of the takeoff and climb is complete, you then return the selector to the "safe" position, in order to avoid an inadvertent drop. We were taking off from Missoula, the landing gear was retracting and the flaps were about to follow. Bill selected "safe," and all hell broke loose. The C-119 pitched up and down violently; one second the windscreen was filled with sky and the next with ground. The wild gyrations were due to the sudden shift in center of gravity and the change in weight. The speed, power settings on takeoff and gear and flap positions also helped change the situation from a normal drop configuration to a deadly combination.

In order to get to know the complicated systems thoroughly and to be ready for my type rating checkride, I rewrote the Boxcar's military manual. I believed that I could present it in a more logical and instructive form for training. As I pounded away on my typewriter much of the summer, former military pilot and B-17 captain, Jerry Sharp, all in good humor, rode me constantly. He chided me about all the wasted effort I was putting in on that silly manual. At any rate, the company liked the manual and purchased it from me. The next season Jerry was chosen to transition to the C-119, and guess what manual he had to study. I got the last laugh!

Bill and I had suddenly been dispatched to Missoula, then to Tuscon, and finally to Ontario, California, this time for forty long days. It was a long way from our wives and children. Several other tanker crews also ended up in the area via miscellaneous dispatches. Chief pilot Reagan decided to treat us all to a popular, and *very* raunchy new movie called "Deep Throat," showing in Hollywood. We all settled down in our seats and Roy brought in bags of buttered popcorn for everyone. Waldman was heard cracking off-color jokes, and as the show unfolded I noticed Roy heading for the door, his hand over his mouth. Later, we asked him where he went. He replied, visibly shaken, "Jeez! I didn't know people *did* things like that!"

Fall finally rolled around and Reagan somehow never managed to give me my promised C119 type rating flight test before I had to leave and fulfill a previous commitment.

Between mid-October of '73 and the new year I flew 180 hours sowing and fertilizing wheat for Watts Ag. Eleven of those hours were completed on the first day after which I staggered back to my motel to rest a bit before going to dinner, but when I opened my eyes again it was morning and time to go to work again! My arms, shoulders and legs carried the soreness of a first-day manual laborer.

There exists an ag pilot rule that new guy always draws the worst airplane. My airplane featured a two-position propeller that vibrated forward to low pitch every time you let go of it. The trouble was while you were holding the prop control in place, the throttle would rattle back to a lower power setting. You had to let go of both of them in order to open the gate to begin broadcasting seed or fertilizer. The boss complained about the excessive noise from your high rpm's but had no idea what you were going through just to control the throttle and prop levers. I was comfortable with the Stearman and managed to get most of the problems fixed in spite of the resisting mechanic. It was hard to warm up to this wrench twister who recently moved to the west from Texas. He whined, "You California pilots are spoiled!"

Five blood-red Watts Stearmans flew into the Capay Valley and landed in formation on a grassy field. This was a *fun* work day. Some days were exciting enough but not so fun. I learned to not be afraid to reduce your load in spite of harassment from your ground crew. They are not strapped to the airplane and they have no vested interest. I was hauling load after load out of a short grass strip in a 450 Stearman with trees at the end, and I was just barely clearing them with maximum power. The rest of the pilots were sailing over them with relative ease, even though they were carrying the same weight. I asked the loader to give me a little less material, but he raised hell and said the loads wouldn't come out even. Stupidly, I continued to abuse my engine and scare myself. If I were to crash into the trees, it would be my fault. The ag operator would be livid with rage and the other pilots would nod knowingly and say, "It figures." The loader would laughingly tell his drinking buddies about the exciting day he had at work at my expense. Maybe it was a sick engine, or an airframe out of rig that caused the problem, who knows? Whatever the reason, I should remember, the loader probably can't do my job.

I made some adjustments to my face plate so that I could scratch my nose. I cut the bottom third of it off. This proved to be unsatisfactory because once you got into the air the wind rushed right under the opening and into my face, forcing seed and stinging fertilizer into my eyes. I suffered through a couple of watery-eyed days until I could buy another face plate. The new one hooked at the top and snapped to the helmet at the bottom. In order to scratch my nose, it was necessary to unsnap the bottom and lift it up. It wasn't very secure. If I turned my head sideways, the wind would try to tear it off. One time I was flying back from a job, and my partner pulled up right beside me. I didn't see him until we were practically touching wing tips. When we got into the hangar, he said good naturedly, "Gee, you don't look around much, do you?" Once the wind actually *did* tear the face plate off. I grabbed it just before it launched into space, but I couldn't get it to snap back in place, so I stuck it down under the seat. I was just entering the field to be seeded and could hardly see. I struggled through the load and congratulated myself for not hitting one of the many trees that surrounded the field. I made my way back to the Woodland Airport managing to land the cantankerous Stearman, even though I was swimming under water. I was almost blind and pretty damn scared. When the boss got back I was crit-icized soundly for a lousy seeding job. My explanation fell on deaf ears, and I vowed to do something about that face plate. The solution was to eliminate the hook at the top and create a swivel with a nut, bolt and washers. That way, when you wanted to get the thing out of your way you could unsnap and swivel it around without fear of losing it. My peripheral vision improved a lot after that!

I landed at a deserted strip northwest of Woodland and shut down to await the arrival of my crew. After some time had passed, it was obvious that they weren't coming. I began the task of starting my starterless Stearman and about twenty minutes of hard hand propping. I was exhausted and concerned. Concerned that (a) did I make a mistake as to where to meet the crew, (b) why won't this son-of-a-bitch start, and (c) what if it does start? At this point, how much fuel had built up in the intake manifold despite low throttle settings? Would it roar into life all at once and (1) kill me, (2) wreck the airplane, and (3) worst of all, would I lose my job and reputation?

The problem was solved when an ag pilot from another company landed and gave me a hand. He handled the brakes and throttle while I propped. After we got the stubborn engine started, he confided that he never shut his Pratt and Whitney engine off from morning 'til night regardless of starter capabilities. This didn't seem like an excessive statement to me.

It was December and I had been flying on bad strips and "hairy" fields. Today my older, more experienced partner and I had been landing downwind on a nice paved airport for about an hour. I landed tail low as usual and tapped the brake, necessary for directional control, when the brake suddenly locked up and threw both of my feet forward onto the sensitive toe brakes. The last thing I remember was a horrible sensation of height as I looked straight down at the runway through the idling prop. The aircraft pole vaulted off its nose and flew upside down and backwards before my helmeted head smashed into the ground. I blinked a couple of times, and what I saw as my eyes struggled to focus, almost stopped my furiously-pounding heart. Oil and gasoline were spreading out on the ground all around the hot engine. The smell of the fumes was powerful. In a desperate flurry of activity I unlocked my safety belt and shoulder straps and slumped to the pavement. Even with my face shield fogged and scratched, I could see that it would be impossible to wriggle out from under the pancaked Stearman through the space under the inverted cockpit. According to witnesses, I was out and away from that airplane so fast, that they wondered if I had even been in it when it flipped! I explained what happened to the boss who didn't believe a word of it. The loading crew, always quick to stomp on the new pilot, swore that I was landing too fast and slammed on the brakes, probably to avoid running into the loading pit. What do you say to someone who has his mind made up? I should have noted how strange it was that my partner had enough room to land over the top of my wrecked airplane, plus plenty of space to stop near the loading area. The truth was that I would have had to add power to taxi up to the loading area. A couple of weeks later, the mechanics took the brake apart, and found the rusted and broken return spring. It was the faulty unit that had caused the self-energizing brake to lock up with no help from me. The boss called for me to come back to work, but by that time I was already working for Bob Nelson in the Capay Valley to the west.

"Boomer" Bob was a long time friend of Harold and Gary Hendrickson, and Gary had suggested that I fly the Stearman that he had recently purchased and leased to Bob's Northwest Aviation. His borrowed strip was just south of the small town of Esparto. This home strip of Boomer's was really something! It was narrow, with crowns and creases, and had a bewildering array of mud holes. Its crosswind length slashed a muddy path between plowed and water-soaked fields. In other words, it was a pilot's nightmare. While landing or taking off, once the Stearman's tail was down on the clay, the narrow strip disappeared under the airplane's nose and you almost needed a sixth sense to guess where it was. I asked Bob if he would fly an aircraft as blind as a Stearman off this strip. He replied, "Hell no, I'll stick to my Agcat!" (built-for-ag aircraft like an Agcat has excellent forward visibility). Later we used George Knolley's ranch farther west in the Capay Valley. George was having Dumont Watson restore a classic Gull Wing Cessna for him in one of his old barns. Remember Dumont, Meta Pool's mechanic from Ukiah? We renewed our acquaintance.

Gary's 450 Stearman was not equipped with a starter or parking brakes. Some operators rationalize that starters are heavy and expensive, and that parking brakes might be inadvertently locked in the air (although I can't imagine how). Gary wanted his pristine Stearman kept in a hangar twenty miles down the road at the Vacaville glider strip, so each day I got up before dawn, drove all the way to Vacaville, dragged the heavy bitch out of its hangar, and propped it by myself. Sometimes it rained, but Boomer said the farmers wouldn't take that as an excuse, so rain or shine I hedgehopped back and forth to work in the weak light of dawn or twilight.

Farmers could be difficult, or downright stupid, at times. One windy day I was sowing seed on a field and the farmer complained to Boomer that I was flying sideways, and that he didn't want me working for him anymore. Bob asked if I had flown in a straight line and crossed the flaggers every time? The farmer agreed that I had, but nevertheless, he didn't like me flying sideways. Of course, I was using proper crabbing technique to fly the airplane in a crosswind but Bob couldn't make him understand.

I had the usual shoestring-type crew, flaggers who got stoned for breakfast and remained that way throughout the day, the loader truck operator was in horrible physical condition. He had a heart attack within the month, and was no help. The loader was an old fellow with a severe drinking problem. It was necessary for me to step out of the cockpit and climb up on the wing to load material or fuel the aircraft, because he couldn't do it.

One cold, wet, winter day the problem was fueling. I had to step up from the cockpit to reach the gas tank with the hose. It was accepted technique to leave the engine idling. Everything went fine until gas suddenly overflowed and caused a slippery condition around the hopper area. While attempting to climb back into the cockpit in my rubber-bottomed shoes, I slipped and kicked the throttle forward. The big radial roared into life, dragging the biplane forward. I flew off backwards and hit the ground rolling as the horizontal stabilizer flashed over me. Sitting up, I saw the whole horrible drama unfold as though in slow motion. The pilotless Stearman churned into the side of Bob's cherished Agcat. Pieces flew in every direction, raining down all around me. The Stearman's propeller became tangled in the Agcat's flying wires and wound it down to a stop. Shock draped over the scene like a cold blanket as the dust settled. The loader truck was already bouncing down the dirt road to fetch Boomer.

The mated airplanes were separated and we assessed the damage; the two wings on the right side of the Agcat were torn to shreds, and the Stearman's prop was bent and damaged. Bob was upset, of course, and wailed about his broken dreams, but insurance eased the pain. I expressed my anguish at what had happened. He exclaimed, "Johnny, the work must go on!" (He was probably thinking, when I run out of Stearmans, I'll fire the bastard.)

First we patched a gouge out of the Stearman's leading edge with a scrap of aluminum held in place with duct tape, and used the rest of the roll to patch various other injuries. We borrowed a propeller from "Slim" Davis which had been lying out in the elements for years. We installed it on only to find that it was frozen in the high pitch, low rpm position. I called Al Ewald and begged him to drive the two-hour distance from Redding to Esparto with his propeller paddle, in the hopes that we could break this bastard loose. Al's and our struggles were to no avail, and we had to look elsewhere for help. I discussed the problem with a mechanic at the Clarksberg strip, some thirty miles distant. Boomer decided that I should fly the frozen prop (installed on the airplane, of course) to Clarksberg where they had the means to loosen it up. The mechanic's advice was, "The runway is a little wet, but if you land about a third of the way up the strip, it'll be okay; Pawnees have been working off it."

The next morning was cold and some of the Sacramento Valley was flooded because of rain. When I arrived over the strip, my teeth were chattering. I noted the brown scar in the wet grass that I was scheduled to land on. The strip was narrow and one-way because of tall power lines on the south end. A strong tailwind didn't make the short runway anymore inviting. I could see mud puddles here and there; but as the mechanic said, there had been Pawnees working here. I could see them parked at the south end. As I made a tail-low, final approach, the runway looked okay. When I touched down at the suggested point, the wheels skimmed over the wet sod with a smoothness that would please any pilot. To my horror, as the full weight of the aircraft settled, the wheels kept sinking. I was slowing down too fast and the tail was coming up in spite of my full aft elevator. Things went to hell in a hurry; the deck was stacked against success. Tail wind, short strip, cruise propeller, and tall power lines looming up precluded the application of power to pull up over obstacles, or to power out of the mud. The parked airplanes were coming at me fast, so bloop! The tail went over the nose and my helmet was buried in the mud. Crawling out of the cockpit in the muddy goo, I threw down the road map I'd been using to find the place, and stomped on it in frustration. I was covered from head to toe with cold mud. The mechanic with whom I had discussed the runway condition came out, slogging through the saturated humus. Stroking his chin and evaluating the situation, he said, "Jesus Christ, I didn't know it was this muddy!" What to do, beat up the mechanic, blame my own stupidity for not recognizing a stacked deck because of the desperation to save the ag season? (If you chose the first option you'd better look for another line of work!)

Soon after the flip over a couple of FAA inspectors just happened by the Clarksberg strip on some other official business when they saw the Stearman. It had obviously been flipped and had a big hole bashed into the leading edge of the wing. The fed's noticed our unauthorized repair on the wing with its piece of aluminum held into place with duct tape. Of course they questioned the airport operators and soon had much of the story. I was called into an FAA office in Sacramento to explain the situation. The office walls were painted a severe white. At a conference table under bright fluorescent lights, I faced several grim agents. They wanted my Certificate, but I argued like a Dutch uncle, painting a depressing picture of a haggard wife and starving children at home, and anyhow, "You know what crop dusting operations are like!" They shuddered and indicated that they did, indeed; and allowed me to go on my way, provided that I report the next incident.

I talked to "Wild Bill" Whitfield and garnered a job for the rice season coming up in April. The only hitch was that I would have to work as a mechanic's helper part-time since all the pilot seats were filled. I was desperate for money and it was the only game around. The pilots began to congregate at the Willows Flying Service strip north of town. As the season began in earnest, I worked like a dog from dawn until dark washing and cleaning airplanes, and helping Joe, a mechanic from the old country. Joe had scars on his shoulder where a Stearman propeller had thrown him twenty feet when he was attempting to hand start it. I learned a lot from Joe, who was not a licensed mechanic, but who knew his stuff. Whitfield was the licensed Inspection Authorized mechanic who gave the orders and signed off all the maintenance and repairs, but it was Joe who did the work.

Jim Lister showed up with a tiny little trailer. Over a beer, I told him that I had 9,000 hours and should be flying instead of washing airplanes, but neither he nor anyone else believed me. I learned that Jim had flown with, and for, someone I had known previously while bunking at "Red" Jenson's place in Sacramento. It was Johnny Anoy, Red's ace mechanic/inspector, who reluctantly signed off the Annual Inspection on my Luscombe more than a decade ago! Jim recalled flying in formation with Johnny in his Agtrucks. He and Johnny had often "punched out" through the fog near Rio Linda and flew to job sites where the stratus was just breaking. Red had begged Johnny to stay with him and said he'd pay him anything, but Johnny insisted on striking out with his own crop dusting operation. Jim said that Johnny flew and ran his business superbly. Nevertheless, he was killed in an Agtruck accident.

Arrival was sort of a joyous occasion for the pilots. Bill encouraged them to warm up. Everyone got their chance to make a "pass" (buzz job) across the strip. Next, a *real* pilot was supposed to pull up into a hairy turnaround to show everyone their "stuff." When I did my pass, Jim said he had to admit that he believed that I had 9,000 hours. Didn't matter, I still had to wait for a seat, but at least my ego felt better.

Fred Gleason showed up tardy. He blew in from Nicaragua. He was a week late because he got on the wrong bus, he said. Just a glance at this character told you that he was different. With his false teeth out and his gray hair worn in a butch, he looked for all the world like the poster entitled, "Sleep Tight Tonight, Your Air Force is Awake." Fred's first task was to get familiar with the Agwagon he was assigned to fly, and check out the local area. He built himself a nest of foam rubber pads and pillows and strapped his body securely in the low winged airplane. Donning his scarred helmet, he taxied onto the short strip, and roared off into the blue, carrying more power than we were accustomed to hearing. He always worked his aircraft at much higher power settings than was customary. A few hours later the operations office received a call from Fred, who said he was stranded at Willows Municipal Airport. He said he was so low on fuel that he dared not make the two-mile jaunt over to the home strip. Wild Bill looked a little bewildered and sent me over there with a can of gas. While I was pouring the fuel into his Agwagon, Fred remarked that he'd seen a lot of short, rough strips but had been afraid to try them. These were the very same strips and road beds he would be required to fly off of every day. The home strip was very short and blocked by giant eucalyptus trees at one end. Fred porpoised all the way from one end to the other. One must be either an expert to fake that maneuver, or simply incompetent and lucky to survive it. The ground crews and pilots looking on all shook their heads in unanimous gestures of disapproval. Undaunted, Fred taxied up to the gas pit and stepped out of the cockpit with an erect and proud bearing as though he had just completed a daring and dangerous mission. Why wasn't this guy fired the first day? The boss was a character himself, and a lifelong outlaw. He found Gleason's antics amusing. Because of his heart attack, Whitfield didn't posses a valid Airman's Medical. That didn't stop him from routinely breaking the rules by flying back and forth in his Navion to visit his wife in Fresno.

The stories began; that is, Fred began telling personal flying tales that seemed so fantastic that no one took him seriously. Soon Fred became accustomed to his Agwagon and began dropping the aircraft in next to the loader with grand flourishes of expertise. Life was one big adventure. The sky became filled with loops, rolls and dog fights. Fred loved to lure other pilots away from the legitimate business of crop dusting, and into aerial combat. Of course, he didn't make much money this way, but he didn't seem to care. He said he had to keep in practice. "For what?" I wondered.

Over a few beers, Fred talked about his past. In WWII, he saw considerable action in P-38s and P-51s. In Korea, he became fed up with government policies concerning the avoidance of attacking certain enemy installations. One night he got drunk and, without authorization, climbed into an F-86, flew into North Korea, and shot hell out of a dam that was on the off limits list. That action drew reprimands, but his superiors were secretly pleased. Still not satisfied, another night while "likkered up" and barefoot, he sneaked into a red-tagged-for-maintenance F-86, and attempted the same stunt again! He had no ammo, and this time the enemy shot back, with the jet sustaining damage. Soon after that the military and Fred parted company, officially that is. I suspect he really never quit working for the government. Afterward, Fred spent years knocking around the world participating in revolutions and crop dusting. He told about how in Central America, he was required to wear an exposure suit, which consisted of a kind of scuba diver costume to protect the pilots against the pure parathion they sprayed.

After an especially bad exposure, Fred had to fly several hours across the jungle to the village where he kept a car. In order to sustain flight for that long he used a low power setting of 25 in hg and 1,500 rpm, an unusual combination. By the time he reached his vehicle, he really felt sick and it was miles out of the mountains to the nearest hospital. He set out in a desperate attempt to drive the bumpy road but soon passed out. A passer by found him near death and rushed him to the hospital where he was recognized. The staff was familiar with the poisoning problems of crop dusters, and Fred had been there before with the same problem. He was promptly treated with atropine in time to save his life.

Back at Willows, Fred flamboyantly swooped into a short, narrow strip with mounds of dirt on either side. Grass disguised the true heights of the dirt piles. Here he came on a low-turning approach. A wing tip swept through the grass and struck the hidden dirt. The Agwagon was yanked around and smashed to the ground. The dust cleared and the gray-haired pilot climbed out of the wreckage, looking around in apparent amazement. Soon the little strip was filled with crop dusting aircraft, their pilots milling around in a convention-like atmosphere, expressing concern and curiosity. The sounds of jokes and laughter floated across the flooded fields in the hot breeze. After some discussion, Whitfield decided that Fred should be flying a Stearman, an airplane he was more familiar with.

The method Fred used to strap himself into his Stearman was based on past experience in, God only knows, how many wrecks. He attached his shoulder straps to a cable that was secured to a strong point on the vertical stabilizer. He explained that this arrangement was arrived at after a couple of mishaps. During an attempt to slow roll his Stearman over the jungle, he suddenly became aware that his seat belt wasn't fastened. While he was hanging on for dear life to the tubular structure inside the cockpit, the airplane crashed inverted. On another occasion, he and another playful crop duster were flying in tight formation when they ran into each other. Both biplanes crashed. Fred confided that he had mangled hundreds of Stearmans in various mishaps, mostly because the foreign mechanics understood little about maintaining them. He also said that military officials usually controlled the crop dusting operations, and were not impressed by a pilot's experience until he had wrecked a few airplanes and had demonstrated machismo. He told about when the local military official would not let him drive his car on a shortcut to town that wandered through a certain piece of government property. First, he must prove that he was really a crop duster by flying his Agcat under a low bridge. The bridge spanned a raging river at the very bottom of a deep and rocky gorge. After squeezing through the dangerous pass Fred added a few rolls for good measure. After that, there was nothing the local soldiers wouldn't do for him. He was treated with the respect of a local folk hero. At another time, in another South American country, a certain generalissimo ordered Fred to take off with a load of sulfur. He was to perform the impossible task of dusting a field, bordered by tall jungle trees at night with no lights. The military man turned deaf ears to his cries of protest. To make certain the operation was completed as planned, the sadistic official announced that he would personally supervise the ground operation. It was dusk and Fred took off. Having no intention of following such insane orders, he located the general's official car in the dim twilight, and during a merry chase, dumped his whole load on the zigzagging vehicle. He returned to the base with expectations of being shot, but was surprised to find the general in a jolly mood despite his furiously watering eyes. He had once again demonstrated his machismo and was not again asked to attempt a job he objected to.

All of this was hard to swallow, but Fred added certain bits of authenticity to his stories when he landed out of loops and hammerhead approaches. Again, Whitfield was fascinated by this guy's abilities and craziness. It kinda reminded him of his own earlier days.

Pilots and workers continued to arrive for the beginning of rice season. Tim was a former Marine jet pilot who, like me, was required to work in the field for a while before getting a chance to fly. Another young pilot, Danny, arrived in his beat up old BT trainer with his girlfriend in the back seat. I'll never forget his grand entrance over the strip doing slow rolls no higher than a hundred feet! Whitfield hired hungry pilots and paid them peanuts. His operation could not afford many real pros.

Tim became known as "Terrible Tim." He began his apprenticeship flagging and loading. He was studying to be an attorney like his dad; but first, he thought crop dusting would be a glamorous adventure. Minutes after the first airplane was wrecked, Tim was in the office trying to get the pilot's job. When that didn't work, he had to go back to work flagging while becoming the butt of sly jokes. Finally his big chance came. He, along with experienced partner Jim Lister, flew off into the sunrise in their Cessna Agwagons. During the course of the day, when Jim's engine suddenly quit, he was required to execute a very difficult dead stick landing on a narrow canal bank. He almost made it; but just as the airplane was about to stop, the bank crumbled, and the craft slid into the waters of the deep channel. Everyone thinks of fuel starvation first. That night Tim spread the news in the local pub that his stupid partner had run out of gas, plain and simple! Upon investigation, it turned out that the mixture control linkage fell off. When Jim heard that his reputation was being ruined by Tim's wagging tongue, there was trouble. Tim somehow talked his way out of a beating. Terrible Tim felt that he was required to do too much flagging and not enough flying, so he quit and went to work for another operator, telling everyone how he had a seat in an Agcat. The only thing he flew was a flag. This really rankled him. Since he was planning to be an attorney, he thought he'd practice by suing his new boss for breach of contract. The end result was that Tim's burning ambition did not endear him to anyone, nor did it speed him on his way to being an ag pilot. The shame of it all was that he flew quite well and would have had his "seat" sooner or later! The gospel according to Fred Gleason was, "One should not blow out another man's candle in order to make yours seem brighter."

Whitfield assigned Jim Lister to a "Bull Stearman," hoping that he could fly it. Lister assured him that he could. A cold front passed through the area and created dangerous wind shear on the tricky Willows Flying Service's strip. It so happened that Jim was inbound for landing and Bill and I were there, watching his approach. As he dropped the 600 Stearman over the tall eucalyptus trees Bill repeated several times in prayer-like rapid succession, "I hope he's a Stearman pilot." Jim put it on the ground in masterful fashion and Bill heaved a sigh of relief, "Yep, he's a Stearman pilot!" No wonder Whitfield had a bad heart, and he died of it a few short years later.

I finally got my chance to fly the low-winged Cessna Agwagons and Agtrucks, and went at it joyfully. These aircraft had much better visibility than the Stearmans, and were a ball to fly, especially in the turns when they got a little light. It wasn't hard to see why Fred enjoyed dog fighting with them. I was also assigned to a Piper Cub and was applying Furdan and Bux low volume dust. I found the 85-horsepowered Cub to be blind in turns, but it was an airplane, wasn't it? It beat flagging.

There were familiar faces uptown where all the ag pilots from the various companies gathered after work. Cliff Anderson was laughing one night about the fact that he almost choked on a piece of beefsteak. We all—Wayne, Don and the rest of us—thought that would be a hell of a way to go after a life of cropdusting and performing dangerous aerobatics for air shows.

The 1974 rice season drew to a close and I was soon wandering around the San Joaquin Valley looking for a seat. I checked Eagle Field, an old military training base that looked like a place where crop dusters would be. Yep, the familiar smell of poison was everywhere. The huge filthy hangar was filled with Thrush Commanders; a few Stearmans and piles of radial engines stacked in the corners. There were rows of Stearmans parked outside in various stages of disrepair. I poked my head inside what looked like it could be an office adapted from the abandoned military quarters. Office workers directed me to talk to the boss, Brian Comfort. Brian was a big, wide guy with cold blue eyes. He asked me where I had been working and I knew I was sunk when he asked, "Ya ever wreck one?" I had to reply "uh huh," and explain the circumstances. I was amazed when he said, "OK, we'll give you a try!"

By the first of June, the family and I were parked at Eagle Field in our little trailer. It was extremely tight quarters. Later, we were allowed to take over a couple of rooms in the old barracks. The water for the shower was drawn from the canal. You dared not drink it, and when you showered, it left a white, chalky substance on your skin that itched like hell. Just west of the administration building were old military housing units used by migrant Mexican laborers. There was a large hall where dances were held almost every night. On the quiet June evenings, bois-terous Mexican tunes danced through the night. The kids, Teri and Jack at thirteen and twelve, were very bored and missed their friends. I missed my friends, too, but we had to manage, and so set about making a new home in Dos Palos.

I was assigned to Number 8, and much to my delight it was a fine Stearman with some interesting modifications. It was equipped with a Pratt and Whitney 1340 engine with the oil tank in the back, behind the pilot. You had to give this baby plenty of time to warm up. The cold oil in the long lines from the oil tank to the engine could flow slowly and result in a lack of oil pressure to the engine if too much power was applied too soon. Number 8 also sported four ailerons with servo tabs on all four of them as well as on the elevators and rudder. Servos were mechanisms that acted as automatic assist trim tabs; that is, the harder one applied pressure against the wind with the control, the more the servo would assist you. It was like power steering; you could fly with your finger tips. The flip side was, you had better have a light and sensitive touch or you would surely stall it out in a turn. It was also equipped with spray lights and turn lights, and, thank God, a windscreen!

The ground crew was quite a mix. There were college students mixed in with fourth-generation welfare recipients who refused to work beyond a certain amount. Some lived and worked only enough to score their next drug fix. Randy and Sandy, my main loader and flagger, began each day with a candy bar and coke. They didn't eat fruit because their rotting teeth couldn't manage it. Edward was a black kid who had struggled through high school barely achieving average grades. Even so, he sacrificed much to take a few college courses in an attempt to improve himself. Then there was "Bennie," a sour-faced, White, high school dropout, who required someone to explain instructions to him because he couldn't read or write. He refused to work with Ed because of his race. He said, "—and besides that he's an IGERNUT M—F—!"

My first night job! This was to be a real rite of passage. Here I was strapped into a blind Stearman, its ancient Pratt and Whitney R-1340 belching flames into the stygian blackness of the night. The crew was busily mixing chemicals and hooking up the hose that would carry the mixture into the hopper that was located forward of the cockpit. Brian was standing by to direct the operation. According to him, I should carry 150 gallons the first try just to be safe. Personally I would have preferred 100 gallons, but since this was my big chance to break into night spraying, I kept my mouth shut.

I held my flashlight on the plastic tube that indicated the level of fluid in the hopper. "Funny," I thought, "it should be filling up." Suddenly, to my horror, the evil-smelling fluid foamed up through the rotten rubber seal around the hopper lid. What a hell of a time for the sight gauge to go on the fritz. Frantically, I signaled for the crew to shut off the pump. Damn it! Two hundred and some gallons of poison when I only wanted half that. I could visualize the tires going flat under the load. This was ridiculous, of course, since I carried that much of a load every day. Day is the key word. This was night and that made a big difference. I thought of the poor devil I had replaced. He had flown many night hours in a Cessna Agwagon, but his first night takeoff in a loaded 600 Stearman ended in disaster. He porpoised off the end of the strip and terminated the departure on his back with his broken airplane's spinning wheels pointing to the stars.

I wondered if I wasn't rushing things a bit since I had flown only a few hundred hours of agricultural-type work, but as the '49ers lusted for gold, I lusted for the increased working exposure night flying would allow. Brian looked at the swollen hopper as it frothed over the top. He shrugged his shoulders and said, "You can handle it." Thinking dark thoughts, I fastened my chin strap and face shield. Pressing the trigger on the vibrating stick I energized my spray lights and taxied to the edge of the strip to perform my before takeoff check list. Controls free, lights OK on required instruments, oil pressure up, altimeter on zero, check turn lights. (Turn lights are spotlights located under the wings and pointing out 45 degrees.) Run up to 1,700 rpm and cycle prop, check carb heat and magnetos, note that the generator is indicating a charge. Release the spray pump brake and open and shut the spray valve to be certain that the pump is working. It is more than just embarrassing to stagger around with no way to spray those 1,600 pounds sloshing around up there.

Taxiing onto the runway I see that no one is landing and that all four of the flare pots on the left side of the runway are burning. Most night pilots utilizing radial engines like the lights on their left because the exhaust is blinding on the right side. If a lot of power is used with a 1340 powered Stearman, the flame shoots right by your shoulder. You can even warm your hands with it in the winter. If there is a lighted airport within range, many experienced night pilots use no lights at all at the strip where they are working.

The runway was paved and of adequate length. The flaggers awaited my arrival in the field equipped with new batteries in their flashlights. I locked the tail wheel and eased the throttle forward. The throttle must have been quite a way forward because the flame was a lot brighter than when I practiced light (that is, without a load). Slowly the tail came up and I began looking forward instead of using peripheral vision. Right rudder must be applied carefully to avoid over controlling the forces of torque, P factor and gyroscopic action on the heavy airplane.

Ah! In the air and committed to the mission, I released the spray light trigger and reached to my left and flipped on the left turn light. Climbing at thirty inches Hg and 2,000 rpm I looked for the safflower field several miles distant that I was supposed to spray. Everything looked different in the dark. Lights blinked on and off as the roaring biplane passed over the farmland at 300 feet. I wondered how I would ever see the flaggers' little lights flashing at me. I hoped they weren't asleep. I surely wasn't. I leveled out and reduced the power to twenty-eight inches of manifold pressure. My turn light picked out the road I was supposed to follow. Up ahead there was an intersection where I would turn left and follow a dirt road to the field.

Suddenly my heavy jacket was ripped open by the wind and filled up like a parachute. I felt as though I would be lifted out of the cockpit. I held the stick steady with my knees and struggled with the zipper. The hurricane ceased abruptly, and the buffeting wind settled down to its usual shriek. "Hmmm," I thought, "where did that road go?" I had turned during my struggle with the jacket, but I didn't know which way or how far. I was totally disoriented for a moment, and it was an ugly feeling. I circled, trying to pick out something I could recognize. Ah, there was an obstruction light blinking, about twelve miles away, near Dos Palos. At least I knew my direction from that point, give or take thirty or forty degrees.

Suddenly a Thrush Commander flashed into view in front of me, its lights flashing and wings rocking. I knew it must be Brian, who had probably seen me stagger off in the wrong direction from the ground. At least I hoped it was he, as I followed him off into the unknown. We made a ninety-degree turn and flew a few minutes in a direction I kind of wondered about. Was that who I thought it was? If it wasn't, could I find my way back to the strip I had left what seemed like hours ago? Before the cold fingers of panic gripped me too tightly, the other aircraft peeled off and buzzed a field. Sure enough, there were the flashlights patiently awaiting my debut as a night spray pilot.

I circled the field several times, making sure it was the right one, and worked up the nerve to go down into that black hole. I had checked the area in daylight and knew there were no wires close, but trees towered in the distance—far enough away, however, that an experienced pilot wouldn't give them a second thought. I swallowed hard, and with both turn lights and my spray lights blazing, I screamed down like a kamikaze from 500 feet. At that altitude your lights illuminate very little except hazy air that reflects back at you. It is better to leave them off until you get closer. Of course I didn't know that at the time. I was tempted to pull up and try some other way of approaching the field, but then the ground began to come into view. I pulled out of my screaming dive as the ground rushed up and a flagger's light flashed beneath me. Because of breakneck speed and inexperience at interpreting what I saw in my lights, I oscillated up and down across the field at heights ranging from two to twenty feet. Unfortunately, I had forgotten to open my spray valve until I was almost all the way across the 1,800-foot field.

Forgetting to spray left me with nearly a full load at the end of the field, so I felt it necessary to extend my turn since I didn't dare turn too tight. This brought the distant trees into the picture. I knew those hundred-footers were out there somewhere, but I couldn't see them, so I climbed. When the altimeter read about 400 feet above ground level, I felt safe and turned back toward the field. My approach for a second try presented the same problems as before. I was too high. Wisely, I reduced the power and didn't turn on my lights until I got closer. What a difference! It was so much easier that I even remembered to turn on the spray.

As the airplane became lighter, my confidence began to build. My turns became lower and tighter, and I worked my spray pass down from fifteen feet to seven or eight feet above the ground. I knew that eventually I would be able to fly on the deck just like the big boys. Increasing confidence was accompanied by a thrill of exhilaration, and I made several passes without noticing that no spray was coming out of the hopper. I cursed myself with two thoughts. The spray pump seal was probably burned out due to the lack of cooling liquid passing through, and the field would have a large colony of hungry bugs where I had failed to spray.

I pulled up and headed back for homebase. By now I was fairly well oriented and could already see the flare pots in the distance. Lining up for my approach, I remembered my first night landing in a Stearman on a strange strip. I grinningly recalled that I hadn't put enough cushions in the seat and could barely see out of the cockpit. On that occasion, I had seen what I thought was the strip in my lights. It looked pretty narrow with telephone poles right on the edge. Instead of circling and checking the situation over I thought, "What the hell, if they can do it so can I," And in I went. How I missed the telephone poles I don't know, but my "strip" had turned out to be a road *next* to the runway. This time I wasn't going to forget which side the runway lights were on.

After a greased-on landing, I switched off my spray lights and taxied with one turn light to the tanker for another load. I felt like a seasoned pro as the crew scrambled to service the aircraft. I probably wouldn't have felt so smug had I known that the boss felt compelled to spray the field over again after my shaky performance.

A pilot may be required to set his flaggers out. This procedure guarantees that the job will be flagged according to his plan. The flaggers must find the right field with semi-accurate sketches scrawled on someone's lunch bag. The pilots often ended up ahead of their crews on a lonely, bug-infested strip, and they had better be prepared with repellent. There were more than pesky blood-sucking insects out there at times. One night, while waiting for the crew, I witnessed a young Mexican couple having a fight. Another car drove up, and the quarreling couple jumped in their vehicle, pealed out wildly, with the second vehicle in hot pursuit. The whole scene had a sinister look to it. Love? Bad drug deal? Who knows! I hoped that I wasn't going to witness a murder, but they soon disappeared. I just sat quietly in my cockpit on the road bed where I had landed, dripping in sweat, the window sealed against marauding mosquitoes even though the air was hot and muggy.

At the Drew strip just before dawn I advanced the throttle. The exhaust glare became brighter and the familiar roaring louder. Just as the Stearman's tail was lifting and the runway ahead became visible in the twin beams of my spray lights, sploosh, my face plate, body, and entire cockpit became drenched with the corrosive chemical, Cygon! I yanked the power off and blindly skidded to a stop, managing somehow to remain within the confines of the strip, and avoiding a flip over. Jerking the mixture control back into idle cutoff, shutting off the master switch and releasing my seat belt and shoulder harness were the work of but a second. I leaped out of the dripping cockpit and ungracefully jumped into the drainage ditch next to the strip, not bothering to remove my helmet. After donning a spare pair of coveralls over my naked and shivering body, I checked to see what had caused the unexpected chemical bath. The small cap on top of the hopper was secured by an ancient, over center mechanism, that had come loose. After adjusting it to its tightest leverage, I prepared to take off again. Down the dirt runway I went, throttle forward and the cool air shrieking past my wet helmet and thin clothing. Sploosh! Son-of-a-bitch! It happened again. I skidded once more to a stop and performed the now practiced routine of shutting down the engine and leaping into the filthy drainage ditch. This time, after borrowing still another pair of coveralls, I made sure the damnable hatch wouldn't open by wrapping the mechanism with plenty of safety wire. The rest of the job went smoothly, even though I was cold.

I was glad the Drew Strip was reasonably wide, because on another night my generator went haywire and my dimming spray lights attested to the fact while I was spraying a nearby field. It was lucky for me that the loader truck left a small light on because I had only that to aim for while landing. The spray lights died just as I touched down, and without some guidance in the dark, I would surely have been in the ditch.

It wasn't long before I began flying a brand new Thrush Commander, a beautiful ag flying machine. The elevator was so sensitive that I only needed the strength of two fingers in a turn, and for good reason. Brian was fond of reversing the elevator servo tabs which in the normal position serve to increase elevator pressure against you. When turned around it contributes to an extremely light elevator pressure thus decreasing arm and shoulder fatigue. When a former military S2F pilot, stalled out his Thrush in a turn and crashed, you can bet the company mechanic quickly made certain that the federal investigators found everything to be in order in the elevator trim tab department.

Getting sprayed wasn't the only hazard waiting for flaggers in the field. Sandy was lucky she was wearing coveralls when a rabid skunk leaped for her face but missed and clamped down on her arm instead. She threw the creature to the ground and started running. Glancing back she saw the skunk scurrying after her, its mouth foaming. I observed from the safety of my circling aircraft as the terrified girl climbed into a pen full of cattle and got away. Another night I set Sandy out on a field in the Mendota area. As the pickup rattled up to the location where she was to begin flagging I noticed a set of eyes reflecting in the headlights. We stopped the vehicle and I heard the yowling of a cat. I walked out and investigated with my flashlight. It was a cat all right, just barely alive and being eaten by huge rats. I hustled back to the road bed and told Sandy we'd start from the other end of the field. I didn't tell her what I'd seen!

One night Judy was flagging for me south of Dos Palos and she had our giant German shepherd named Schazam with her for company. When that canine saw that eight-thousand-pound Thrush Commander coming at him with fire belching out the exhaust and stuff spraying out behind the wings he panicked. When the winged beast bellowed over him, he sprinted, terrified, to the pickup a half mile away. The window was only half open but the hundred pound dog got in anyway! Judy decided that Schazam might not be the best bodyguard for her. Nevertheless, on another night she wished that she had him with her. She was on a road bed next to a deep ditch overgrown with trees and brush. The spray job was about halfway completed when a vehicle stopped on the edge of the field. Two men stepped out and walked toward her. I watched them from my Thrush Commander. Neither Judy nor I liked the situation. We didn't know who these two were to be wandering around in the middle of the night. I rolled over into a turn on pylon, where the pylon was the two men, and focused my turn light on them. The blinding light allowed Judy to slip down into the ditch as they walked by. As they moved on, she ran like hell to her pickup and drove away. We didn't go back until we were certain those people were gone and Judy had someone to accompany her.

Hazards for flaggers ranged from abductions to dog attacks. Some got nervous when they were forced to work near bee hives. One bunch of workers plunged into a deep canal early one morning when the fatigued driver went to sleep after partying all night. The driver was known for his drug habit and for stealing welfare checks out of mailboxes. You could tell when it was about time for a fix, his eyes would bug out!

One of my college student flaggers backed her pickup into a small cement drain ditch one night. At first I thought she was only stuck, but it turned out that the drive shaft was broken and hung up. Since the pickup was blocking the drain ditch, the water was flooding the surrounding fields. The pickup couldn't be dragged out of the ditch until the drive shaft was removed. This was a trick in the middle of the night with the vehicle half submerged.

Back at the base when the flying is done, the flaggers and loaders are assigned to the dirty tasks of servicing and cleaning the aircraft and other equipment. If the pilot knows what's good for him, he'll stick around and supervise. Just when you are least expecting it, the crew may not complete their clean up and service assignments properly. The pilot had better check *everything* to be sure.

After the Willows rice season, Jim Lister landed himself a seat at San Louis Air, based at Los Banos, some sixteen miles northwest of Eagle Field. We saw each other often in the countryside. Eventually, he came to work for Agair and we began flying partners.

The day before, Jim had instructed his crew to flush out his hopper after having baited a melon field. They were also told to convert the aircraft from a duster to a sprayer. The conversion means removing the spreader and clamping on the spray pump, the spray booms, and other equipment. Since these operations had been accomplished successfully by the same crew many times before, Jim wrongly assumed this occasion would not be different. When he arrived at the strip near the field to be sprayed he discovered that his spray pump seal was burned out as a result of it spinning without any cooling liquid passing through it. Although he had placed the pump fan brake in the ON position in the cockpit, the crew had neglected to hook up the cable to make it work. Next, the crew didn't flush out the hopper as instructed. The result was that the entire spray system was plugged with bait. In order to get the load out without dumping the expensive chemicals and screwing up the environment, he could manage only one pass on the field before he had to land and have the booms flushed out. Each one of the forty or so nozzles and their diaphragms had to be cleaned individually. Ironically, the only ones who made any money that day were the ground crew who made the mistake. But, of course, the pilot bears the final responsibility.

The pilot must understand the loader's job and its difficulties in order to run the field operation. Being a versatile mechanic and a diplomat is good. Holding a black belt in the martial arts would be useful in certain labor relations. One day I had to face down Jessie and his crew to get them to work for me. Jessie usually worked for Brian, but this day he and his crew of cronies were assigned to load for me, but he didn't feel like working. Jessie was a bona fide, card-carrying member of the Mexican Mafia, and had only recently been paroled on a rape charge. After a few unpleasant words I told him and his crew that they could walk home if they didn't want to work. Bottom line—they worked. Jessie with the long black hair and flashing black eyes soon returned to prison, this time the charge was murder. He shot a couple of guys and burned them up in their car, but one lived to testify.

It was a black bastard of a night when I got my first chance to fly the Thrush Commander at night. The Hoag strip was rough, down hill and downwind for takeoff. There was a deep ditch on one side and a plowed field on the other. The strip was no big problem even though it was unlighted. What bothered me was the field we were going to treat. It was a long, narrow strip of cotton that lead uphill into the mouth of a canyon. About three-thousand feet west of the field lurked giant transmission lines that sagged across the canyon in the darkness. While sweeping the area with my spray lights, I concluded that it would be best to make a right turn out of the field in order to avoid an uphill climb into downdrafts. Brian countered my reasoning saying that the hill wasn't that steep and that a left turn would save time. Hell, I did it my way, (sounds like a song, huh) and things went smoothly. No sudden deaths tonight! Later Brian admitted, after a few drinks, that he tried a left turn only once and staggered up the hill almost to the wires. By the time he could turn around, the tail wind rushing down the canyon carried him beyond the flagger and time was wasted.

Jim and I were loaded and ready to fly on some oats and vetch near Eagle Field. Since there was no radio available, Jim waited long enough for the flaggers to get into their positions. Then he taxied out onto the windy strip and took off. I tried to keep warm while sitting in my Stearman with its engine idling slowly. As I watched the Thrush struggle I was surprised at the severity of the turbulence. The heavy airplane was having difficulty maintaining a safe flight attitude. Watching him being knocked around gave rise to thoughts of a warm place and a hot cup of coffee, so I taxied back to the ramp. Meanwhile, back at the ranch, the flaggers found that the first of the two fields they were to flag hadn't even been plowed to receive the seed! Meanwhile, back at the airport, I waited with increasing anxiety, noting the rapidly-changing wind conditions. Suddenly my partner's Thrush Commander appeared on a downwind leg in preparation for landing. His ground speed was astounding in the tail wind. When he turned into the wind on final approach his ground speed slowed to a crawl and the heavy airplane oscillated up and down like a yo-yo. The strong wind had now reached the ground, and I could feel it whipping at my own controls as I sat idling on the ramp. A well-executed wheel landing brought the matter to a close and we both taxied to the tiedown area.

I noticed that ten degrees of flaps helped the Thrush Commander into the air on takeoff and allowed a steeper bank when turning around to reverse directions. I began lowering my flaps before the beginning of my takeoff rolls. Brian asked me if the strip was so short that I needed flaps to make it into the air? Embarrassed, I replied to the question, "No, of course not." Later I observed his takeoffs and noted that about the time his tail came up, his flaps came down! Why do people do this to you? More sick duster pilot humor, I guess.

After performing a satisfactory run up and magneto check in my Thrush at the homebase, I flew to the strip that we would be operating out of. On the way I noticed that the rpm's were fluctuating slightly. "Nothing to worry about," I thought, "the tachometer is probably sticky." After filling the hopper for the first load, I began the takeoff run. (In a duster operation you don't check your mags before every takeoff.) Halfway through the takeoff roll, the round engine started backfiring and shooting flames out of the exhaust stack. I skidded to a stop at the very end of the strip, taxied back and investigated. The problem was in the right magneto, which was digesting some of its parts. I was lucky that the trouble became obvious when it did. Farther down the runway, or once in the air, I could only have dumped my load and hit the ground. In another case, a pilot of some fifteen-years' experience forgot to turn on his fuel selector. The result was that his Stearman assumed the traditional wheels up attitude of defeat just off the end of the runway. There's just not time to troubleshoot when flying a heavy airplane close to the ground and your power suddenly fails.

Taking off holds special hazards when two or more airplanes are working together. Two of Spain Air's Stearmans crashed at a strip near where my partner and I were spraying a field. We had been dodging them as they flew to and from their own job like busy bees. Suddenly we had the skies to ourselves and later I found out why. One Stearman pilot was on his landing roll when his partner began his takeoff, evidently without looking. The landing aircraft was blind straight ahead and had no room for evasive maneuvering. The result was two mangled airplanes. The pilot landing was very lucky since a strut poked through the side of his aircraft and lodged under his seat! A few years earlier a similar accident occurred but one of the pilots wasn't so lucky and was gored to death. Another time, one of Spain Air's pilots had another interesting takeoff in a Stearman. Shortly after becoming airborne, the propeller parted company from the airplane and he managed a survivable crash. In yet another takeoff incident, the Thrush pilot taxied his aircraft out onto the runway thinking that his partner had already taken off. The conditions were patchy fog. The other end of the runway was shrouded in the gray mist. Wisely, not wanting to take off into the blinding fog, the pilot decided to taxi to the other end in order to size up the situation from that angle. As he cautiously poked his nose into the dreary curtain of mist, another Thrush Commander roared overhead so close that he could count the rivets. With pounding heart, his first thought was, "That was really stupid buzzing me in the fog!" Later he found out what really happened. His partner was taking off, hopefully into the sunshine. At the last moment he saw the airplane in his way and just barely managed to clear him by pulling on the flaps and yanking back on the stick.

One veteran pilot lifted off in his eight-thousand pounds of Thrush Commander gracefully, except that a main gear wheel fell off! The pilot, being unaware that he was missing a wheel, flew to the field and began to put out his load. After a while he noticed the flaggers jumping up and down and pointing at the airplane. Unable to find anything wrong (the low wing configuration hid the wheel from his view), he finished the business at hand. On the way back to the airport he decided that the only thing he couldn't see that the flaggers could, was probably the landing gear. Unable to see a shadow, he chose a convenient canal and skimmed the undercarriage through the water. Noting that there were two trails in the water, he prepared to land. Still suspecting landing gear troubles, he made his touchdown, slow with power and flaps. It didn't take long to determine which side wasn't working right. The big airplane skidded to a stop with a minimum of damage, thanks to the skill of the cool headed pilot.

In an "almost takeoff" incident, Firebaugh-based Bob Vance was hand propping his weak batteried Thrush, when it roared into life, its throttle set too far forward. The parking brake was not set, nor were the wheels chocked. The big, low-winged agplane lurched out over a bumpy plowed field that was bordered on all sides by ditches and canals, its red-faced pilot running and stumbling in trail. As the pilotless aircraft approached a canal at a pace faster than Bob could run, it suddenly changed course and described a circle as it struck a clod of dirt. This fortunate event occurred several times, thereby saving a crack up. Finally the out-of-control machine hesitated in a rut long enough to allow a heroic (and nimble) loader to leap aboard and yank the throttle back to save the day!

In a tail-heavy Stearmans handling characteristics both on the ground and in the air are lousy. Some operators have cleverly enlarged their hopper capacities in order to haul larger loads of light, bulky material. To make this possible they move the cockpit aft eight inches and may change the location of the oil reservoir aft as well to accommodate the heavier and more powerful engine. Sometimes a lighter engine ends up perched there. Look out! You can expect decreased forward visibility. Control pressures feel a little different when flying from a rearward-located cockpit. Because you are sitting nearer the tail, the nose appears to wobble around kinda like a tail gunner in a B-17. Although you can get used to the position and higher-appearing nose attitude, I always thought a flip over would be violent. You are sitting farther from the protective cabane strut and closer to the vertical stabilizer, which always gets creamed. Wheel landings have you sitting up high and produce interesting sensations. In one tail-heavy model I flew, the nose actually came up by itself when you throttled back for a three point landing! One pilot told me that he stalled a tail-heavy Stearman in a turn and crashed. The airplane was not wrecked too badly, but there were flames in a small pool of gasoline. The pilot told me, "I could have put it out but I hated that God damned airplane so much that I just walked away and let the bastard burn!"

There is a tricky little technique for going around poles without banking or straying too far from your desired spray path. The procedure involves very good timing and a skid, first one way, then the other. You may wish to pass to the right of a pole, spraying as close as possible. You are passing under wires that do not allow room to bank. Using precise timing, first skid right just before you reach the pole, then skid to the left. You will fly sideways by the obstruction looking right at it (definitely not for the faint of heart). Be especially careful with this maneuver when upwind of the obstruction. I once used this technique to save my own life and that of a flagger who was not paying attention. I couldn't bank into a turn, and if I climbed, it would be right into power lines. His eyes opened up as big as banjos as the big engine and whirling propeller looked straight back at him as I skidded by him sideways!

When spraying a field with a line of very tall trees at the end of it, one must plan a pull up to allow a safety margin. Caution! Begin your pull up early, but not too early. A long, gradual pull up may put you into a tree near the top if you have misjudged your speed loss in the climb. On the other hand, pulling up too late may necessitate such a steep climb that you are forced to do precarious aerobatics at the top. Begin the pull up sooner with a tail wind.

Flying in a field near a strange crop duster is more hazardous than when flying with a partner. Partners have a game plan whereas you have no idea what the stranger is going to do. You know when to expect your partner to arrive and depart, but you have no idea when the stranger is going to take a lunch break. Could be he'll come back and maybe he won't.

Stalling and hitting the trees is not the only danger existing when you pull up over an obstruction that hides whatever is beyond. Remember Danny from Willows Flying Service? He landed a job flying a Stearman near Tracy. This day he was applying sulfur in a field adjacent to another pilot also applying sulfur. Somehow, they lost track of each other and both pulled up over a line of trees at exactly the same time and collided in a spectacular crash. Both pilots were killed instantly.

One night I was spraying a field in old Number 8, when a very large barn owl flew up out of the grain and crashed into my flying wires. It died with its eyes wide open and fixed on me. It was very distracting with this big bird staring at me accusingly. Its eyes were saying, "You killed me." I tried to shake the image out of my mind and concentrate on pulling up over the tops of tall trees in the darkness. Every time I dove back into the field and energized the spray lights there was that bird again. I was relieved when that load was completed and we could pry it off the wires.

Sulfur is commonly applied to cotton to control mites, and to grapes to prevent fungus. Applying sulfur has inherent hazards. Soil sulfur is much heavier than the dusting kind. Once I made the mistake of overloading because I didn't know the difference. I nearly paid with that lack of knowledge with my life as I staggered around the countryside, the Pratt and Whitney up front bellowing, and the pilot in the back dodging obstacles he couldn't climb over because of the unexpected weight.

We dusted sulfur at night sometimes because of the cooler

temperatures. This night the crew had set out three smudge pots for landing guidance. They were helpful because the 450 Stearman I was flying was blind looking forward, and without the lights I would have had to taxi quite a ways doing "S" turns for visibility when approaching the loader truck. As I was landing, I noted the flickering fire pots. Down went the tail and I counted one, two and suddenly I sensed that something was terribly wrong, but I didn't know what. I slammed on my brakes and skidded to a stop. When I looked around the nose, there was the loader truck just inches in front of me. I shut the idling engine down and climbed out, noting the pile of bags burning beyond the truck. I told the frightened helper *never* to burn bags until he had received an OK from me. I had mistaken the burning pile for another runway light and had been tricked into believing that the truck was much farther away. We both pushed the aircraft back so it could be loaded up again.

As the day gets warmer, pilots and crew watch the other airplane for a stream of fire coming out of the spreader. To fly sulfur in temperatures exceeding seventy degrees Fahrenheit is to court disaster.

The wind should be stronger than five mph and should be a crosswind. No wind, or a shifty wind condition makes the job miserable and lengthy. The pilot is either going to fly through some dust or wait for it to settle. Flying through sulfur dust is a good way to get killed because of the lack of visibility. Getting the stuff in the eyes will make them burn and tear, especially when exposed to wind or strong sunlight. The burning sensation will come in waves. I wondered how anyone could possibly fly in this teary-eyed condition? Believe me, you can if you have to, you must force yourself to see should you have an attack of tears at the critical times during taking off or flaring out for a landing. To combat the eye-burning sulfur, the best antidote is to cry a lot!

In the cool of the morning at a short sod strip, I stood back watching my crew choking and crying as they loaded bags of sulfur into the 450 Stearman. Bags were strewn everywhere, and as the last sack was loaded, I donned my open cockpit flying togs and strapped myself in. The bags, I reasoned, would be blown out of the way when I applied power for takeoff. This logic proved to be incorrect when a bag blew up and lodged on my left horizontal stabilizer. Picking up speed down the short runway laden with 1,500 pounds of flammable material, I was committed to the takeoff before I realized that something was wrong. The tail wasn't getting light. I pushed the stick forward hard and forced the tail into the air. The throttle was wide open and there was a ditch just ahead. I opened the gate wide, but sulfur doesn't dump very fast. I relaxed my straining triceps just a little and allowed the stick to come back slightly. The crippled Stearman limped into the air just barely clearing the ditch.

Once airborne, the nose would have pitched straight up if not for my crushing grip on the stick. Quite a spectacle when farmers looked up and saw a bellowing biplane staggering around at forty feet above the ground in an apparent attempt at skywriting. I very carefully banked the airplane to the left, then gradually around to the right in order to get pointed back at the runway. I was getting lighter now, but it still took slightly less than maximum power and almost full-down elevator to avoid a pitch up and stall. The not-very-long runway was rushing up at me at over 100 mph. I hit the ground in a wheel landing configuration and chopped the power. The tail dropped immediately and I skidded to a stop with little room to spare while the loaders scattered. I shakily climbed out of the cockpit and examined the bag plastered to my horizontal stabilizer. It was difficult to believe that a little sack could raise so much hell with the flight characteristics of that rugged old biplane. Don Hale further illustrated what a small disturbance to the airflow over the elevator can do. He took off from Five Points area headed for Raisin City in his Thrush Commander. A tear in the fabric on the top surface of the horizontal stabilizer had been repaired with duct tape. On the way home to Raisin City the tape tore loose on the leading edge and stood up in the air stream so as to act as a stall strip. The result was that the 240 pound pilot had to alternate his hands in order to hold the nose down during the ferry to his home strip. He also mentioned that the landing was "interesting."

Stearmans have a glass fuel gauge that hangs down underneath the top wing. A float in the gas tank located in the top wing center section is attached to a wire that extends down into the glass, indicating the fuel level in the tank. Seems foolproof, doesn't it? One night I preflighted Number 8 in a rush. Quickly shining my flashlight on the glass, I was satisfied that it read full. Later, as I was making my second spray pass, I caught a good look at the fuel gauge quantity indicator in the reflection from the spray lights while crossing light-colored ground. Egad! The indicator was resting on the bottom of the glass and wasn't even jiggling. I discontinued spraying immediately and pealed off in the direction of the Eagle Field with teeth gritted, trying not to think of what might be awaiting me in the darkness below. I made it with nothing to spare. Damn it, *always look into your fuel tank. Don't trust gauges!* Another point learned from Anthropology training: perceptual screening, you will see what you want to see. I wanted to see a full tank because I was in a hurry. I believed that the crew had fueled it as they had been instructed to do.

Brian was a veteran of fourteen-thousand hours in Stearmans alone. He related a tale of when he was spraying a field one night and noticed his low fuel condition the same way I did. He figured that he might as well spray out his load and make an emergency landing since there were no strips within his current fuel range. He was just finishing his last pass when the engine quit. At that moment, luckily, he had a landable spot in his spray lights and made a successful touchdown. The flaggers saw the unscheduled stop. They drove over with their pickup equipped with fuel and a pump, and added fuel. Now, with enough gas to make it back to the strip, and this field completed, it was time to move to the next job. All in a night's work!

Remember Fred Gleason? Well, there he was reporting for work at Agair, and that night we were to fly partners! He had been assigned a 450 Stearman and I a 600. Despite the unequal power plants and equal loads, he was out turning me. How that old guy could fly! (Of course he later admitted that he was running his poor engine wide open most of the time.) We finished the field with headland swoops in perfect unison. Our grand finale was poetry in motion.

One day Fred got drunk and took a radio-equipped company pickup to parts unknown. He began to recite poetry and limericks which continued on into the night. It had the irritating effect of blocking our attempts at operational chitchat. The company searched for the drunken philosopher, but to no avail. At about four in the morning, I was still flying and he was still going strong. As day wore on, Fred finally tired of the game. He began giving clues as to his position, and the chase was on! All available company aircraft searched from the air while the ground crews scoured the local towns for some sign of him. Finally, he voluntarily turned his pickup at a local bar. Much to my surprise, he was back flying the next day. When he showed up for work as though nothing had happened, Brian was caught off guard at his audacity and even a bit amused. Since he needed pilots he didn't fire him this time.

Next, Fred showed up inebriated to an FAA safety meeting. They were in the process of showing movies about propeller vibrations. Fred had a degree in aeronautical engineering, and it was only natural for him to stagger down the aisle, face the camera and proceed to deliver a lecture on propellers. Someone ended his evening as a public speaker by yanking him down into a seat.

Brian's skill as an ag pilot was superb. He had a great comprehension of the job, having been a farmer himself. I questioned his risk management approach, though. One foggy day Jim Lister and I were instructed to land on a road bed near the field we were fertilizing. The road was just wide enough to roll our Thrush Commander's wheels in the tire tracks. On the north side of the questionable landing site, there was a deep ditch, and on the south side, a freshly-plowed field that lay soggy and sloppy. Straight ahead a concrete pipe was sticking up which forced you to slip around it during taking off and landing. The crosswind was horrendous, requiring a high speed wheel landing and sometimes full application of the controls. To turn around after stopping, you had to hold the brakes and apply a lot of power, lift your tail over the ditch, swing around 180 degrees, and drop it back down on the narrow road bed.

I asked Brian if he thought it was worth the risk, that maybe a brake would fail or something. He said, "If you can't handle it, I'll do it myself!" (He probably had started his day with a little "royal" in his coffee.) My pride left me no choice but to carry on. If a brake did fade, you can bet who would be blamed for losing control and/or exercising poor judgment, but you have to manage the risk against how hungry you are.

One night I was spraying a deadly chemical combination of methyl parathion and phosdrin when I began to smell the stuff. It was blowing up from the floor right into my face. Many pilots and operators of the day would pooh-pooh the possibility of poisoning and continue working. I elected to carry the one more load it took to finish so we wouldn't have to go through the rigmarole of having to set the job up all over again. I held my breathe as much as possible. After landing back at Eagle Field, I found myself walking three feet off the ground on an organophosphate high. There was a crack in the fiberglass hopper and the deadly poison had blown right into the cockpit.

I knew that your liver must process this poison. Unwisely, instead of going to the hospital and getting some tests, Jim and I went out and had drinks that evening, all evening. We visited Don at his duster operation at Raisin City and recounted old times. Naturally this made my liver work overtime processing poisons. I staggered home around 4:00 a.m., only to learn that I was supposed to report to work at 5:00

I ferried a load of paraquat, a deadly poison to both plant and animal, about ten miles to apply it to weeds in an open field. The flaggers were in their places on each end of the field. As I approached the field to be sprayed, it seemed as though my mind were elsewhere (gee, I wonder why!). I zeroed in on the flagger on the far side of the field and sprayed a mighty swath right across a barley field on the other side. When I realized what I'd done, I felt like crashing on the spot and ending it all! As I expected, the boss didn't buy the "poisoning" explanation, and I was in the dog house. Even though you try hard, you occasionally screw up. Fred Gleason suggested chanting the following ditty under your breath when under pressure:

Here's to me as I gamble, sin and drink.
Here's to me as I ramble, sit and think.
When my flying days are over,
And my death has come to pass,

I hope they bury me upside down,
So the whole wide world can kiss my ass!

I needed to leave the valley. I longed for the mountains and forests of Plumas County and was sick of looking at endless rows of defoliated cotton. I told Brian that I was going to fly the rice season in northern California during Agair's slow season. He said, in an attempt to discourage me, "If you do that, you might as well keep going." I resigned myself to the idea of keeping going. It was in April that I tackled the new challenge of rice season in Chico Aerial Applicators' 450 and 600 horsepowered N-3-Ns.

Dutch, a part owner of Chico Aerial Applicators, sneered at the abilities of big airplane pilots, claiming that they could never master the N-3-N like he had. He said that in twenty thousand hours of flying dusters, mostly N-3-Ns, he had never come close to having an accident. While that may or may not have been true, the "N" was a formidable beast. The 600 hp version offers little forward visibility. I was asked if I wanted the cockpit canopy installed, or not. I replied, "Naa," remembering that visibility had been good from Stearmans with open cockpits. So, for the first job I headed into the fields with no canopy. There was no problem until I was loaded with seed and the stuff found its way under my face plate and into my eyes. It was a complete surprise! While struggling to see, I remembered that Watts Ag had opened holes in the fuselage and eliminated the windscreens on their Stearmans just to get rid of this problem. Bottom line, my first day was abysmal. While I was struggling to see with seed chafe in my eyes, Dutch said I looked like a salmon going upstream. No explanation was sufficient for him, but by the next day, I had that canopy on that airplane.

I was ferrying a heavy load of fertilizer from the strip to the field and not able to climb very high. With the nose so high you had to "S" turn now and then to make certain that there was nothing in front of you. Sometimes the hot exhaust located on the right side could distort your look ahead when S-turning to the left. Motoring along in the cold morning air, my eyes and nose were running a little. Then my heart almost stopped as a live oak tree sailed by on the right, its large canopy higher than I was. I thought in a moment of panic, "Christ, I could have flown right into the middle of that!" Later, I learned that some pilots have done exactly that.

Much to my delight, my former C-119 captain Bill Harndon was flying with us. He was a great help in giving me insights on how to best fit into the organization. I fit in pretty well, while flying some 130 hours in a month and a half. Len Parker was flying with us, too. He was a huge, exuberant guy. Len loved to do "whoop de doo" buzz jobs on the strip and showy turnarounds to landings, as did most of us. One day he whooped a little too high and the doo part smashed him into the ground short of the runway. He came limping into join the pilots and crews for an after- work beer and explained that he simply didn't know what happened since he had done the maneuver hundreds of times. Such was the nature of the beast. As the stick begins to shake, no amount of power will allow you to increase your bank and you had better not ignore that pre-stall signal.

Al Hirt and I were flying partners. I couldn't believe he kept hauling such heavy loads of fertilizer as the day grew hotter. I was struggling off the ground and almost stick shaking around turns with the engine bellowing to keep up. We didn't discuss it because there was a lot of work to do and nobody wanted to be the one to hold up the parade. Later, we laughed at each other when it came out that we each wondered why the other didn't down load when the density altitude got so high. It was the old ego thing, "If he can do it, then by God, so can I!"

Chico Aerial Applicators used dozens of strips all over the

north valley, some better than others. One landing area required you to arrive and depart under large power lines. There were bear pits, as Bill Harnden called them, on both sides. The technique in the blind N's was to do a wheel landing followed by judicious braking. Any excursion to the right or left would result in a disastrous wreck in a bear pit. One time after a whole day of working out of this awful strip the pilots were laughing about what a mess it was. Joking I said, "I think I can, I think I can," referring to the moment of transition between tail up and tail down when you couldn't see forward at all and you relied heavily on your brakes. Dutch was listening to all this with a frown. He looked at me and said, "It's just a matter of time," meaning that I would surely prang an airplane. What could I say? Barring mechanical problems, I had never lost control of any airplane. Actually, I was getting to like the N-3-N a lot and felt very comfortable on short strips in the wind. Dutch didn't believe that I was only teasing. In fact, before he hired me, he called Brian for a reference. Comfort's terse reply was, "He won't wreck your airplane." That was not a bad endorsement from a crop dusting operator.

Good brakes are important. Some operators will push you to press on in spite of the warning signs. To operate with flakey equipment is just plain stupid. Because of this attitude, many expensive airplanes have ended up in a drainage ditch with the pilot's abilities in question. About once in forty flight hours, the "N" that I was flying showed it's insidious brake problem. The left brake would suddenly fade on landing, forcing me into a hairy power and rudder shuffle to keep control. Then, the problem would disappear, and you could continue working. One day, near the end of the season, I was in danger of hitting something because of the damn brake. This time, I wisely told the field boss that I'd better take the bird back to homebase and get it fixed before something serious happened. He agreed. When I arrived at the shop, Dutch was waiting for me. I explained that the brake faded on me every once in a while and needed attending to. he jumped in the cockpit and tested the brakes that, at this point, were fully pressurized. he climbed out and said, "There's nothing wrong with these brakes. Collect your pay, you're through!" The next day Bill Harnden was assigned to my airplane, and the problem showed up again right away. He taxied back and told the mechanic to fix it!

We were now homeless and camping in the little trailer at Round Valley Lake. During May and June I traveled back and forth to Lovelock and sprayed for Chuck. Besides ag work, I gave some flight instruction and even flew charters in his Cessna 185.

In August we finally found a place to live near Quincy, in Meadow Valley. The transaction required the entire amount of the equity we had retrieved from the Dos Palos house for a down payment. I didn't think it would be a problem since I had arranged to fly a season for Agair at Gustine.

The Gustine operation carried Agair's name but Ed Wilcox was essentially in business for himself. I was confident the money was there since Ed's former pilot, the handsome and smooth-talking Chance Davis, spent a great deal of the season entertaining various women. He also wrecked a Stearman. Even so, he still managed to make $14,000 in a month and a half. I thought I was looking forward to a pleasant time in Gustine, but the season turned into a financial disaster! There was a cannery strike and they weren't buying tomatoes. Besides that, there was a scarcity of bugs to spray. Ed had to take all the flying he could himself, which put me in an awful financial bind. I was in desperate straits, running around the valley, living on credit cards while searching for another seat. Finally acting upon a suggestion from Don Hale, I looked up Dave Miller at Kingsberg. Dave's strip and home nestled among orchards, vineyards and was just south of the Kings River. (This was not the crook, Dave Miller, nor the brother of gas boy and entrepreneur, Steve Miller; this was the pilot, Dave Miller, who once flew head-on into a palm tree.) Dave needed help. I began spraying in his Pawnee, and soon graduated up to the "Blue Goose," a nickname for the early model Thrush Commander that was painted blue. Dave had worked hard for years and now enjoyed the situation where I was out making money for him while he was spending time on the golf course. During slow times I could drive home and return just for certain jobs. Life was pretty good working for Miller Aviation until early in October, when I learned how treacherous the fog could be around the Kings River.

A telephone pole suddenly materialized out of the fog. Yanking back on the stick, I watched it flash beneath the big white and blue ag plane. Desperately, I nosed down until a small patch of farmland reappeared. How had I gotten into this mess? About five minutes ago, I had climbed into the Blue Goose. As the big Pratt & Whitney radial warmed up, I scanned the horizon. I decided that the fog had lightened enough that I could ferry the duster to a strip four miles to the south where we would begin a long day of cotton defoliating. I wiped the windscreen clean of the dew that had blown onto it, cinched my helmet strap tighter and carefully fastened the shoulder harness.

Yesterday we had worked farther to the east and the fog hadn't been a problem. Conditions looked about the same as before, so time to go. I brought the 1340 to thirty-six inches for takeoff. Just before liftoff, dew from the crevices around the hopper lid spattered onto the windscreen; and, as the Goose rolled out on a southerly heading, the hazy sun made it difficult to see. No matter, I thought, I can see out the side windows. Since I was taking off without a load, I was easily able to clear the wires that I usually ducked under at the end of the seven-hundred-foot strip. When loaded, it was not only necessary to fly under the lines, but you had to skid around the edge of an orchard at the end of the runway. You couldn't take a very heavy load out of there.

Following a highway that leads to my destination, I failed to notice that conditions were rapidly worsening. At first, I was relieved that the sun was out of my eyes. But wait; the fog was getting lower. Still not realizing the extent of the trouble into which I had blundered, I decided to turn around; but as I banked away from the highway, the ground was lost in gray nothingness. Quickly, I turned in the opposite direction, but that was no help either. I was locked onto the road for my only visual cues whether I liked it or not. Due to the thickening fog I was forced to fly below the level of many obstructions between the airstrip and me, still a mile and a half distant.

My mind was racing. Should I pull up and climb for the sun? No way; the Thrush had no gyro instruments, and the wet compass wasn't even working properly. Land? There were open fields around, but I couldn't see far enough to determine if a field was safe. The road was lined with telephone poles that would never accommodate the Goose's forty-four foot span.

Water condensing from the soggy fog was streaming along the windscreen. The only way I could see the road below or the trees and power lines coming at me was to fly in a violent slip. Twenty feet below me, a car slammed on its brakes, the driver staring up at me incredulously. "I don't believe it either, buddy," I thought.

A set of wires flashed into view just above eye level. I darted under them, hoping there were no lines or guy wires low on the poles. My heart pounding furiously, I skidded around a mist-shrouded tree. "Christ," I muttered, "how long can I keep this up?" I lowered the flaps halfway and increased the rpm to 2,000. The dirt strip lay somewhere just ahead, parallel to the road, and I hoped that I might clear the wires at the end and throttle back for a straight in landing.

Wires ahead. Up I went into the gray hell and down again. There was the strip, right next to me, outlined in the fog. A tree flashed past. I'm too far to land; I'll have to go around. I turned away from the strip and headed out across a featureless alfalfa field, nudging the prop control to full rpm and extending full flaps. I could see straight down only if I remained just a few feet off the ground. I tried to visualize the location of the power lines and big concrete silo ahead. I knew that my pattern would have to be tight. My only directional guidance came from water checks on the ground lined up east and west.

Around I came, hoping to arrive at the strip in a landable direction. The runway flashed into view, but my angle was too great. In desperation, I forced the right wheel and wing tip onto the ground, hoping that their drag would turn the airplane in the right direction. The craft was too heavy to be deflected, though, and the wing tip and wheel dragged across the runway as the spray boom splintered. A tree flashed into view, and I applied full power. The wounded Thrush staggered into the swirling gray mist, and the ground disappeared.

The stick was jammed. I wrenched the ailerons loose just as the ground reappeared at a crazy angle. Hanging on the edge of a stall with full flaps and full power, I forced the damaged Blue Goose into a right turn. Power lines flashed into view and I staggered over them. With deliberate resignation, I lowered the Goose's long nose and throttled back for a landing. Forward visibility was zero. Straining my eyes through the wet windshield, I glimpsed a cotton field. Flaring carefully, I felt cold despair. The wheels and flaps defoliated cotton for a good 200 feet, then the ride became rougher. Finally, the tires dropped into the rows deeply enough to start the 8,000-pound craft over in a horrifying forward flip. Slowly and with great violence, the Goose crashed onto its back. A cotton row crunched through the overturned structure, forcing my helmeted head forward. All I could see were cotton stalks and dirt. Gasoline was pouring out of a ruptured tank. I unbuckled my seat belt and shoulder straps, braced my feet and charged through the Plexiglas like a fullback out for a bonus. Moments later, I staggered onto the road to flag down the crew, who were groping their way through the mist.

The cockpit roll bar broke and split in such a way, that had it not been for the shoulder harness and the Calmill helmet, my brains would have been splattered all over the place! Missing in most ag aircraft are the most basic instrument flying aids such as an electric turn/slip indicator. That's all I would have needed to confidently climb up through the fog layer.

Although Dave was very understanding, there was only one Pawnee now and I was the odd man out. I hitched up the trailer to the tired Dodge pickup and headed north on 99 with a heavy heart. As I was driving I noticed an air show going on at Merced. I really wasn't in a mood to stop and watch.

I had seen Cliff Anderson perform in his Pitts at a little air show in Firebaugh. Involuntarily I had sucked in my breath as I witnessed the most spectacular series of high-speed rolls I have ever seen, which began immediately after the wheels parted with the runway. The daring maneuvers were topped off with an outside immelman. Wow! Sadly, the next time the name of Cliff Anderson came up was when Don Hale showed me the blackened wreckage of his Pitts where it was stored in his hangar. Cliff's charcoaled shoes were still there. The accident occurred at the Merced Air Show which happened to be in progress just as I was driving away from Kingsberg. He had pulled straight up from the deck and then flat spun back to earth. Don speculated that he could have passed out from the g's.

Judy was working for minimum wages at the Ten Two Restaurant nearby in Meadow Valley. She was an excellent and cheerful waitress and received generous tips from grateful customers. Unfortunately, Jerry, the cold hearted bastard of an owner, made her turn them all over to him. Nevertheless, any money she brought home helped as winter closed in. I did some freelance instructing at the airport and managed to land a job driving a beer truck.

Spring was approaching and son, Jack, was helping out with the household food by fishing in the open ditch above the property that served as our water supply. A call came through from Al Hirt whom I'd met while flying for Chico Aerial Applicators. He was now running a satellite base in Wray, Colorado, for Top Flight Ag Service headquartered at Imperial, Nebraska. He said that they needed help. We worked out a strategy where I would fly airlines to Denver and they would fly over in a light aircraft and pick me up. It sounded better than whatever I was doing. Late in April of '77 I hit the road again.

Ron, the owner, maintained an apartment in Denver so he could conveniently make the rounds at all the hot spots. I was required to accompany him in a night or two of revelry, and was tired of it by the time we finally arrived in Imperial to go to work.

At first I bunked in the bottom floor of Ron's large two-story home, but soon I was assigned to an abandoned office where my bed consisted of a mattress on the floor. The shower was very strange. It was a large, tiled room with a shower nozzle sticking out of the wall like in a gymnasium. The place was full of stored furniture. Since I didn't have a car, I occasionally borrowed the state-sponsored "airport loaner car." It was lucky to get out of the parking lot. One dreary, overcast morning I had planned to drive to town for breakfast. I cranked the engine over and heard a terrible "yowl!" I jumped out and popped the hood to discover a poor cat, still barely alive that was chopped to pieces by the fan; ugh, so much for breakfast! I wished that I could go home!

Top Flite had two Thrush Commanders, and much to Ron's credit, he gave me the new one that seemed to turn tighter and burn less fuel than the older one. I thought I was a real hotshot until we traded planes one day and the fuel/oil burn situation was reversed! I followed Ron around to different strips and we worked together for a while to let me get the feel of the area. I was less than secure though, while following him through blinding rainstorms since he knew every little strip to put down at, and I didn't have a clue! Ron wanted me to fly near the Nebraska base for a while before sending me to Colorado on my own.

Soon I was venturing far from the homebase. I'd top the fuel tanks with 106 gallons and the hopper with spray to be put out in low volume. I wasn't to come back until it was all gone. I ventured over thirty miles, located a number of fields, sprayed them using "automatic flaggers" and returned before running out of fuel. Automatic flaggers are rolls of toilet paper you release from a canister on the wing to mark the point where you entered the field.

The farms in southwestern Nebraska are composed mostly of circle irrigation systems. There are thousands of them and they appear identical. They equipped me with a county map that showed thousands of crisscrossing roads at ninety degree angles to each other. In addition, I armed myself with a sectional chart and watched for the names of towns on water towers to help locate the proper field.

I pulled up out of a field to ferry to the next job. Suddenly, while pointed skyward, the whole windscreen of the Thrush was filled with the belly of a giant B-52 bomber! I could even see the rivets! I rolled into a turn and expected any second to be smashed into the ground by the twin tornadoes from the bomber's wake turbulence; but, thankfully, it never came. This area was part of the Air Force "Oil Burner" routes. These four-engine war machines were practicing low-level bombing runs at barely subsonic speeds!

It was so flat in Nebraska that it was difficult for me to judge the height of a low overcast. Once, I took off thinking I had hundreds of feet to climb before encountering the base of the overcast, but was in it almost immediately after liftoff. I carefully lowered my nose and skidded around the pattern with wheels almost touching the dirt around the airport, and my head almost in the fog!

The most difficult time for me was when there was not a lot of work to do, and yet I couldn't afford to go home. I visited a rare prairie dog town and enjoyed observing the social little beasties. Once, I went to a dance in a neighboring town and ended up playing and singing with the band. They wanted me to travel with them, and it was tempting. I gave dual instruction in Top Flite's Rockwell Aero Commanders. Joe Weiss was preparing for his Commercial Certificate and I was able to recommend him for the flight test. I didn't know that he was also getting ready to take my job.

Al Hirt decided to move on, so I was reassigned to take his place at the Wray satellite base to do small seeding and fertilizing jobs. My field person was a disgusting character who spoke about women as though they were cattle. He would say crap like, "I challenged her but she broke for the gate," or "I covered her!" I have never liked male chauvinists.

Although I met interesting people and saw new country, *all* the money was burned up in travel. I dreamed of home and family. The kids both played sports and Teri was a cheerleader. Judy had her horses and I was missing it all. I also dreamed of creating a flying business of my own. I even whiled away the lonely hours creating a logo that consisted of a circular pattern saying, "Sugarpine Aviators of Plumas County." I drew a bald eagle in the center. I had always admired the huge sugarpine trees of home. There certainly were none here!

The job was over. I took a bus from Imperial to Denver and spent more on food than I intended. I didn't arrive in Denver with enough money for the air fare to Reno, nor did I have enough to buy food for several days on the bus. I called (collect) to my old friend John Metzker and requested that he wire me some money for the flight. Fortunately, I had enough money for a motel room that night.

Part II
THE PROMISED LAND

Chapter 12
Sugarpine Aviators

While back in town from flying in Nebraska, I dropped by the airport and Curt and I would talk. He was *the* airport manager and *the* Fixed Based Operator, but he was mostly interested in fooling around with antique cars. He told me the story of the hot summer day when a group of three FAA officials was getting ready to takeoff. The wind, as usual, was out of the southwest and the pilot said he would be departing in a westerly direction on runway two four. Curt said that a westerly takeoff would not be advisable due to the uphill gradient of the runway, higher terrain in that direction, and downdrafts. The pilot retorted, *"I'm* the pilot and *I'll* make the decisions." Five minutes later he and his two passengers were dead! Curt described the 150-horsepowered Cessna Cardinal struggling by the end of the runway with its engine running poorly, probably due to an excessively rich fuel mixture. Soon, it was just barely missing the trees in the valley. When the pilot tried to turn around at the narrowing west end of the valley, the stall speed increased as the angle of bank increased, and suddenly they fell straight down into a gravel plant.

The manager's style of flight instruction was interesting, to say the least! Pete owned a Cessna 150. He soloed in under four hours and was soon taking scenic flights all the way to the coast by himself without benefit of cross-country instructions or the required formal sign offs. After all, it was his airplane, wasn't it? Curt grumbled about one of his students by the name of Frankie Dee. Frankie was a red hot carpenter, but when it came to flying, Frankie was on another planet. According to Curt, he flew his rental two-place Cessna 150 OK, but he swore that he could *not* check him out in his four-place 172. Frankie, frustrated, purchased the 150 he had learned in, and he and his spouse proceeded to fly it all over the western United States camping. He just knew the couple was doomed.

I returned home from spraying in Nebraska in July. Curt asked me if I would like to buy his trainer and take over the flight instruction. Personally, he was more interested in flying his Twin Commander on a Forest Service Air Attack contract. I went for it. I again called John Metzker for help, and he came through immediately with the $5k purchase price. Curt allowed me to operate out of one drawer of his desk in the airport office.

The little 150 was well into its second top overhaul (which means that only the cylinders had been overhauled but not the "lower end"). If we were to survive, it was going to have to work, and work it did as the word got around that an enthusiastic instructor was in town. To my amazement and frustration, after I had bought the plane and began training students, Curt did his level best to run me out of town! I lost my desk drawer privileges. He seemed to become jealous when he saw the sudden increase in activity. I must have struck him as an irritating young upstart. After a short battle of wills between us, though, he lost interest and minded his own business.

Janet worked as a waitress in Bob's Cafe, and she was a delight to teach. You told her something once and she never forgot it. Curt was the pilot examiner, and I had worked hard with the enthusiastic Janet to get her ready for her flight test. She couldn't wait to show him her stuff. The big morning arrived and I accompanied her to the office. She was grinning from ear to ear. Patronizingly, Curt signed her off without even a flight. You could see the disappointment draped all over her. It was heartbreaking. She had been cheated of that wonderful knowledge that she had really earned that certificate. She got married, moved away and, to my knowledge, never flew again. Next I recommended Roy, who was a very nervous individual. He was looking forward to his flight check though, and I felt that I had prepared him well. Curt did not like Roy. The appointed time to fly came and went while Curt found other things to do. Roy became more and more nervous and eventually just plain pissed. The smooth air of morning was replaced by the rough air of afternoon. Of course he flunked!

I formed the Sugarpine Aviators Flying Club, which was a little reminiscent of the Enterprise Flying Club, and produced a newsletter that listed those business names who signed up to advertise themselves as Flying Club Boosters. The names were collected by selling the advertisement door-to-door. Slam, of Slam's Country Store, yelled at me to "take my scam and get the hell out of his store!" Too bad, Slam, you're gonna miss my beer and gas purchases for the next twenty or thirty years!

The fledgling company had to have an office, so I rented a corner of Terry Reeson's hanger which was one of four connected airplane stalls. The area serving as an office and the hangared airplanes were separated only by skeleton walls of two-by-four studs. There was no electricity, telephone or heat and a dirt floor. I placed an old scarred dresser in the corner by the side door, and a couple of chairs around it. A battery-operated lamp served as a light. It was miserably cold as fall turned into winter. Much of the flying was done by appointment, but I still spent a lot of time in the cold office, or in my car with the heater running. The trainer was tied down just outside the door. It was necessary to cover the wings with frost-proofing tarps if you expected to fly in the morning. Fortunately, the usual heavy snowfall was missing due to the drought conditions. Sometimes I couldn't help thinking that, if only I had I had taken that teaching position at Butte College, I would have had a nice cushy life and be a leg up on retirement by now. As it was we had *no* retirement fund, *no* health insurance, and *no* savings.

My friend, Dr. Denny Mansell, bought a brand new turbo Aztec. Now he had one less lung, lost to cancer, and the probability was that the "big C" would eventually win all of him. He still hadn't taken the time to obtain an instrument rating. This day he needed all six of his seats, so he didn't call me to fly with him. He attempted to return to Quincy from Washington in bad weather. Witnesses said the Aztec fell out of the terrible storm in pieces. Aboard were his oldest son, his youngest son, his wife and his mother and father.

On a rare day off I met Perry Jones, mountain man, at a bar. A person of about seventy, he had an impressive white beard and bragged about how he could whip anybody in the place. Of interest to me was that he was the owner of a patented mining claim that covered 160 acres on and around the Middle Fork of the Feather River. That meant that he had one of the very few Jeep trail accesses to the designated wild and scenic river. I wanted to be able to go down and swim in it. "Perry Jones' Cabin" was a locally famous landmark. We struck up a friendship and he told me to come down anytime, but remember to remind him of who I was because he always had his .44 handy.

Judy and I had a chance to get away for a day and bounce down the four-wheel drive Butte Bar Trail to Perry's. The first time you do it scares the bajeezus out of you, but Perry assured me that I'd have no trouble. That was true provided you didn't get a wheel off the edge. We finally emerged at the bottom of the four-thousand-foot descent and were greeted by an open gate, but with signs on the trees saying things like, "Beware, Blasting!" and "Trespassers Will Be Shot!" I remembered Perry mentioning his .44 and I fingered my own .38.

The tall pine trees gave way to huge moss covered oaks at the lower elevations. There was the old cabin surrounded by years of accumulated cars, motorcycles, rusted mining equipment and plain old junk. A radio was playing music somewhere. We walked up to the cabin cautiously and called out Perry's name. He answered with a roar from the hill above and behind us. He looked impressive with his huge, white beard and big gun slung across his forearm, his eyes a little wild. I reminded him who I was and where we met. He finally let Judy and me hike down the precipitous trail to the river for a swim in its cool, emerald waters flowing over smooth white granite bedrock. That was only after we were forced to chugalug a couple of straight shots of his best whiskey. We decided to make the trek often.

Curt decided to return to the Sacramento Valley. He informed me that if I wanted to take over as Gansner airfield airport manager, I would have to buy him out. According to him, and the county, the manager position *and* the FBO went together.

Tracy was the manager of the Wells Fargo Bank and he owned the house that was once home to my mother, father, and me. He felt some sort of connection there, and granted me an outrageous personal loan. It had to be that way because I had no equity in anything for the bank to attach. The loan covered Curt's fuel in the ground storage tanks, and an old military preheater that leaked and was dangerous beyond belief. One day a spark from jumper cables caused a battery explosion and almost blew my head off. I gave the damn contraption away.

I wanted the manager's job for practical reasons; the title included some pay and medical insurance. This was OK'd provided that I turn over the fuel concession to the county. With agreements concluded, I took my place as the latest of a long line of FBO/managers at Gansner Airfield. Most of them had failed to make a living and had quit, or like the Wardmans, had come to a bad ending. Curt sold his twin, which incidentally, blew an engine on the way to its new home.

Chapter 13
Airport Manager

Judy said that she got goose bumps every time she explained to somebody that her husband was the airport manager. She was so proud of me and pleased that I had achieved a desire that had been lurking in my subconscious, although I never really admitted it.

The airport manager job consisted of keeping the fuel pumps open, and plowing the snow off the runway and ramp area in the winter. The plow the county provided was the same 1950s Chevy dumptruck that Wardman, and all the managers in the ten years after him, had operated. Having ridden occasionally with Herb in the ten-wheeler, it didn't take long to learn the tricks. The old plow blade required moving by hand, and the pins that held it in place would shear off with very little jolting. It took a lot of patience to plow the runway, taxiway and ramp and to dig everybody out of their hangars. It took foresight to keep from getting stuck in the two-wheel-drive rig. We kept the fuel pumps open seven days a week, sometimes dawn until dark in the summer. The county benefited with each gallon we pumped, and I was determined to pump more gallons than anyone ever had. I was sure that I could be a positive force for aviation in the community. Unfortunately this didn't leave time to join Rotary or other social clubs.

The restaurant building our office was located in was built around 1948 and then sold to the county for a pittance, so that the airport would have a pilot's lounge and meeting place. I noticed that the roof of the historical building was leaking badly, and I believed that the general structure and fine knotty pine woodwork inside would be ruined. In my official capacity, I complained incessantly to county officials. It was an uphill struggle. Finally in October, they relented and replaced the roofing. Then they hiked the fuel cost to pay for it. Since we bought most of the fuel, I guess we paid the lion's share of it!

John Metzker called, wondering if I might accompany him to fly with him in his P-210 to the Yucatan Peninsula to investigate an Inca ruin that had recently been excavated. He said he'd pay all my expenses. Sadly, I had to decline. Expenses paid or not, I simply could not afford to be away from the struggling business!

It was New Year's and Judy and I were having a few drinks at the bowling alley. It was close to midnight, but we had no more money. We got up to go but an old high school friend, Mickey, caught my arm and told me to sit down as he slipped me a twenty! Another time, Judy and I had a couple of drinks that we *could* afford in the Capitol Club. A Hollywood troupe was filming an episode from the series, "Lucan, the Wolf Boy," and they needed extras to sit at the tables during a bar scene. We were chosen, and the pay was several free drinks of our choice. Since it was a day off, I had a couple of straight shots of Crown Royal.

I read with interest in November of '78 that Carl Hunn, the Chester airport manager, had been accused by the Supervisors of various discrepancies. They involved the lack of certificates of insurance and not collecting tiedown for the county as his contract required. He was living in Southern California while allowing his son to run the airport, and this, too, was contrary to his contract. Hunn had a grandiose plan to create a scheduled airline between his home in Orange County and Chester. His company was advertising on-call *guaranteed* 24-hour, all-weather airline connections to Chico, Reno and Sacramento, and on weekends you could "share expenses" to Los Angeles! I couldn't imagine how he planned to guarantee service to mountain communities that are plagued with storms or low-ceiling fog all winter, and where instrument approaches weren't possible.

Sometimes we took off from Gansner Airfield with the fog lying in the valley. There was always the possibility of engine failure with nowhere to go. Also, instruments were known to fail. I remember one day I was just about to enter instrument conditions for an approach into San Jose International when my attitude horizon suddenly rolled over. I was forced to cancel the procedure.

At Gansnser Airfield, I made instrument departures on runway six because the rising terrain was a little farther away than it was to the west. Even there, the terrain rose steeply on all sides. I favored waiting for enough ceiling clearance to get the landing gear and flaps retracted before entering the blinding gray stuff. More often though, I was lucky just to attain rotation speed before running out of forward visibility. Next, I would climb at the Best Rate of Climb Speed on a heading of 040 degrees and intercept the 300-degree bearing outbound from the local AM radio station. Typically, the stratus was about a thousand feet thick. Cold air complicated the situation; at twenty-seven degrees Fahrenheit, the first problem was to start the engine safely. Without engine preheat a fire was a good possibility and engine abuse a probability, even though we used a lighter weight oil in the winter. Once the engine was started and the aircraft was out on the ramp idling, the airframe would frost up. The back side of the propeller would become heavy with ice and would shake so badly that you had to shut down the engine. If you were determined to climb through the dangerous fog, there was only one way to do it and hope to survive. You had to complete the before takeoff checklist with your tail pointed out of the hangar, shut down with a hot engine and slather the airframe and propeller with isopropyl alcohol, push back out of the hangar, immediately start the engine, turn on the pitot heat, and GO! Customers never knew the trouble we went to in order to meet our appointments.

I discovered a previously-unanticipated hazard on a predawn takeoff in the fog. Just as I rotated and disappeared into the blinding stuff, I saw something that made my heart skip a beat. The angle at which the overhead panel light shined down on the plastic instrument panel overlay caused a black shadow to obscure the top half of my directional gyro display. It was absolutely critical to hold the appropriate heading, while maneuvering on the NDB departure procedure. It forced me to continually calculate the reciprocal of what I was reading on the bottom of the DG. That very day I removed the offending plastic outer panel cover and painted the metal that actually held the instruments a flat black. It looked more businesslike anyway (like a C-46).

My immediate boss in the county hierarchy was the airports coordinator, Cliff Brown. He read somewhere that "public aircraft" were not required to comply with the usual rules required by the FAA. An airplane owned and operated by the county would be considered a public aircraft. He had dreamed up all kinds of schemes to bid on, and acquire cheap, public aircraft to make money for the county, and to transport officials around.

Furthermore, he planned to use the county-owned hangar that I was leasing in his plans. I told him, "I think not!" Fortunately, those schemes went by the wayside To my horror, next he had all the beautiful cottonwood trees cut down. They had stood on the west side of the hangar and had shielded the structure against the intense summer sun. I asked him why he did that and he replied, "So that interlopers won't have a place to hide." Enlisting the aid of some other county employees, I did my best to reverse this mentality by creating narrow "green belts;" that is, planting fir and pine tree yearlings donated by the County Agriculture Department. Next, I asked an old time pilot, Bob Cotter; who worked for the county Road Department, to dump a bunch of gravel in the sun-fried, west-facing yard of the restaurant/administration building. He secretly donated county gravel. (Bob and my mother were contemporary pilots. He was the first person to reach her deadly crash at the Quincy Sky Harbor in 1944.) Others in the community helped, too. Merv Hanson had leased the travertine quarry at the Soda Rock. He graciously agreed to let me have a couple of giant chunks of the precious rock. I sneaked over in the unlicensed airport snowplow/dumptruck where they loaded me up. I dumped the several tons of the beautiful chunks on top of the gravel. It made a very interesting landscape study. To round it out, we planted some donated low-growing ground cover that took off beautifully with an occasional watering. I planted a pretty little white fir behind one of the travertine rocks and it grew like a weed. I knew it would eventually protect the west-facing part of the restaurant building from the burning sun when it grew out from behind the protective rock. On the south-facing eaves of the building, a white climbing rose flourished after a watering and trimming treatment. It was the same one I had planted when first learning to fly here eighteen years ago. Virginia Creepers were getting established on the chain-link fence and the harsh lines of the place were gradually beginning to soften. There were birds singing in the trees and shade to rest under.

A family of five disappeared in the LaPorte area in a snowstorm. Ernest Ortiz stumbled into LaPorte with a harrowing tale of several days and nights of survival in the snow while going for help. Meanwhile, his family was still out there buried under snow in their car. I took off in the Cessna 150 and sighted their vehicle marooned in Onion Valley within fifteen minutes. The woman and kids were afraid that they wouldn't make it home for Christmas, or maybe not at all, but they did! I was happy to donate my services.

It was May when Judy's brother, Tom Rahn, came to work with us, leaving his cushy job as a Wildlife Biologist with the California State Fish and Game. His primary reason was that he wanted to return to Indian Valley and get away from the Sacramento Valley. Just like me, he tossed away the security of a good job to pursue aviation and the promised land! I was glad that I had started him out flying in my old Luscombe in the early 1970's. Now Sugarpine Aviators had a "chief pilot!"

Beginning on Fathers Day, 1979, the Sugarpine Aviators Flying Club sponsored "Airport Days," featuring the famous Jim "Red Baron" Lister. My crop dusting partner performed death-defying aerobatics in his Pitts Special. Les Waterman, now the owner of his own duster operation at Willows, thundered in astride his North American P-51 called "The Straw Boss." We would line up all our airplanes and sell rides.

Lister liked to warm up the day before the air show. All he asked was that we pay for his fuel and provide a place to sleep for the night. FAA Inspector Bill Hughes was here the day before the event to issue the permit for the aerobatics. The paperwork had just been completed when Jim in his cherry-red

Pitts roared down the runway in a "knife edge" configuration, a highly-illegal maneuver unless sanctioned for an air show. Bill pivoted toward his car in the parking lot muttering to himself, "I didn't see that, I didn't see that!" Some of Jim's most dangerous moments in the old Pitts were not at the air shows but practicing for them. He had to dead stick it in twice for a landing, due to engine failure while practicing some stunt. Jim says that's why he always practices near an airport. Landing a Pitts Special, even at an airport, without the use of power, is no easy task. Jim had been taking time out from crop dusting to perform at several air shows throughout California. As a measure of how good he was, one day he entered the Reno Air Races for the first try in his unmodified Pitts without a sponsor. He had no crew and slept on the ground out in the desert. When the dust cleared, he flew away with the silver trophy in his class!

When Curt left the area, the FAA appointed me the Designated Pilot Examiner in his place. The fees I received from offering that service came in very handy. I was asked to conduct flight tests for the Private, Commercial and Instrument ratings. I accepted only the Private Designation for our own students. I wanted to avoid any unnecessary entanglement with the feds. I learned later that I might as well have accepted the designations anyway. I was required to attend a meeting each year, and every other year it had to be a renewal from a roving FAA blue ribbon troupe. The renewal procedure included a difficult written exam on pilot certification procedures covering all pilots from Private to ATP. If I should fail a test, I would be required to travel to Oklahoma City, on my own nickel, to be retrained as a Designee.

I soloed son Jack, and the following article appeared in the *Feather River Bulletin:*

THIRD GENERATION OF FLYING MOORES SOLOS
"The third generation of the flying Moore family of Quincy made his first solo flight recently.

Jack is a third-generation Moore to learn to fly at Quincy. His grandparents, the late Dr. John Wesley Moore and Gail Rogers Moore, both learned to fly at the Old Quincy Sky Harbor. (Actually Dr. Moore already had a Commercial Pilot Certificate.) His father, Johnny, learned to fly at Gansner Airfield.

It was noted in the April 6, 1944, edition of the Feather River Bulletin; "Dr. Moore put Quincy on the air map." There was no airport here when he started flying back in 1936. He and Fred Russell, who had an airplane here rented the ground from Henry Lee and spent their own money to grade it."

The article goes on to say that the project became so important that responsibility for managing the airport was assumed by the Plumas County Board of Supervisors.

"In the late '40s the airport was moved to its present site on donated Gansner land. Jack's great grandfather, D. N. Rogers, was chair of the Gansner Airfield airport committee until his death in 1970. Jack's father, Johnny has been the airport manager since February of 1977. Other flying relatives of Jack's include the late Byron C. Moore, a former senior captain for American Airlines; Mickey Hudson, Captain for Eastern Airlines; the late David H. Rogers, former military flight instructor; Tom Rahn of Indian Valley, charter pilot and flight instructor; the late John Thomas, former airport manager in Sonoma County; Joe Ross, a private pilot; and Jack's mother, Judy, who soloed in 1962."

Lance Brennan, high school student, wrote this paper for a school project. *"His cigarette glows in the choking darkness of the fall evening. He grabs his old, torn denim jacket and walks out of the hangar to greet me. He climbs into the small, beat up trainer and we taxi to the runway. The plane lifts softly off the light bordered strip. I level out at our usual practice height and glance over for instructions. Usually, we practice maneuvers of flight till I shake or get nauseated, but tonight he seems content to watch the scenery like a first time passenger. I circle the valley looking down at the yellowed diamonds and gazing up at the dark sky. The green marker light of another craft flashes off to the right. I descend smoothly to earth and throttle off the engine and the whistle of flowing air becomes apparent. She flares delicately, playing with the gusts, then settles onto the runway. As the plane rolls out, I look over at the wise, old "first time passenger" who knew it was time I experienced some pure flight. Sometimes we are so intent on the means that the cause becomes obscured. I was lucky in my flying that I had someone who would not let this happen."*

I loved the story, but shuddered to recall how many years I had wasted smoking cigarettes. I'm pleased to say that I threw 'em away for good shortly after Lance wrote his soliloquy. That took more guts than anything else I'd done in my life so far!

A dry cold front was passing through and I was in the pattern with a student in the left seat. It closed in suddenly and we found ourselves wallowing around the sky, being tossed all over the valley. The tremendous wind shear was pulling us down from pattern altitude, almost to the pastures below, and then kicking us back up again. I was desperately maneuvering into position to enter a base leg for runway two four. It was necessary to slam the throttle forward and then back in a largely unsuccessful attempt to control our altitude. All controls were being worked at their limits when a call came in from a Cessna 182 saying that he was downwind for two four. I announced that I was on base leg for the same runway, but that didn't stop him from cutting in front of me for the landing and forcing me to circle in the severe turbulence. On this circle we barely escaped hitting the power lines that crossed the valley as the bottom dropped out. I pointed toward the runway again and flew through the cascading air at full throttle, then slammed into the runway blowing a nose-wheel tire. The commercial pilot and his passengers were sitting at a table in the restaurant when we finally got in. I was fighting mad when I confronted him saying, "I think you had a little more going for you in your bigger airplane!" He just nodded sheepishly and I let it go at that.

In 1980, Plumas County Fair Manager, C. W. Adams, took over as airports coordinator. A pilot, he was also a charismatic former champion bull-rider-womanizer, and full of bull shit! He was good enough looking to pose for the cover of a magazine, and he did. His game was power; that is, political, financial, and personal power. If you weren't part of his power base, you were his enemy! He demanded, and received, full autonomy in the running of the airports. It didn't take him long to notice that I wasn't the "yes" person he wanted in an airport manager. One of his first acts was to threaten me through a local business person. First, he told me how I should be offering package deals with my student program. The next day a local businessman told me that if I didn't offer him a "package deal" to learn to fly, he would bring in his own instructor (an acquaintance of C. W.'s) who would run me out of business.

The airport restaurant had closed. I gave C.W. a written proposal to take it over as part of our operation. We already shared our office with the restaurant with only a display case dividing us. It seemed like a natural to me. I wrote of how I would like to maintain a decor that emphasized the local area and aviation history. I wanted to begin with fresh soup and sand-wiches and gradually expand to all the other services; you know, the old fashioned honest grow-into-it approach, just like we had handled our flying business. The new coordinator threw it in the trash without a second thought. The cafe contract was awarded to someone from Southern California, who never even bothered to show up.

Sierra Pacific Industries' MU-2 prop jet was a regular visitor to Gansner Airfield, bringing its owner in so that he could personally supervise his far-flung forest products empire. Bob, his pilot, was very good at getting him where he wanted to go, come rain or shine. While the runway was under construction and part of it was torn up, I was amazed to witness the high-speed turboprop approaching runway six on an unusually low glide path in an attempt to land short. Highway 70 runs perpendicular to the runway, and fewer than a hundred yards away. The MU-2's extended landing gear knocked a stack of firewood off the back of a pickup. Then, the aircraft smacked down right on the yellow "X" covering the white "6" painted on the end of the runway. It The 4 by 8 feet sheets of plywood flew everywhere! Even though the Mitsubishi stopped before running off the usable part of the runway, and even though the boss got to his appointments on time, Bob had to explain to the FAA why he hit the truck while landing on a closed runway. He found his wings clipped for a while.

Soon it was time to get a bigger rental airplane, and I worked out a pretty good leaseback for use of a late model Cessna 172. Not long after that, John Metzker offered to lease me his 182. The Forest Service supervisor decided that it might be safe to fly in a single engine aircraft. We were now doing business with the Forest Service, providing both transportation, and fire and timber reconnaissance.

As more students completed their flight training; the number of aircraft renters continued to grow and demanded more airplanes to fill their needs. We started drawing renter pilots from surprising distances. We also conducted air ambulance flights at all hours of the day and night. They were flown in a Cherokee Six-300 that I managed to purchase for nothing down.

The big "Six" was bought in Chico. It was the same aircraft that I had flown the nurses into Sacramento Metro on the night the electricity failed at the airport. The deal was that all systems were to be working. After they fixed the avionics glitches, they presented me with a bill amounting to $700. I explained to avionics department that those items were included in the deal. The boss said, "Yeah, sometimes the sales department promises things like that." I continued to receive threatening letters. I finally got sick of it and paid, but they lost thousands of dollars worth of my future business.

There was something about the "Star Of Life" logo on the side of the Six that drew attention, some not so good. I taxied out from an FBO at Clearlake and the operator ran out shaking his fist screaming, "That is an illegal insignia on your airplane!" I gave him the finger, turned my tail around and blew dirt in his face. The truth was that the District Hospital Ambulance Service had placed it there themselves, and they were our official providers with a five million dollar insurance policy to back it up. Our equipment and documents had been FAA inspected and certified, so to hell with him!

One day Chester manager Hunn showed up at Quincy and asked me if I would like to manage the gate for his airline. In other words, he wanted me to be his ticket agent. I respectfully declined. He added that soon he would have *all* the business in the county. A few days after that when I was picking up an ambulance case at Chester, he ran out of his office, interfering with the loading operation of a very sick patient. He shook his fist at me saying, "Enjoy it while you can because soon I'll be doing this instead of you!"

One dark and overcast night on an ambulance mission at Chester, I learned that when you rotated the long nose of the Six up for takeoff, it blocked out everything straight ahead. Above, the overcast blocked out any reference from the stars and the tall trees on either side stopped any lighted ground references from those directions. In other words, from the point of rotation you were on instruments, and you better not allow *any* turn to occur or you would be into the trees in a heartbeat.

There were memorable air ambulance flights, such as one when a large former Marine and his motorcycle collided with a logging truck. In an attempt to save his life, I was descending at high speed into Reno after midnight. The patient was in his death throes, slinging both the doctor and the nurse around the cabin and kicking a rear window out. I gritted my teeth and left the throttle wide open, intent on saving my *own* life!

A casket will fit into the Cherokee Six. I was called upon to fly a recently-deceased loved one over to Eureka, an hour and some from here, over on the coast. How could I refuse when the bereaved relatives asked me to take along all the flowers that had been at the service? I found out why I should have! The sweet fragrance of lilies and other flowers were overwhelming in the tight cabin. I had every vent open and I was gasping for air with my mouth and nose sticking out the storm window. It was hard to get a breath with a 160 mph wind tearing at my face.

Early in the spring I tried my hand at flying a twin engine Hummingbird ultralight. I was bundled up against the cold, but it was still freezing. Try as I might, I couldn't get the damn thing to climb over the tops of the trees. I was forced to fly around them, and I felt the control that was accomplished mostly by warping the wings wasn't very positive. I could easily imagine running into a pine tree at the hundred-foot level and falling the rest of the way. I thanked its owner, Harry McKenzie, for the flight, and walked away unscathed The next would-be Hummingbird pilot, Mark Whitney, MD, almost broke his back by stalling it out in a landing attempt.

I was asked to administer a retest to Edward Wibbel, owner of a French biplane, a Stampe SV4-C. His particular problem was in the area of navigation, according to his pink slip. My first action was to get some instruction from *him*, since I didn't know the first thing about this open cockpit French flying machine. After following him through a thorough preflight, I felt satisfied that at least I knew the basics of its systems. There was no way to communicate between the tandem front and back seats except for hand signals.

I gave candidate Wibbel an easy route from Quincy to Reno. Most pilots followed Highway 70 until they climbed high enough to proceed direct. We took off and headed due north, about ninety degrees to the left of Reno. I thought, "Jees, where the hell is he taking me?" I let him continue for a while to be certain that this wasn't some altitude-gaining maneuver. Finally, I shook the stick to get his attention. Through sign language I indicated that I wanted him to return to the airport. Wibbel executed a snappy turn and unerringly returned via direct course, and landed.

We climbed out of the biplane and I asked him to show me on the sectional chart the exact route we had taken. He did just that. I said, "Why were you taking us north when Reno was more than ninety degrees to our right?" He replied, "I believed that the route I had chosen would be the best one." Well, the route was *not* the best one but I couldn't dispute that he knew exactly where he was at all times. I threw up my hands and issued him his Private Pilot Certificate!

Jean, a wealthy woman, was taking lessons in the 150. Her

long cross-country would take her north to Alturas, then southeast across the wilds of Nevada to Lovelock, and finally, west and back to Quincy. She arrived in Alturas expecting to fuel up, but the airport manager was busy talking to someone and ignored her. For some unknown reason, the normally assertive Jean gave up and launched for Lovelock, but became disoriented and ran out of fuel. Somewhere north of Lovelock she dead sticked the little trainer, landing safely on a dirt road far from any civilization. Against all odds, someone happened along in a car and she was able to hire him to take her to Lovelock. She got enough fuel in cans to return to the aircraft, fuel it, and proceed to the airport. She thought it was funny, but I failed to see the humor. She made a bad decision not to fuel at Alturas and thereby put herself and my airplane in great danger. The cost of that little airplane, which carried no hull insurance, meant nothing to her and everything to me! I've gotta give her credit though, she knuckled down and continued on to achieve several pilot ratings.

On a warm August day, Judy noticed a suspicious-looking operation down near the end of the tiedown area. A Grumman Tiger had parked and a white pickup truck was there to meet it. She could see a man and a boy climbing out of the aircraft, and that the back seats and baggage area were crammed full. As she watched, they and a woman and a young girl unloaded camping gear and food into the back of the pickup and drove off. Judy remembered when an Inyo County official had called, warning that a stolen Grumman was probably in the vicinity. Oroville Aviation had just notified us that some jerk in a Grumman had filled up his fuel tanks and had taken off without paying! Yesseree, that was the stolen aircraft! We notified the Sheriff's Office who decided to stakeout the airplane. After a couple of days of no action, the officers began to take time out for lunch.

Naturally, it was during one of those times that the pilot returned and prepared to fly away with a juvenile. I called the cops, and suddenly you could hear their sirens wailing from miles away as they headed this way at top speed. The airplane thief failed to realize that those sirens were for him. He methodically strapped himself into the Grumman and prepared to start the engine. The unmarked police sedan skidded through the airport gate, a hubcap flying off in the violent turn. Several patrol cars were in hot pursuit, their lights flashing and sirens blaring. They all closed in on the surprised suspects.

The young man had stolen a Cessna150 from Quincy and flown it down to Inyo County. There, he swiped the Grumman and returned to Quincy. His accomplices were his son, daughter and wife. The pickup was also stolen. Judy received flowers and a note from the owners of the 150. It said, "Thanks so much for your sharp eyes and mind!"

Crystal was a vivacious young woman with raven black hair and a yen to fly. Fly she did, with me teaching her in her Aeronca 7EC. She completed her Private Pilot training and flew often. One day while landing her taildragger downwind at the short Calistoga glider port she lost a brake. With the aircraft mostly out of control, she managed to steer clear of a group of frightened people but was unable to stop before clipping a glider. There was no structural damage and the FAA man said there would be no trouble about the incident. Nevertheless, Crystal soon received a call from Tom Howell of the Reno FSDO who demanded that she take a recheck in her Aeronca. Tom was the same fed who busted me for wrecking "The Blue Goose" in the fog near Kingsberg. I flew with her and gave her the works in the way of recurrent training in takeoffs and landings. I accompanied her to Stead Airport in the Aeronca to meet Howell. Enroute, a most interesting thing happened. I was leaning forward from the rear seat to yell out some instruction when my left knee wacked the ignition key that shared a ring with ten other keys. The result was that the magnetos shut off and the whole ring full of keys fell to the floor. The engine suddenly became silent. Crystal wondered, "What the hell is he going to do to me now?" She looked back to see me on my hands and knees, desperately trying to prevent the key ring from disappearing through one of the spaces in the wooden floor board and into the belly, where they would be irretrievable. I managed to snag the ring, find the right key, and turn the mags back on before we hit the ground. After the successful flight re-check, on the way home a snowstorm barred our way and we had to land at the Beckwourth airport. The strip was deserted, and the wind was freezing. I called Judy from a phone booth to come and retrieve us, saying that we'd be at the Beckwith Tavern, a mile or so down the road. We tried hitchhiking, but nobody would stop. I laughingly told Chrystal that someone might have picked us up if she didn't look like such a hippie! Judy found us laughing about the whole situation and joined us at the bar.

By the time the 150 finally got a major overhaul it had 3,500 hours on it (1,700 hours over the manufacturer's recommended time between overhauls). Frank Nervino, the old engine master, said that it had been a shame to tear it apart because the little 0-200 Continental was in beautiful shape. I also had the propeller overhauled, polished and retwisted to a climb configuration; that is, a flatter pitch for more rpm's and power for takeoff.

John Metzker called me and said he was interested in buying a Fixed Base Operation at the Truckee Airport and would I move over there and run it for him. He suggested that I would probably be set for life if I did. I was frustrated and retorted, "Damn it John, why didn't you call me a year ago before I had so much sweat and blood in my own business?" I told him that I appreciated the offer, but no thanks. I was determined to make it at the backwaters of Quincy even if there was more business potential near Lake Tahoe and Reno.

The addition of two seasonal pilots was necessary to meet the summertime demand as we added a co-op fire patrol. It was a patrol much like the old days with Wardman Flying Service, but almost three times as long. One part-time pilot was Herschel Beail, who owned his own body shop and was a Private Pilot and an A & P Mechanic. Once we trained him through his advanced ratings, he would slip away and fly a charter for us when he wasn't too busy at his own shop. Dan English, too, was a Private Pilot and had been working as an assistant aircraft mechanic in Alaska. We trained Dan all the way through his Instructor rating and hired him to fly and perform maintenance.

I was tired of leasing. It seemed like throwing money away and we were gaining no equity. Ran Slaten acquired a 1957 "square tail" 172, and on speculation, offered it for sale. It fit the bill for us, and I bought it. Its tail number was 8023 B. It soon acquired the colorful handle, "Bucko" from the students. We used it for scenic flights and patrol, too.

We were equal opportunity fliers. On one day we flew dope growers on scenic flights, ostensibly to enjoy the scenery, but actually to see if their marijuana gardens could be seen from the air. The next flight might well have been with the authorities looking for the illegal plants. One day we would fly environmentalists around who invariably would be shocked at the state of the forest, and the next flight would be for a forester conducting timber cruises in preparation for logging. It was best to remain tight-lipped about politics.

I first became aware of the airport restaurant when I was receiving my initial flight training under Herb and Loraine Wardman in 1959. It was a cozy place with a cheery fireplace, surrounded by overstuffed chairs. On the north side of the open-beamed room was a bar complete with a grill and a refrigerator. Loraine, being of Seventh Day Adventist persuasion, would fry me up vegaburgers. The airport manager and Fixed Based Operations office, the pilots' lounge and the food bar were combined in one room that had an open-beamed ceiling and a knotty pine finish throughout.

Eighteen years later, Bob and Peggy Gorton operated a cafe in the same building. I mentioned the breadboards and solo boards that I had wood-burned the names of the first solo students at Tahoe and Redding into. They allowed me to put up solo plaques on the open ceiling beams. I located old barn wood planks and cut them up into 4 by 9 inch pieces. The routine was to take a picture of the student as he or she got out of the airplane and glue it to the plaque. When a Private Pilot Certificate was earned, a gold star was glued onto the picture. Each additional aviation rating merited another gold star. The student's name and the date of solo were wood-burned into the plaque.

The supervisors put out a bid to build an airport administration office upstairs in order to create more room in the restaurant. It was a tiny little space, but I was able to get enough materials donated to add on a deck, thereby making it more tolerable. At least the office had big windows and a good view of the runway. Meanwhile, downstairs, a dozen of the precious solo plaques had been ripped off the wall in the reconstruction and were lying in a heap of trash destined for the dumpster. I rescued them at the last moment.

Coordinator Adams was quite the salesman, for sure. In a foolish gesture meant to improve my relations with him, I bought his old Oldsmobile station wagon that he said had just been overhauled. We immediately began having problems with the engine. I found out that it had been overhauled all right, but that it been run out of water and it had been severely overheated. We sold it at a loss.

A day in the summer of '81 became less humdrum for Tom as he was giving dual instruction to Coy. While they were practicing stalls, a vacuum line connecting gyro instruments with each other had worked loose and had entangled itself with the yoke mechanism behind the panel. Tom could only pull the elevator back about halfway. He and I discussed the situation over the Unicom. I suggested trim, flaps, and power for maintaining pitch control. Down was no problem, just up! Coy suggested that when they got close to the ground, they could jump out and hit the ground running! Tom approached with flaps and power while Judy and I watched with our hearts in our mouths. A good landing, to be sure, although we prefer 'em with the nose off the runway. I decided that since Tom walked away from it, we'd let the less-than-perfect touchdown go this time!

Frankie Dee decided to sell his 150 and purchase a much more powerful and complex model Cessna. The square tailed 182 needed a lot more maintenance with its six cylinders and constant-speed propeller. Virtually *none* of the radios worked right and there was no transponder. Frankie said that the compass lied to him a lot and so did his VOR. One day Frankie taxied out, and as he rounded the corner to takeoff, a tire blew. I helped him push the wounded Cessna off the runway. I was shocked by the ragged tire concealed under the wheel fairing. I investigated the other side and noted that several layers of cords were showing, and the tube was bulging through a hole! Frankie had chosen to buy insurance for his new airplane, but I wondered if the insurance company would pay off in case of an accident. The aircraft had not had an Annual Inspection in many years, nor had he subjected himself to the required Biennial Flight Reviews. Maybe that was because he had not kept up his required Third Class Airman's Medical either. He did scavenge my old Jeppessen instrument approach plates though. He said he kept them in case of an emergency!

Frankie was flying home to Quincy one night. The trip from Palm Springs was 500+ miles over some of the highest mountains in the United States. Both the distance and required altitudes were near the limit for the aircraft and his physical ability. Since his compass was inaccurate and his VOR didn't work right, he had a little trouble navigating. I reconstructed his adventure like this: It was a very black night due to bad weather, but Frankie figured he had the lights of Inyokern in sight. He was surprised that Inyokern was such a big town with such bright lights. As it turned out, they were actually the lights of Las Vegas, some 150 miles due east of where he imagined he was. He had just blown through the Edward's Air Force Restricted Area and the Las Vegas TCA without a clearance. They probably didn't see him anyway since he didn't have a transponder.

Frankie figured he might be getting disoriented, and tried to land at an unlighted airstrip he could just barely make out in the gloom. It did have one small light at one end but he decided against the landing. Upon analysis, I figured that this strip probably lay somewhere in the Yucca Flats Prohibited Area. Climbing out and reaching for the stars, he continued on. Now, with fuel getting low, he cleverly switched to single-tank operation so he would know exactly how much fuel remained before starvation. He was on top of an overcast with the moon coming out. The engine sputtered and coughed as the right tank went dry, and roared into life again when switched to the left. Suddenly, a large hole in the overcast revealed a smooth desert floor illuminated by the moon. But wait! Those flat places that at first had appeared landable were actually flooded alkali flats. Lights glowed in the distance and Frankie thought, "Maybe there's an airport up there." He wisely headed for them. He heaved a sigh of relief when he saw runway lights. One fuel tank was definitely empty and the selected tank's gauge had stopped bouncing off of "E."

It was after midnight at the Wendover airport when the on call fuel attendant came out and topped off Frankie's plane. Its usable fuel capacity was fifty-five gallons and he took fifty-three. He had found a landing place with six minutes to spare! After calling his wife, he took off for home "IFR" (I Follow Roads) via Interstate 80 to Reno and Highways 395 and 70 into Quincy. A major Pacific cold front slammed into Quincy only a short time after Frankie exited the runway, patting himself on the back!

The silver haired Lieutenant Colonel (retired), secured the Forest Service fire contract for air attack at Gansner Airfield. His maroon and white Aero Commander 500B occupied a corner of the ramp. We made a little money selling him fuel, but he took most of our Forest Service fire detection business. "The Colonel" spent his summer evenings in the bars around Quincy. He told tales of the days when he had eight throttles in his hand as captain of an Air Force B-52 bomber. At the end of the season, he would takeoff in his Aero Commander, turn around and make a low pass over the runway and follow it with a showy roll. His winters were spent far to the south in Pheonix.

He decided that I would make a good Air Attack relief pilot for him, and in the spring of 1981, he proceeded to check me out. He and I were in front, with Judy way in the back, as we took off for Pheonix in the Commander. The weather was mostly IFR. His military-style of instructing was brutal. He shouted commands and insults in a continuous stream. He would yell out stuff like, "You think you're such a big shot but you haven't shown me shit yet!" I gritted my teeth and settled down to business, ignoring all but whatever information that made sense. The first order of business was to sharpen up my instrument proficiency which was pretty rusty. For some reason, the colonel decided not to file IFR through the Los Angles basin and we found ourselves weaving our way between large cumulus clouds in the San Gorgonio area. The peak of San Gorgonio loomed ahead 11,502 feet high and we were being forced to climb due to rising terrain. Finally we were boxed in, and I glanced back at Judy who was clearly worried. I recognized the terrain, and so did she. The Colonel believed a pass lay to our right, but I knew only big rocks were hidden in the clouds in that direction. I got a glimpse of the valley to the north of San Gorgonio and pointed it out. My mentor shouted, "Go for it!" I transitioned from a climb configuration to landing gear down, flaps down, and approach power. (The maneuver reminded me of Buzz Dyer's plunge into the Sagwon strip on the North Slope in the C-46.) We dove through the small, layered opening, emerging out of the clouds and into the lower valley. The fluffy, terrain-hiding killers became more scattered and were easier to navigate around. The Colonel was a little quieter after that.

The colonel based the 500B at the tiny airport at Glendale, northwest of Phoenix. It was a big airplane for the short runway with power line for obstructions at each end. I was taxiing, and he kept telling me that the airplane had hydraulic nose steering actuated by a slight touch on the toe brake. I kept having to use brakes and differential power to steer the craft. My military instructor got pissed and said, "Here, let me show you!" When he took over, he found that the hydraulic nose steering was inoperative! In the several days that followed, we shot approaches at all the instrument facilities in the area. Then we flew cross-country to the high altitude Snow Flake airport for short field practice. The last time I was there was by mistake with a student in Meta Pool's Cessna 210. The strip had improved dramatically since 1962. Then on to Taylor where the Colonel's Aero Commander maintenance guru had his operation.

Judy and I brought the Aero Commander home to Quincy, and in the next few days I passed a multiengine ATP and FAR 135 flight check with the FAA. The next test was a U. S. Forest Service IFR Air Attack and IFR competency check at the North Zone headquarters in Redding.

The most fun was Air Attack on a campaign fire and watching the whole drama unfold. I listened to the ground chatter of Forest Service people setting up camps and strategic operations according to their Incident Command system. I watched the lead plane dive and swoop and the big air tankers drop. The most difficult operations were when taking off from Quincy with a heavy load on a hot, windy day. Sometimes I had to insist on downloading in the interests of safety. If you took off uphill and upwind on runway two four, all the advantage of heading into the wind was lost by the lay of the land. The uphill grade and terrain guaranteed that obstructions, downdrafts, and turbulence would be in your path to force you to do some fancy maneuvering. Conversely, if you took off downhill and down wind, all the runway would be used and only a flat angle of climb could be achieved due to the increased ground speed. In any case, if you lost an engine while heavy in those conditions, you might as well plan to skid it in straight ahead. Any other choice would be even more deadly, probably resulting in an inverted crash.

Sometimes adverse weather arrived at the airport at the same time I did. One day, returning home with a load of Forest Service people, I was flying on the leading edge of a classic cold front. On final approach, the Commander pitched and twisted. We were all over the place, with every flight control smashing to the stops and the throttles doing the same. Differential engine power helped the big rudder to maintain directional control. A missed approach into the canyon to the west would be very dangerous. I touched down at high speed and barely managed to stop at the end of the 4,100 foot-long runway. Another evening I flew the Commander to the Reno airport and picked up the colonel, who had arrived from Pheonix on the airlines, and who was profoundly drunk. He had a buddy with him who knew nothing about flying. I made the colonel strap in, in the very back seat, while his friend occupied the copilot station. The visibility was dropping rapidly, but I knew exactly where I was from familiar ground references. I proceeded toward the airport one house light at a time. You couldn't see the runway because Radio Hill was in the way. My former student, Greg Hockenson, happened to be in the office at the time. I asked him via the Unicom to operate the controls on the office wall and change the intensity of the runway lights from 10 percent to 100 percent. He gave me a running dialogue of the wind and visibility. There was no rain yet. The black clouds were closing in fast, and down the final approach, we flew hanging from our seat belts with the colonel looking very sick in the back. It was the same situation as the last cold front: no go around, control movements and throttles to the stops, high-speed touchdown and barely stopping at the end of the runway. Large droplets of rain began pelting and powerful wind gusts were blasting us as we rolled onto the ramp. The bleary-eyed rear passenger slurred his thanks to me and the two pals headed downtown to the Capitol Club for a nightcap.

My next encounter with the FAA was with Inspector Howell for our company FAR 135 (Air Carrier) check ride. I was apprehensive, considering our previous contacts, but we got along well enough, and the summer season was underway.

Bart, my old high school mate, arrived from Idaho in his Cessna 172. He topped off the four- seater with fuel, and he and our schoolmate, Dick, and their wives took a flight, or rather a fright! Bart, being unaccustomed to flying out of Quincy, took off uphill toward the west, into the wind, and into the resident downdraft. I saw the underpowered craft struggle over the threshold, only a few feet into the air. It took remarkable courage for him to hang in there and fly the narrow canyon up Spanish Creek until finally, eight miles distant, it opened up into Meadow Valley. I honestly don't know how they made it. Dick's first flight was with me years ago when I demonstrated a snap roll to him. He almost barfed then. This was the second flight, and I wondered if there would be a third.

Occasionally I thanked John Metzker for helping me out by giving him instrument instruction in his pressurized Centurion. We were practicing instrument approaches at Reno and I asked him to disengage the autopilot, but he declined to do so. The conversation turned to the cost of various instruments and gadgets that adorned the panel. He waved at the $20k panel and said, "I told my avionics person that I considered this minimal instrumentation!" While all this was going on, he didn't notice that the autopilot failed to hold altitude. I tapped the altimeter and noted, "Money does not solve all problems, so let's turn the damn autopilot off and practice without it!"

Dennis had purchased a nice '75 model Cessna 172. One night he had business at the Columbia Airport. I accompanied him in the role of instructor. It was an exceptionally black night due to a forest fire nearby. I asked Dennis' friend, who claimed to be a pilot, which way was best to takeoff in the dark. He said, while blowing a liquor-laden breath my way, "They always takeoff that way, without exception." He waved toward the north. I was skeptical since "that way" was uphill, with rising terrain beyond. We lined up on runway three-five and commenced the takeoff. I didn't like it at all, especially as hot and smoky as it was tonight. After breaking free of the ground, I flipped on the landing lights and all I could see were rocks and trees coming up! Having recently flown as a night spray pilot, the next maneuver wasn't too much of a stretch of the imagination. I slipped to one side of the runway, lowered the nose to pick up speed, and reversed course in a wingover that began at pavement level. We were now pointed down the runway and downhill. I don't think Dennis ever quite understood what happened, and I never tried to explain it. As we left the area I was happy just to be alive.

During the months of September and October of 1982, six people died in two separate, and unnecessary, aircraft accidents. Four individuals disappeared after taking off from Colusa enroute to a golf tournament in Nevada. It was stormy weather and the pilot, who had previously had his Pilot Certificate revoked, decided to try sneaking up the North Fork of the Feather River, a deep V-shaped canyon, but the aircraft disappeared. Searchers suspected that the wreckage must be in the Belden area of the canyon. They had found a piece of an elevator about fifty yards up on the north side of Highway 70. Another remnant was found near the top of the mountain rising three-thousand feet vertically on the north side of the highway. Yet another piece of aircraft aluminum was spotted on the south side of the river. The terrain that direction was even steeper and higher than Red Hill on the north side. The search and rescue team called me in for my opinion. I climbed up to the ruined elevator and noted where the other pieces were. From that information and other accounts, I concluded that the aircraft must have ricocheted off the mountain above us, sailed across the chasm, its engine still screaming and vital parts flying off. Residents of the area reported hearing the engine sounds. I lined up the evidence and pointed right at Fern Canyon just upstream from Belden. That narrow canyon was a searchers' nightmare. Some of them suffered injuries from falling on the steep slippery, moss-covered rocks. It was hard to see more than a few feet in the tangle of wet trees and brush. Nothing was found immediately. A few days later I fueled a Civil Air Patrol O-2 search plane. The guys said it was great to have a weekend outing and get the fuel paid for! I was flying the day they got killed and I can tell you that it was nasty and windy, scary even to the most seasoned pilots. Nobody had any business flying low in the area of Fern Canyon. It was down on the lee side of the mountainous Bucks Lake Wilderness, right where the worst downdrafts and turbulence would be, but that's where they vanished. I spoke to the CAP commander about advising non-professional pilots not to fly low in mountainous areas, especially in those conditions. His reply was unbelievably stupid. "Oh, no, if they see something they *gotta* go down there and check it out," he said with military sternness! Their bodies were found in Fern Canyon not far from the crash victims they had been searching for.

Spring semester was partly over at the local community college. Previously I had taught the first of several aviation courses and was gratified to have fifty-some students complete each one. Jazzed about teaching, I thought about trying an Anthropology class, too, if there was ever an opening. I hit the books with some current Anthro study material. During this particular course, I had given seventeen students the actual FAA Private Pilot Written Exam. Usually, I charged thirty-nine dollars a pop for those, but I thought I would do a community service and give them for free since they'd paid the college for the course. Those who passed the test would receive an "A." The result of the FAA written test took at least ten working days to get back through the mail. The college officials insisted that I must have my grades in by the next day, in spite of the fact that there was a month and a half of the regular semester left. Mine was a concentrated course. They threatened to hold up my pay check because the grades weren't in according to their little rules. I just laughed at them and the stupidity of it all, especially since they had already paid me! It was coming back to me why I went back to flying instead of teaching college. Incidentally, all seventeen test takers passed the Private Written.

On a cold and dark February evening, I was called upon to accompany a rescue team up the side of Hospital Hill that rises abruptly just north of the runway. Non-Instrument-Rated Gary had taken off on runway six into fog and followed other untrained pilots to a sudden death. My theory was that he thought he could easily pull up through the layer of fog and get home to Redding that night. The bartender at the restaurant said that he had his strobe lights flashing brightly as he disappeared into the fog. The flashing strobes would contribute to spatial confusion. In a steep climb, the Centurion would have had a left-turning tendency due to the asymmetrical thrust of the propeller, among other things. I theorized that when he looked away from the attitude horizon in order to retract the landing gear and adjust the power setting, it probably rolled over into a left bank. Pulling back in a banked attitude would slam the high-performance aircraft right into the spot where it lay burning!

Quincy can be a deadly place at night with fog present. To the south the terrain raises 3,500 feet within three miles, and to the north, 600 feet within a mile. Fog was forming at Quincy this night. Judy said over the Unicom that she could see the end of the runway, but could not tell what the ceiling was. I asked her to flip the runway lights on and off in a steady pulse, and I would fly under the stuff from a couple of miles out, aiming for runway two four. Soon I was at full flaps in the Cherokee 180, just a few feet off the ground, with my landing light blazing. I could see some yellowish lights but they were not pulsating. I initiated a missed approach from ground level and transitioned from a critically slow airspeed with full flaps to a maximum flaps up, climb configuration. Every ounce of my experience came into play as I carefully worked the "Johnson bar" flap handle and watched the attitude horizon and directional gyro. While turning off the confusing landing and strobe lights, I had to be careful not to turn off the all-important panel lights located nearby. My heart was pounding and I was breathing deeply. I knew the unforgiving nature of the terrain, both to the right and to the left of the straining Piper and it's frightened pilot. When I broke out of the mist, I saw that the fog had risen above the top of Hospital Hill in just a matter of minutes. I headed back to Chester for the night feeling lucky!

The charter business was booming and we got our share of weirdies. One day Tom loaded up the 182 and headed to Wendover with a scruffy looking guy, two scruffier looking women, and a dog and a cat. They had kitchen utensils, sleeping bags, but had to leave the kitchen sink. They took their case of beer, however. We got our money *before* the flight commenced. Tom said the cat threw up during the takeoff and soon one of the women had to piss in a can, and it went downhill from there.

We flew for the County Mental Health Department. One day I transported a huge man out of Quincy, who was restrained by only soft cuffs and a foot length of chain between them, just right to use as a garrote! He was seated right behind me. The youthful cop with me stood about 5' 2" and I suspected, like Barney Fife, that he was allowed to have only one bullet for his gun. The patient was being flown to Napa for a more-or-less permanent stay, but he thought he was going home to Oroville. The kid cop let it slip that we were going to Napa State Mental Hospital, a place the giant in the back seat right was plenty familiar with. He started shaking. In fact, the whole airplane was shaking. I told him to calm down, that we were only going there to pick up someone else and return to Oroville. I told him to enjoy the ride. That did the trick, but I wouldn't want to try to gain his trust a second time. When they hauled the huge person away in the white paddy wagon I tried not to make eye contact! On another mental health flight, the woman insisted upon removing every stitch of her clothes, but otherwise was a model passenger. I worried a bit about liability. The paddy wagon boys at Napa got her dressed again, but I could see through the window as they drove away that she was starting all over again.

Sadly, the Hummingbird owner, Harry, made the mistake of flying with an former Air Force pilot in his hot, twin-tailed pusher Varieze. There is something seductive about the flight characteristics of this little home-built airplane. The pilot was fond of hot dogging the aircraft, and was seen buzzing ridges and peaks all over the northern Sierras. One day he and Harry went for a joy ride and a miscalculation was made. They were found scattered around Haskell Peak. Soon after that, I accepted a ride with another Varieze owner. He was fond of doing rolls and insisted on showing me a few on a rough and windy ride to Beckwourth. A few days later, he took off from the Spaulding strip with a first-time passenger. Shortly after takeoff, he started a slow roll but, while inverted, plunged straight down into Eagle Lake! On my back seat ride I noticed that the Varieze has a side-mounted control stick. Could it be that the panicked passenger grabbed it for support while inverted and pulled the nose down?

A local good ole boy decided to rent the Cherokee Six and fly his buddies to Mexico. I was elated to have the business, and to promote some good will. All went well until the return trip when, high over Southern California, the tachometer needle suddenly began dancing around, and then went to zero. The air was rough and they were flying in a powerful tail wind. (I remember one cold morning consulting with Frank Nervino about my Luscombe's tach dancing around and making funny noises. I had wondered if there wasn't something wrong with the engine. He just laughed, and oiled up the cable, and after that the engine seemed just fine!) Two miles high in a Cherokee Six, the throttle is set wide open and the propeller governor is set for cruise, so why not sail right on home to the other end of California? Instead, this pilot elected to make the long descent and land. He called and told me how pissed he was that this happened. He and his friends were taking the airlines home, and I will damn well pay for their tickets. I did so, and also paid a pilot and his airfare down to Realto to retrieve the Six. Over the phone, I discussed the tachometer exchange with the proprietor, Paul Mantz (the famous stunt pilot) and he confided, "You'd better watch these guys. I overheard their conversation and they plan to screw you good!" It seemed that he was right because the renter pilot didn't even want to pay for the ferry flight home. My elation over any good ole boy business" evaporated!

John Metzker was now the president of Fitzgerald's Hotel/Casino in Reno and had purchased for his personal aircraft a Cessna 421C Golden Eagle, easily a $200,000 hunk of metal. He asked me to accompany him to the Flight Safety Institute and be his co-captain for the training period. He was paying, and I couldn't resist. There was a hitch, though. I had to pay a pretty penny in recurrent training expenses to get a substitute pilot ready to take my place on the Forest Service Air Attack contract. Only then could I go off and play 421 pilot. It wouldn't have been necessary if we could have waited a week, but John had his schedule.

I arrived in Reno expecting an early start, but then had to wait for John to finish some business and his daily gym workout. After a late start, we departed Reno in the 421 with an instructor. We flew over the Rockies and into the stormy Midwest. Our IFR charts ran out short of Wichita. The final leg was completed in the dark, side-stepping thunderstorms, with only the aid of a WAC chart. It was late at night and a couple of time zones' difference when we finally got to bed.

The Golden Eagle training began at dawn. Ground school sessions discussing aircraft systems and performance concepts lasted all day. Systems such as electrical, fuel, powerplant, propellers, pneumatic, pressurization, air data, and anti-ice, were laid bare by the instructors. Subjects ranging from descent profiles to the function of each circuit breaker and switch on the airplane were covered in detail. Next came cram course, full-motion simulator training, during which John and I swapped seats every four hours. The instructor manipulated a large bank of controls and instruments in a separate compartment. He could create any flight scenario and cause any instrument to malfunction. He was attempting to make me crash by dialing in severe turbulence and heavy icing. Next, he caused an engine to fail, but I continued to hang on. Finally he despaired of shaking me loose, and we heard maniacal laughter behind us as he assumed control of the simulator and crashed us! He shouted, "Nobody gets away without crashing!" In the final few hours, we were allowed to fly the simulator any way we pleased and were encouraged to experiment. I learned to roll it right after takeoff and to fly under bridges inverted. The simulation was supposed to be true to life. I thought I would skip flying under bridges in real life, although my old friend and air performer, Chet, mighta tried it! The total simulator time was sixteen hours plus two hours training in the actual airplane. I felt very checked out!

After work we dined and toured around Wichita. I would have preferred to go to bed, having not yet caught up to the time change. John caused pretty waitresses at the restaurants to breathe hard and flush when he teased them, telling them that he was a big time casino owner and that he could make them into stars. I thought it was hilarious, especially since it was true! He even pulled that routine on a female FSS weather specialist. She looked a little dreamy-eyed before she pulled herself together.

After our return to the west, John and I brainstormed a scheme for a charter operation at Reno, using his 421, his pressurized Centurion, and later, a leased Conquest turboprop. The scheme continued to evolve and became ever more intricate under John's creative genius. He had the resources and the contacts to make it a reality. The idea was to create a full service charter operation to fly people to places like Cabo San Lucas, provide them with lodging, fishing boats, or whatever they needed. Part of the job would be to hang out in paradise. I was going to attempt to run both operations; that is, Sugarpine Aviators as the proprietor and Golden Eagle Aviation as the managing partner. John said that I would never have to worry about money again. (I'm certain I'd heard that somewhere before.)

I traveled to Reno daily and hammered out an acceptable plan with FAA Inspector Howell. The documents required to comply with the Federal Air Regulations that deal with the international charter operation were extremely complex, and took time to produce. Finally it got to be too much. John insisted that I must scrap my operation in Quincy and move to Reno. I said no. He hired another pilot and proceeded with his plans without me.

In a previous magnanimous moment, John suggested that we let RenoFly and do the Annual Inspection on my Cherokee Six. The purpose was to see if they were trustworthy, or would they rip us off, before we let them have at the bigger planes. The new company, Golden Eagle Aviation, would pay for the experiment. The maintenance outfit managed to run the bill up to over $4,000 and sent it to John. He forwarded it to me saying, "I can not bankroll an operation that is not producing any revenue." I couldn't afford the huge bill along with the payments and insurance too. I *gave* the airplane away and leased it back! I learned the hard way that you do *not* play with the big boys unless you *are* one.

Since there were no flight services being offered at Chester, I organized a training program for students from surrounding areas. The missionary effort was reminiscent of the old Enterprise Sky Park days when John Johnson and I traveled all around to give flight instruction. We proceeded to give lots of lessons out of the Chester airport. In the fall and winter months, Quincy was often socked in with fog, while not far to the northwest, the Chester Airport and nearby Lake Almanor, remained sparkly clear. As often as three days a week we had to takeoff from Quincy, IFR in Bucko, if we were to get any of the flight instruction done over there. Fortunately, the 1957-model Bucko was equipped with a Continental 0-300-D engine. This was a conversion to a later model powerplant that included an engine-driven vacuum pump, as opposed to an outside venturi. This was significant because the directional gyro and attitude horizon were spinning their gyros at satisfactory speeds *before* you plunged into the blinding fog. Those instruments were needed to maintain directional and attitude control when the horizon was not visible. We gave instrument training in Bucko too, and sometimes it was in actual cloudy conditions. I decided that it was past time to add a heated pitot tube and an alternate static source to the airplane's equipment list. If those two items were to become plugged by structural ice with no alternative venting system, several important instruments wouldn't work; namely, the airspeed, the vertical speed, and the altimeter. I was grateful for Bucko's excellent Mode C equipped (altitude reporting) transponder. Once I was being vectored to the final approach course on solid instruments when my transmitter refused to function. After an inappropriate silence on my part, Oakland Center casually suggested, "23B, if you can receive me but are unable to transmit, IDENT." When you push the ident button on the transponder, it shows up on the controller's screen. So we communicated just fine this way all the way to the landing. We just couldn't tell jokes!

Occasionally a stray cat would wander into our lives and become the airport kitty. The first calico took up residence in the upstairs office draped across the window soaking up the sun. She lasted about a year. She had a bad habit of climbing into strange aircraft baggage compartments. When we were between kitties, a squirrel took up residence in the shop, entering and exiting through the doggie door. Also, a huge bull snake lived under the stairs among the ferns, and occasionally would make itself visible and scare the hell out of customers. Several times I captured it in a garbage can and transported it over by the river; but invariably it would follow me home. Damnedest thing you've ever seen, almost like a puppy!

We heard about a litter of free puppies in Meadow Valley; and yesseree, there were six or seven black and brown squirmy little things in a basket. Mom had no specially distinguishing characteristics. Amelia squatted over in the corner; her black glittery eyes said, "Leave me alone!" The rest of the puppies begged to be taken but I grabbed Amelia Airheart, (named after the famous Earhart, of course), and we brought her home, much to the disgust of the rest of our animals. Amelia simply took charge of our lives. She had the most compelling and powerful personality I had ever seen in her species. She was low-slung, about twelve inches at the shoulder, a poodle-like head and a long tail that curled up when she was happy and droopy when not. Her ears flopped down like a spaniel and she was black as sin.

When we went on wood-cutting excursions, I would try to get her to ride in the back of the pickup on top of the wood rounds like the rest of the gang. She would stare daggers at me until I finally relented and let her sit on my lap and help drive. Amelia's first flight was in a high-winged Cessna. Everything was fine while taxiing out and for a while after takeoff. Then she stared down at the ground for a few seconds and, suddenly in a panic, she scrambled to the baggage compartment and could not be coaxed out. When the wheels touched the ground at the other end of the flight, she bounded back into Judy's lap and everything was fine again. That was the drill on each flight from then on!

One of our favorite summer outings was taking friends in the Jeep down to Perry Jones' Cabin. We'd say "Hi" to Perry and have a swim in the river. Al and Jerry Ewald went with us for their first time down the steep trail. It was amusing to see their eyes bug out as we hung from our seat belts going downhill. Perry was home and, as usual, there was the insistence that we have a libation. (I always brought something with me to replenish his supply.) The Ewalds were impressed by the twenty or thirty coyote skins hanging from the ceiling. The smell was overwhelming too. Perry told us the tale of how he accidentally rubbed the wrong kind of mushrooms on his skin one day and went plumb psychedelic for almost a week!

It was in 1983 that I went to Fresno to a required Pilot Examiner meeting. I was accosted with the stupidest edict ever issued by the FAA! It was their official view that all landings, other than emergencies or aircraft Pilot Operating Handbook limitations, were to be accomplished with full flaps. No exceptions, period! I thought back through twenty-four years of flying, nearly fifteen-thousand hours, and only one thought came to mind, "B.S.!" The other Pilot Examiners jerked their heads up and down and agreed with anything the feds said. I alone objected vehemently, asking, "What about strong cross winds? What ever happened to the technique of reducing the crosswind component by using a higher landing speed? What about the advantage a tail dragger has when executing a wheel landing in gusty air?"

I was met by dogma, "That's the official policy and that's the way it is, and that is what you are to teach. That's what you are to insist upon during a flight test. Those are the *official flight standards*!" Happily, the FAA later dropped that particular dogma. Damn it. I just think some things are worth arguing about!

The Colonel's Air Attack contract had not been renewed, but he still wanted to spend his summers in Quincy. First he tried to buy the fuel concession from the county, but it wasn't for sale. Then he asked if he could work for me and use his Skylane on a leaseback basis. I agreed, but pointed out that the scheme probably wouldn't be very profitable to him. He insisted that it would be fine and that he just wanted something to do for the summer. The crafty former colonel had more up his sleeve than that. He tried to relieve us of our precious Forest Service business. He would say, "All right now you take everything else and leave the Forest Service work to me, OK?"

I kept saying, "Not only no, but hell no!" Then he slipped over to Forest Service Headquarters and tried to get them to switch away from our contract to his own. (He had failed to mention that he held a "Call When Needed" Forest Service Contract that could be used anywhere in the United States.) Even though this action on his part was legal, the Forest Service could smell a rat. He eventually left after not receiving any calls for his services.

I checked on three brothers from Redding and it was all good

news. Steve Miller, who was once Alma Hind's gas boy at H &
H. Flying Service, had became the owner of the place and called
it Hillside Aviation. His brother Dave, who once had been a pro-
phylactic purchaser (the rubbers were used to test for glaucoma)
had swung a huge and profitable deal. He sold a carbon processing plant to Exxon and was now independently wealthy. He was
enjoying his favorite hobby, building airplanes. Brother Paul was
a department head for Peterson Tractor. Pretty good for a laid-
back hippie!

Sometimes Amelia Airheart didn't mind very well. One day
Judy and I were walking her along the Bucks Lake Road when
she strutted out on the pavement with a logging truck coming
fast around a blind corner. We both yelled for her to come but to
no avail. She just looked at us as though we were stupid.
Suddenly the logging truck was upon her, and right over her. She
crouched and was miraculously untouched. There was no time to
move before a car that had been following the truck also ran over
her. We gathered up the terrified, but untouched dog. She reeked
of exhaust fumes. We took her home and she never ventured into
the road again.

Bill Harnden had gone to work for a company at Stead
Airport, near Reno, rebuilding and refurbishing exotic war birds.
He flew into Quincy now and then and inspected our airplanes
for their Annuals. He was pleased with his life and having fun. I
was shocked to the bone when I heard how he died. He was in
Idaho working on a PBY, a huge WWII aircraft that had been
converted to fire bomber work. He and a mechanic were taxiing
down a strip that dropped off on the sides and at the end. When
the brakes failed, Bill sent the mechanic scurrying to the tail of
the aircraft for his safety. He was still struggling for control as the
amphibian lumbered off the runway. In the valiant attempt to
save the airplane and his passenger, Bill was crushed. The PBY's

nose struck the ground with brutal force and the cockpit wrinkled up with Bill inside. It was determined that improper fluid had been introduced into the brake system by persons unknown.

It was the Christmas season in 1984, when Wayne gave us a dubious present. He had landed the 150 and was taxiing back when he allowed the left main wheel to wander off the taxiway and into the snow. Wayne poured the coal to the engine with the intention of powering back onto the blacktop, but instead the craft flipped over onto its back, smashing the vertical stabilizer and bending the prop. Wayne blamed the large moon boots he was wearing for his loss of control. On one hand we were all sad to lose the little trainer that had seen us through thick and thin but, on the other hand, it was due for a major overhaul again. The insurance paid up with no questions asked. Still, I felt a lump when the high bidder arrived and stuck new tail parts on and a new propeller, and flew the 150 away. As it disappeared into the cold winter sky, I wondered when the crankshaft was going to disintegrate after the probable sudden stoppage that occurred during the flip over incident. For years we saw it parked in places around northern California. Someone once asked the owner how it was doing and he replied that it had flown its wings off and had never been overhauled!

I had been studying hard for the Airframe and Engine Mechanic written exams. Al Ewald had kindly signed me off for the required practical experience to be able to take the tests. Dan English had been working under an Inspection Authorized Mechanic in Alaska, and also had the required credentials. In March of 1984, we drove Dan's car to a school in Long Beach. En route, I bored us both to tears with recordings of me reading regulations for mechanics.

Long Beach is an awful place for mountain people like us. It was the kind of place I have always tried to avoid. There were bars on all the school windows even remotely accessible from the ground. The school recommended a rooming house located near them in Signal Hill. I had very little money to spend, and the $75 a week split between the two of us sounded good; that is, until we met the landlady, who started out on us immediately with all the house rules. These were followed by a tirade of how we would be thrown out at the slightest infraction of her regulations! The room was equipped with sway-backed beds and one naked light bulb dangling from the peeling, yellowish ceiling. The window looked out on the nearby railroad tracks. Just across the tracks stood the Western Bar that attracted sirens and red lights in the night. The procedure for taking a shower was to go down the hall with your personal towel and soap. Step in the shower, remove your clothes, hang them on a hook, and pull the curtain across. After taking your shower, dry off, and get dressed while still standing in the shower stall.

Dan put up with that for a couple of nights and then traveled across town to stay with relatives. I had to spring for all the cost of the room from then on, and rent a car too. Dan finished up his exams first and escaped the city while I had a few more hard days to put in. Just before leaving the rooming house, I stole the poster off the wall with all the house rules scrawled on it. Seemed like a perfect keepsake to me! I turned in my rental car at LAX and could hardly wait to get on the jet that took me out of there. Judy picked up her exhausted A & P Mechanic in Reno that night.

It was time to have some fun. Judy and I loaded up the Cherokee Six with water and camping gear, leaving all but two seats home, and headed south for a much needed vacation in Baja. The idea was that it would be a complete write off since we were checking out various destinations in order to advise our rental customers.

The first stop was Alfonsina's, about an hour and a half south of the border. Alfonsina's lies in the Bahia de San Louis Gonzaga, a protected harbor. The strip is on a sand spit parallel to a line of private beach shacks. According to our information, the runway is flooded during high tides. I looked it over carefully and landed the heavily-loaded Six toward the north where the bar was supposed to be located. Alfonsina's was changing managers and the place was in a mess. (I suspected that this was an ongoing situation.) In order to pull our airplane up onto the sand above the high water mark, they made us rent a hideous plywood shack. We cooked in the shack and slept on the beach. There were *no* toilet facilities, only a few well-used bushes. Bottles of beer were available, three for two dollars American money.

We stretched out in our sleeping bags and I gazed at the full moon rising over the gulf and looked down the line of beach shacks that sat on leased Mexican land. The hodgepodge structures were owned mostly by Americans. I couldn't help think how difficult it must have been to get building materials to this isolated place and I wondered what happened to their sewage. (Actually, I had a pretty good idea where the slime on the bay floor was getting its nutrients.) Except for those few negative thoughts, the scene was gorgeous and I drifted off to sleep, only vaguely aware of the warm ripples lapping on the sand twenty feet below us. I had felt only slightly nervous about the unidentified men strolling aimlessly back and forth around the shacks and on the shoreline. I awoke suddenly to the sound of water lapping the sand right next to my ear. The tide had come in with a vengeance! We checked out the Six and were relieved to see that the tail, which was downhill in the sand, was still out of the water. Later, the tide was finally down and the sand dried out quickly. I taxied to the south end, applied power and turned sharply on the packed sand. The 300 horsepowered Lycoming roared its loudest and we lifted off with only a few feet to spare at the end of the strip which plunged into the waters of the bay. I climbed out right over a Cessna 310 that was resting in the salty brine, an aircraft whose pilot couldn't wait until the tide receded.

We turned south toward Mulege, over two hours distant. The isolation of pristine beaches was guarded by savagely-rugged mountains. Here and there, the beaches looked landable by small aircraft, but if you disabled your airplane, you'd better have food and water. The Serenaded Hotel owned the airport next to it and advertised that fuel was available. It wasn't, nor were there tiedown ropes. No matter, we had enough fuel and the Six was unlikely to blow away. In the town of Mulege we went uptown to a restaurant for lunch. I caught the waitress switching menus on us and asked for the original one back. Much to her disgust we ordered a fine meal at non-tourista prices. It was a nice walk along the Mulege River, and we enjoyed a fun night at the Serenaded Hotel bar. Outside, the rain came down steadily.

The next day we set out for Loreto; but en route, we encountered the tail end of the retreating hurricane "Tiko." Tiko had just devastated Mazatlan on the mainland. It was raining hard and we were getting short on fuel. Fortunately, there was a strong signal from Loreto VOR that helped guide us in to the airport. After breakfast the next morning, we experienced the most dangerous part of our journey, the cab ride to the airport! Chickens, little children and dogs fled in a panic before the madman behind the wheel. It was full throttle to the stop sign and then slam on the brakes! We careened by a group of military men who looked like children. They carried automatic weapons and the cabby said they were searching tourista cars for guns and contraband. We saw swastikas and the Communist hammer and sickle symbols spray painted on fences.

We took off from misty Loreto with assurances of excellent weather ahead. The sun shone brightly on the fabulous white sandy beaches and fantastic colorful and rocky mountains. The abruptly rising ridges appeared to have been formed in sedimentary layers and then uplifted and twisted into bizarre shapes. It was a bad place for an engine malfunction. The WAC chart showed a landing strip at Tembabiche. I observed that it was deeply rutted and probably dangerous. Strangely enough, it did not show the fine runway at San Jaun located on the Bay of La Paz. We flew over them all and continued to the city of La Paz.

At La Paz International Airport we staggered toward the terminal with our bags. It was not at all clear where we were expected to egress. It was not at the military installation guarded by the soldiers and their ever present machine guns. Finally, after locating the proper gate, we rented a Volkswagen and headed for town, peering at the landscape through the broken windshield. For lunch, it was a wonderful shrimp salad created by the restaurant, El Taste. After dinner we walked hand-in-hand on Paseo Alvaro Obregon, the main street that followed the contour of the bay. There were bright lights shining out on the water to attract fish. Pelicans sat in large numbers on the small boats anchored in the harbor.

Judy was to drive the VW around the block and meet me at a hotel where I checked for price and cleanliness. Instead, for the next couple of hours, she became lost and wondered all over the city of La Paz. The narrow, one-way streets forced her farther from the brightly-lighted Malacon Highway. Later, the darkness had an even more disorienting effect. It was an empty feeling to be separated from your loved one and traveling companion in a strange city, much less in a strange country! Suddenly, I saw her in the middle of the traffic looking one way and then another. I yelled, "Judy" and leaped over and across car hoods to get to her in the slow-moving mob of cars! I ran alongside holding onto the doorjam until she could pull off and let me in!

We finally decided to pull out the stops and stay in the gaudiest high rise hotel in town, the Gran Baja. It towered above every other building and was located in a beautiful setting with jungle all around and the Bay of La Paz in its front yard. After some investigation, it looked as though flying was the safest aspect of being in Mexico. OSHA was definitely missing. While climbing the steps to the eighth floor, we noticed that there were no railings on the spiral staircase. It would be a simple matter to step off the edge to your death. Also, in the room, the huge windows opened wide with the window sills only about a foot off the floor. The view was fantastic, but there was nothing stopping you from stumbling over the door sill and out into space! Better go easy on the tequila with the window open.

I stripped down and stepped into the shower. I was looking forward to the hot water cleansing away the frustrations of the day, but only a little dribble came out at first, and then just a hissing sound. I called the desk and they agreed that that it was a bad thing and that they would have it fixed right away. Later, at dinner, we found out that the lack of water pressure was the case more often than not! Next I had to track down the cocktail waitress who disappeared with my twenty dollar bill, supposedly looking for change. This was quite a tourist trap!

The next day we began a Volkswagen tour that took us all the way to the city of San Jose Del Cabo. There, not far from the southern tip of Baja, I got bruised and scraped on the rocks while snorkeling in the ocean still riled up from Hurricane Tiko. At that point, the car began to leak oil at an alarming rate and we decided to return to La Paz before something dreadful happened to the junker. I bought some cheap oil to pour through it enroute. Back in La Paz, late in the evening and exhausted, we settled on the motel Castel Palmira for a night's rest. We both looked scroungy, and when I told the night man that we would pay cash he nodded, but asked how I would establish credit? Meaning, did I have a bank credit card? I explained again that we were paying cash in advance but he only shook his head. Coldly, he calculated that we could pay a deposit of $107 American dollars for a $20 room. I turned as if to walk out, but he quickly agreed to take the cash if we promised to make no phone calls.

Flying northwest from La Paz at the thousand-foot level, we could see a lot of cactus, rolling hills and no civilization. We encountered the Pacific coast south of Bahia Magdalena and flew low over some interesting sand spits. The Pacific coast of Baja was raw and windy, with a rough ocean, very much the opposite of the Gulf of California side. There were miles of inland estuaries protected by the sandy barriers where wildlife abounded. A few isolated fish camps could be seen and farther north there were boats participating in a local regatta. Between Boca de la Soledad and Boca de Santo Domingo, I noticed that the long and narrow sand islands did not connect with the mainland. Call me paranoid, but I could picture us starving (right after we died of thirst) on these deserted places in the event of a forced landing. I picked up the altitude and moved a little closer to the mainland.

Next we flew over Bahia Magdalena and could see a good highway to Madero Amarillo. At Puerto Adolfo Lopez Mateos there was a fair sized village and a nice strip. Another thought popped into my mind as I a story I had heard about a pilot and his wife from Redding who were sailing these waters on vacation. The couple had been befriended in that town by the son of the sheriff. He and his friends partied at the town bars. Later, the young man and his friends boarded the vessel and killed the pilot and tried to rape his wife. The woman escaped and the sheriff was notified. According to the teller, the sheriff brought his son to justice. I guess the point is that one shouldn't become *too* relaxed in unfamiliar areas even if they seem friendly.

We passed by Puerto Adolfo Lopez Mateos and continued on by Estero San Gregorio where we noted a huge array of solar collectors, the purpose for them being there unclear. They were many miles from any large electricity users. Farther north, the highway grew to be a beautiful four lane dream road intersected by unexpected chasms caused by huge washouts. There were *no* warning signs on the highway. If driving, you could suddenly find yourself flying before you knew what happened! Further north around Laguna San Ignacio we saw inland estuaries where the tides created rapidly moving rivers. I spotted several large fish, small whales, or large sharks? I couldn't tell.

After consulting our outdated leather bound *Baja Traveller* book, we decided to land at Bahia de Los Ballenas. The photos showed pretty grass buildings. Looking down at the strip, I decided it was OK. It was like landing on a sandy road with a few little dips. My concern mounted, though, when as we taxied to the end of the strip expecting to see the bar and the cute little grass huts. Instead we saw some really *ugly* plywood shacks and hungry-looking indigenous types running toward us. I turned around and blasted off. I was reminded of the time in Texas when I had landed in someone's field to remove the tiedown clip from the wing of the Luscombe. I took off again because I didn't want to be at the mercy of people whose intentions toward me were unknown. Mostly, I didn't want to put Judy in that position. The law might as well have been a million miles away. It would have been different if I had been traveling with a bunch of guys.

Fifteen minutes later we spotted the Punta Abreojos and landed. While rolling out on the big sandy strip we were accompanied by three pickup trucks who drove in formation with us.

They sped off as we parked. When we stepped out of the Six we were greeted by two youthful Navy-boys carrying machine guns. They demanded to see our documents and attempted to copy everything on the flight plan. It was obvious that the writer was nearly illiterate. To break the tense moment, Judy showed them a picture of son Jack in his Navy uniform. They said they'd heard of San Diego and we said, "That's good, and good-bye." The two military kids nervously eyed the official looking Star of Life logo on the side of the airplane with its snakes wrapped around each other, and I think they wondered who we were, exactly. That logo was noticed everywhere we went. Officialdom in this part of the world was regarded with great seriousness. We casually walked down the glass littered sand to the airplane smiling and waving. With all 300 horsepower we said adios to Punta Abreojos, again, a good place for a bunch of guys to camp on the beach and eat lobster in town. I had been trained as a pilot not to dive into something without knowing what I was getting into.

While flying east of Sierra Placeres, I spotted a road heading the same way we wanted to go and straight as an arrow. Although it looked vulnerable to the shifting sands, I kept it under me like a long runway. Crossing the Laguna Ojo de Liebre, a famous whale mating area, we looked for the creatures in this desolate salt recovery area, but nobody was home.

Guerrero Negro lay on the border of Baja California Norte and Sur. Although there was a 7,200-foot-long paved airport a mile or so north of town that had been there for ten years, it still had no facilities. Instead, we stopped at the smaller strip next to town to fuel up. A late-model Turbo Centurion had just taken on fuel ahead of us. Its Mexican pilot threw his empty bottle of beer into the bushes and popped open another. On takeoff, as the gear was retracting, I could see him tilt the bottle up to his lips for a long, satisfying swig.

We flew northeastward to the Gulf of California side, and assessed the terrain enroute. I wrote in my notes that an engine failure over the broken and rocky terrain would be worse than just disappointing. However, only forty-two minutes after takeoff from Guerrero Negro, the dependable Cherokee brought us humming into Bahia de Los Angeles. We were greeted by a long blacktop runway and a van from the Hotel Villa Vita. Our outdated Baja Traveller book showed only the now closed dirt strip in town.

The Villa Vita had an inviting swimming pool, bar and restaurant. The pool water was furnished by an underground lake located miles away. The rooms were clean and neat and the Baja weather was reported every evening by radio. As evening approached, two groups of motorcyclists rolled in; one group had highway machines, while the others rode rugged cross-country machines designed to take on primitive trails and roads. The cross-country bunch said that they carried tools and had the know-how to fix anything that could go wrong. Their biggest problem was finding fuel to purchase from ranchers. Usually, native farmers or ranchers had some of the precious stuff to spare, but sometimes not. The same went for flying when off the heavily beaten track.

I held my breath at Tijuana when checking in with customs, but no one even glanced at our Cherokee Six with no back seats (a perfect dope hauler). I did kinda wonder about a Mexican based DC-10 that took off and disappeared into the distance with its wheels still hanging down. Did the pilot forget? I remembered the time twenty-four years ago when I had watched a Mexican DC-3 taxi out for takeoff with its external rudder lock still in place. The copilot had to climb out and remove it while they parked at the runup area with the engines idling.

Back in Quincy, I had long hoped to create a fly-in campground down at the east end of the airport. It was a quiet place where soil had been scraped out for the runway extension. It had left a depression that held water for much of the year. Around it grew willows, cottonwoods and mixed conifers, and it was full of wildlife. I talked C.W. into letting a contractor dig the hole deeper with an excavator in order to produce a really scenic pond. Tom (our very own wildlife biologist) planned to construct a nature trail where people could see the great blue heron, warblers, kingfishers, red-winged blackbirds, and deer. The pond would be stocked with blue gill and gamrusia to eat mosquito larva. The area needed some big rocks to make it more interesting. I talked to club member, Kent Karge, about the granite rock quarry owned by the company he worked for. Could we get some big rocks? He said, "If you'll leave the county snowplow/dumptruck overnight at the quarry with a six pack of beer under the seat, I'll see to it that it gets filled up with big granite rocks. I left two six packs, and thanks for the donation, guys!"

My second ten-year airport manager's contract was finally approved. Political controversy in the county was continuous. C.W. Adams was flying county officials hither and yon in his airplane. They decided that tax money should be provided to buy insurance for all county employees with pilot's licenses who were using their own planes to fly themselves, or other county employees, to business meetings. In effect, the move created the unofficial position of county pilot who charged less than the local air charter service; namely, us. The supervisors were laying out $3,600 in annual insurance premiums to cover four employees. I just sighed in frustration at our phantom competition. The county would never have spent that much if they had simply hired Sugarpine Aviators to fly them anywhere they wanted to go!

I started a diary for recording dates and times of things that happened at the airport. It was hard to put my finger on the feeling, but I suspected that in the future I would be called upon to provide information about what I do as airport manager. Except for my pilot logbooks, I had never kept a diary before. I felt uneasy and paranoid. The thought crossed my mind that maybe I didn't really want a job that required me to keep a diary just to cover my backside.

Jim Brock, Director of Public Works, began assuming the duties of the Airports Coordinator from the departing C.W. Adams. Referring to my agreement with the county regarding a fuel flow fee, he stated, "I can't understand why we are paying you to pump gas into your own airplanes." He didn't believe that such an agreement should stand. Our relationship was off to a rocky start! The next clash was when the aviation women's organization, The 99s, offered to repaint the numbers and the name, "Quincy," on the runway. They also were willing to paint one of their special, and beautiful, blue and white compass roses on the ramp. I asked Brock if he could get paint from the Road Department and the customary lunch for the girls. He replied, "The county will supply paint for the runway markings, no paint for a compass rose and no lunch." I objected, saying that was pretty cheap on the county's part. He retorted angrily, "Moore, you'll *never* get anything out of me!" I was once again appalled at the negative effect I had on Airports Coordinators. As he promised, paint was supplied for the runway markings only. I personally bought coffee and donuts for them. I felt ashamed of the county's official position when the girls said that our airport was the only place they *ever* had to buy their own lunch.

I attended a mechanic's seminar in Reno. At break time, I gave John Metzker a call just to say "Hi." He suggested that it might be more fun for me to skip the mechanic thing and go with his pilot and him on a training mission in the company King Air C-90. I agreed. I was startled by the scene flashing by in the windscreen! There I was, standing in the door of the twin engine turboprop, while John was receiving touch-and-go instruction at the Minden Airport. Glider crews were desperately trying to drag their long-winged craft off the edge of the runway and out of the way of the King Air charging through their midst. After the second touch-and-go with gliders on the ground, in the air, and all over the place, I politely suggested that maybe it would be prudent to go elsewhere. The instructor looked at me like I was stupid, but complied with the suggestion. It only took a short time to hop over to the deserted Lovelock airport. I don't think the pilot cared for the idea when John suggested that I fly copilot in the King Air 200 for them occasionally, just for a little variety and $75 a day.

I was pleased with the challenge of learning a new airplane and getting a little taste of corporate flying. I studied the manuals with a vengeance and even drew a large poster-sized picture of the panel and the location of each instrument. I made a cassette tape, reading out procedures that I could replay when I had a little time. Finally, I had a chance to fly copilot on a charter to Las Vegas. I learned how to turn on the coffee pot, but that was about it. While we waited in Las Vegas for our charter passengers, the pilot told me the tale of when he had flown John and Jean south to Culiacan, and they experienced engine problems. The Metzkers went on their way leaving him to find a way to get it fixed. After the fix it, job he took off. When the engine failed again and had to be feathered, he just kept his mouth shut and flew it all the way north to an American port of entry.

On the way back from Las Vegas, we flew through an extremely ugly thunderstorm. The charter customers in the rear all looked sick, I thought we could have deviated around it, but then I wasn't the captain. The next King Air flight was just a little hop over the hill to the Baron Von Hilton ranch. (I don't know whether Baron was really a "Baron" or a "Von" or not, but that's what they called him.) John didn't go because he and Baron were not the best of friends. The little paved strip didn't appear on any charts. It was located in the middle of a valley that Baron owned. The parking area was full of expensive corporate aircraft. Our little King Air 200 looked like a piker. The Baron's ranch house rambled on and on. The guest quarters were located in a restored, beautifully rustic, and historical rest stop. It was to be an outdoor affair with fifty or more tables surrounding the sparkling pool; their double white and burgundy table cloths crossed tastefully. All the eating tools were *real* silver and the linen was expensive, too. Stewing under twenty-five pure silver warming trays were tender cuts of roast beef, pork, and every other imaginable hot delicacy. The aroma was divine! Drinks were iced down and cold water filled the glistening crystal goblets on the tables. Wine flowed like water for everyone but the pilots. Gorgeous showgirls from all over the Hilton empire rushed to serve one's every need. It was quite a bash and we sat down to eat.

With my mouth full of scrumptious roast beef, I listened to the classical music and watched the glider perform its graceful aerobatics. It eventually settled to the earth in perfect harmony with the ending crescendo. It was a wonderful show and everyone clapped. I was settling into some serious eating when suddenly I heard a "whoosh" sound. I looked up just in time to witness a Shrike Commander Buzzing us from east to west, inverted, with both engines feathered. The Shrike executed several slow rolls, restarted its engines and proceeded with a dramatic aerobatic show. You guessed it; after landing with both engines feathered, the famous Bob Hoover stepped out and joined the party!

One day Judy had given Edwin Anderson, a balloon pilot, a new logbook because he had forgotten his own. He kindly repaid us the next day with some balloon instruction. It was a 560A Raven Hot Air Free Balloon in which I logged liftoff, contour, level flight, and a landing approach. It was quiet except for the occasional burst of flame to create the buoyant hot air that kept us aloft. The experience was nothing like the relative quietness of sail plane flying in where the sound of air passing over and around the craft was the only sound. While floating in the balloon, you could hear people talking on the ground and cows mooing in the fields under us. The flamboyant and vibrant colors added to the spirit-lifting effect. The warm early morning summer sun felt wonderful. We touched down in Bresciani's field and joined in the traditional first flier's champagne ceremony.

In February, the snowplow broke down and the county refused to fix it anytime soon. Our flight operations were halted. Finally, Sierra Pacific Industries brought in their own equipment and cleared the runway and ramp so that their owner could land. That was a sad thing to witness after I had worked so hard for twelve winters to do a neat, clean plow job on the runway, taxiway, ramp, and around all the hangars, plus the restaurant parking lot.

It was still freezing when Bob showed up. I walked into the outside bathroom one morning and discovered a pathetic little Manx that looked for all the world like a baby bobcat. When I tried to pick him up, the little bastard tried to rip me to pieces. I ran and got Judy and a pair of gloves but Bob eluded us for a while. We finally cornered him by a hangar and grabbed him. The veterinarian said that the emaciated critter was only hours from death. We took Bob home and he soon became the "lion on the verandah," always trying to be tough and independent, but giving into purrs when picked up. He slept with us every night and disappeared every day, but showed up in the evenings for our sojourns to the pond.

Skip Kobel just looked like a screwball! He claimed that he was an electronics genius and proceeded to engage in one failing business venture after another. He seemed to enjoy setting up situations that would lead to confrontations. He possessed a Commercial Pilot Certificate and had acquired most of the required time for it at night. That fact fit in well with his shadowy character. He always insisted on owning tail draggers although he was hopelessly incompetent in them. The bird he showed up with first was a Piper Pacer. On his first attempt to land at Quincy, he wandered off into the weeds and wrecked it. The air was perfectly calm. The second was a Bellanca Cruisair. I felt sorry for the little guy; and, as airport manager, I officially suggested that he move his trailer over to the airport security trailer spot. I told him there would be no charge in return for him keeping an eye on things. I also told him he could tie down his airplane in one of my spots by the hangar at no charge. He said that he'd had experience as a security guard and nothing had ever been stolen under his watch. His eyes bulged and rolled around as he spoke. I was a little uncomfortable at the intensity of his statement. By June of '86, Kobel's trailer occupied the airport security site. I hoped that the fuel thefts and other mischief on the airport would cease. They did not because Skip disappeared for a month without a word. I wondered if he was dead, but he finally returned, saying that he had been on "business." I wondered if it was in Transylvania. He stayed in his little trailer all day with his German shepherd as his only companion. Soon Skip began chasing phantoms in the night and almost catching them. One late evening, I taxied in with a student and was met by Skip, the shepherd, and an Uzi semiautomatic assault rifle. He said he was patrolling. I thought he was kidding and told him that the whole thing was a bit of an overkill! A couple of weeks later, Skip threatened a couple who was parked by the restaurant watching a lunar eclipse. He stuck his loaded Uzi in their faces. Of course, I heard about it right away. Skip was crestfallen when I told him he couldn't carry his Uzi on airport property anymore. One warm Sunday afternoon the boys of Rotary were having an unofficial get together in one of the hangars. There was beer and food and—a porn movie! Skip was lurking nearby and his sensibilities were outraged. Instead of coming to me, he went directly to a female county supervisor who was also outraged and demanded a public apology from the whole Rotary organization. (Of course the Rotary organization really had nothing to do with the situation.) I, in turn, took a lot of heat because I had appointed this character to play "airport guard." After checking with county counsel, I relieved Skip of all guard duties and told him to take his trailer and his airplane and get out. The trailer didn't move, and neither did the Bellanca. I couldn't seem to get rid of this guy, so I began legal proceedings. Meanwhile, if any airplane was left unlocked, its microphone would disappear. The office door was mysteriously opened in the middle of the night. Of course, Skip knew where the key was hidden.

It was summer and I was eight years into my airport manager's contract, when I agreed to also manage the Chester Airport for a three month period in the summer to help the county. At the time, Coordinator Adams thought he could hire any bozo off the street to manage an airport because, after all, they were only gas boys! Bob Silvera, his hire of a year ago, possessed a long criminal record. (Nobody had bothered to check his background.) He had apparently reverted to form when he disappeared with a large sum paid to him in cash for county fuel. He was apprehended in Kentucky and put away in the slammer for a while, but the county failed to follow through with charges and let him out.

Ray was a Private Pilot with a military background. He had served as a crew member aboard hurricane-penetrating aircraft. He possessed a likeable, funny personality and boundless energy. He wanted the job of Station Agent for us at Chester and conjured up a scheme whereby the government would pay half his wages. He was so insistent that I finally gave up and hired him but, as I suspected, involvement with both him and the government were more trouble than it was worth. Ray's tenure was short and crazy. I thought for sure a guy with a teaching credential could do math and write legibly, but no. He was always in a frenzy—a virtual whirlwind of activity with little productive results. Even so, we remained friends. He really meant well. Dan English took over and also began flying our daily Fire Patrol.

The county expected me to iron out the chaos left by Silvera, especially in the area of fuel sales, which was a mess due to poor or non-existent records. I also found out that a number of local pilots were pumping their own fuel and charging without supervision. I began by stopping any charging and instituted a night "call for service" system. Soon, though, the pressure was on me again to charge to local aircraft owners and out-of-town, large-volume purchasers. A strong push came from the operator of the Chester based air tanker (fire bomber) and the Air Attack Skymaster contracted to the Forest Service. They went over my head to Jim Brock who, at the direction of the supervisors, directed me to allow these, and certain other prominent users, to charge fuel. Later, a Forest Service representative from the Chester area, and former Chester Airport Committee member, remarked that these companies that were contracted to the Forest Service should pay like everyone else. He complained aloud and couldn't understand why *I* allowed them to charge fuel!

318 | JOHNNY MOORE

One hot summer day at Chester, a company pilot gave in to the demands of his boss, and took off in a Cessna 180 to show off its new STOL (Short Takeoff and Landing) kit. He took off uphill and downwind toward the north with only about half the required runway available. It was ridiculous! He plowed through the fence at the end, bounced across the highway and into the trees. Miraculously, between him, his boss, and two passengers, there were no serious injuries. I was notified and immediately hopped into an airplane at Quincy, arriving at Chester not long after the dust settled. The pilot told me what happened, blamed his boss, and then asked me to lie for him. Ha! I hope he's looking for a job in some other field of endeavor.

Jack Farrell was trying to sell his Cessna 175. Jon Taborski and several would-be partners were trying to buy it. The deal included an Annual Inspection to be signed off by John Coffelt, the new airport manager at Chester. To save money, the menial work was to be done at Quincy by the buyers and John C. planned to drop in and check on things. One of the items accomplished was an oil change. I was asked to begin Taborski's Biennial Flight Review while ferrying the aircraft over to Chester where its Annual was to be completed and signed off. Chester is less than a half-hour away from Quincy with rugged mountains and canyons between. Almost half way on our journey, I noticed the rpm's slowing down. At the same time, Jon pointed out that the oil pressure gauge was indicating zero. I immediately grabbed the controls, executed a very steep 180 and pointed the nose toward the nearest field north of Quincy. The end of the runway lay a mile or so beyond that.

I instructed Jon to call a "Mayday" to Quincy Unicom. I left the throttle wide open and watched as the oil temperature rose steadily and the propeller turned more and more slowly. There was nothing under us but tall trees and big rocks. Finally, we arrived over the edge of the meadow with the runway in sight. A west wind rolling off the lee side of Hospital Hill was creating wind shear and wave action that had to be navigated through. Suddenly, we were too high in spite of the slowly turning propeller. I throttled back and wasn't surprised when the engine seized up. The prop stopped and you could have chinned yourself on it without it budging an inch! I used the manual flaps liberally to create and eliminate drag in a hurry, much like using spoilers in a glider. The sharp up and downdrafts had to be dealt with effectively in order to maintain a safe glide path to the airport. I thanked the gods that the early-model Cessna wasn't equipped with slow-operating electric flaps! I demonstrated "S" turns and slips to Jon while on final. After all, I was supposed to be giving him a Biennial Flight Review! The last part of the descent to the runway was traversed in silence except for the sounds of the wind. I felt confidence from having flown gliders and arranged to have just enough speed to make the turnoff at the far end of the runway so that we didn't have to push the inoperable hulk very far.

When we uncowled the engine, the problem was obvious. The oil drain consisted of a hose attached to the oil sump with a cap threaded at the *end* of it. In other words, the whole tube was full of hot oil. Whoever had completed the oil change had screwed the cap on with feather fingers and had not safetied it. The whole arrangement was strictly a "Rube Goldberg" setup and quite illegal. The cap had simply unscrewed itself, fallen off and all the oil ran out.

Potential trouble followed the incident. I soon received a call from FAA George "hatchet man," Eicher, who told me he had received a complaint from an anonymous source, and that I was in plenty of trouble. I told him to go to hell! Next, Jack Farrell's attorney considered suing me since I was Pilot-in-

Command, but I suspect Jack put the kibosh on that. Eicher eventually called me back later and told me that I was off the hook for any blame in the incident.

One night the phone rang late and I struggled out of a deep sleep. The voice on the other end said that he was in a telephone booth at the Tonopah Airport (250 miles southeast of Quincy) and needed a charter to Oakland. The voice said he'd pay double my regular charter fee for the inconvenience. I made it a practice to never pick up strangers at some far off place without the money in my hand first. I sleepily replied, "Why don't you call my competitor, Verman Charters, he's got an 800 number." I hung up and went back to sleep. Verman took the bait and picked the guy up and flew him to Oakland where the police were waiting. The charter "customer" turned out to be a fugitive and the pay for the flight was zero!

Fred Gleason paid us a visit. He was driving a Cadillac with the entire driver's side wiped out; no door, no windows. Plastic Visquene-like stuff was taped on to keep the wind out. He told me how he had pulled into a crop duster operation at Knight's Landing to check on a job when a loader truck ran into him. He just drove away without pressing the operator about his insurance. Later that night at the Capitol Club, he had a limerick contest with another patron. He lost when he drunkenly fell off the bar stool and was asked to leave. Ya really gotta work hard to get thrown out of the "Cap!"

Bill Budney was a very personable character. When I checked him out in several of our airplanes, he flew well. The only problem was that his checks were no good. Bill was a con man. I was especially impressed when he talked a sales representative with a turboprop Cheyenne into picking him up at Quincy and letting him fly the airplane to the coast for a demo. He made him believe that he might buy it. Bill generously shared with us the fresh shrimp he had purchased at a coastal market when he returned. Soon after Budney checked out in the Cherokee Six we heard rumors that he might skip town because his bad checks were catching up to him. We were concerned that he might steal the airplane, so we began a stakeout. About eleven at night I decided that this was a bunch of B.S. and disabled the airplane so that it couldn't be flown. I knew that Bill liked to hang out at the Bank Club, so I went after him clutching one of his rubber checks. Yep, he was at his favorite table buying a round of drinks. With very little force I traded the bad check for cash. The next day they hauled him off to jail and a lot of people in town got burned, but I wasn't one of them!

Once in a while an FAA-induced maintenance headache pops up at the most inconvenient times. It was June and we were busy as hell. Unfortunately one Cherokee had arrived at the 5,000 hour airframe event and Airworthiness Directive 87-08-08 required that the wings be removed and certain parts be checked for cracks with a dye penetrant. Chief mechanic, Dan, dove into the job and soon I was looking at the horrifying sight of the Cherokee in three distinct pieces. He didn't find any cracks; and I was hoping that it would go back together as well as it was before. Not to worry, Dan had it back together in record time and it only cost about $1,000 plus lost revenue due to down time. Two weeks later, I received the official notice from the FAA that the AD had been rescinded!

It looked like we needed another airplane suitable for charter and Forest Service recon, but we didn't have much money. I spotted a '60 model Cessna 210 in the Trade-a-Plane advertisements, that was located at Fresno. Only $11,900! I wondered what was wrong with it. The owner said that he'd bought a newer model and this one was just sitting on the ramp neglected. I flew down with a cashier's check and took a look at the bird.

There was nothing specifically wrong with the airplane other than shabby paint, ripped upholstery and antiquated tube-types radios. Also, the wings were full of bird nests. I paid the owner the price of a Cessna 150 and flew the 210 home.

The "new" 210 served us pretty well during the first summer season. It was awhile before I could lay my hands on the appropriate operations manual that instructs the pilot to turn the fuel boost pump on before switching tanks. (The only selection choices are "Right," "Left," and "Off.") There were power interruptions before we realized that there could be air in the fuel lines. They needed the additional fuel pressure provided by the boost pump to eliminate the possibility of fuel starvation when switching from one fuel tank to the other. One day I was flying a real estate lady from Sacramento to Quincy, and when I switched tanks the engine quit cold! I switched back so quickly that she never realized what happened. I knew it happened, but I didn't yet know why, and it didn't happen every time. Oh yes, the 1960 model Cessna 210 fuel system was a nightmare! Holding only fifty-five gallons of useable fuel, the fuel feed in the tanks will unport when in an extended slip if the fuel selector is feeding from the wing down tank. This was amply demonstrated one afternoon when I was flying with a Forest Service recon observer. I was showing him a suspicious lightning strike area near the bottom of a drainage. While holding my heading with the rudder, I kept the wing down with the aileron. (I held a bank without a turn so the observer could see better.) The engine sputtered and died! With fuel three quarters used in the selected tank, the line from the fuel tank to the engine was sucking air. The engine will also starve for fuel if the airplane's deck angle is tilted too far up, such as on a takeoff, a go around, or pitched too far down, on an approach for landing. You always try to use up one tank in level flight so that the other one will have sufficient fuel in it to allow for any maneuvering. The FAA requires placards to be placed near the fuel gauges warning against prolonged slips with less than half tanks of gas.

It was a clear day enroute to Orange County, flying in as straight a line as possible to ensure plenty of fuel for maneuvering on arrival. Upon entering the Los Angles Basin, the landmarks were obvious due to the unusually clear air. The FAA accused me of crossing a tiny segment of the LAX TCA (twenty five miles from Los Angles International) without authorization. I pointed out to the inspector whom I contacted that I was directly over a VFR checkpoint and descending clear of the TCA. At an informal hearing at the Reno FSDO an FAA attorney heard my story and recommended to her boss that they drop the case due to lack of evidence. No such luck! I was accompanied by my attorney when I attended the kangaroo court in Los Angeles. The FAA couldn't even name the controller who complained of the alleged infraction, nor did they have the usual videotape of the incident depicted by radar. The copy of the audio sounded like an excellent example of pilot/controller interchanges and useable for a training course. In the formal administrative hearing, Air Traffic Control claimed that I was at the same altitude and location on three different occasions, minutes apart. This was an unlikely scenario since I was tracking 180 knots over the ground and descending at 1,200 fpm. That didn't stop them from suspending my ATP Certificate for sixty days! It encouraged me to instruct my large ground school class as to exactly what happened, even using the recording the FAA had used against me as evidence. They became a generation with a bone to pick with the FAA's abusive and unfair enforcement practices.

Not to leave out some fun times, I vividly remember a wonderful flight in the slim little 210 around the Smoke Creek Desert. It was a horse-counting mission for the Bureau of Land

Management. My official passenger was content to allow me to cruise through the canyons looking for wild horses at low level and at my discretion. It must have been a picture to see the 210 with its long sleek wings quietly slipping through the crisp mountain air at minimum power settings and sipping fuel at the rate of only five gallons per hour. The narrow fuselage and long wings and gear tucked up made for a wonderful flying machine and I loved to fly it, especially like that!

During the winter we refurbished the 210 with an expensive paint job, copying Cessna's dazzling 1960 scheme. Just before painting, the engine was overhauled and a landing gear door modification kit was installed. After spending all that money on improvements, we began to experience mechanical problems with the airplane.

It was a hot day and chief pilot, Tom, had a load of Forest Service personnel in the 210. He was about to takeoff on runway six, but then had to taxi back to the ramp to pick up some item that had been forgotten. By the time he taxied back for takeoff the Cessna's fuel-injected IO-470 engine was as hot as a pistol. He lifted off with a quartering tail wind, and as his hand moved toward the lever to retract the landing gear, he noticed the engine was gradually losing manifold pressure. He left the landing gear and flaps in the takeoff position, and as per manual instructions; Mixture-Rich, Fuel Boost Pump-On, Fuel Selector-Switch Tanks, all to no avail. In the critical moments after liftoff and too late to stop on the runway, it was obvious the engine was going to continue to lose power. In a gutsy maneuver, Tom retarded the throttle, extended full flaps and landed in the only hay field that was available. Not a scratch on the plane or passengers! Talk about a "Cool Hand Luke!"

Naturally there was a Forest Service investigation into the incident. After they looked things over, we towed the high-winged aircraft back to the airport via road beds between the fields and ditches. When we finally got her dragged home, we checked every fuel screen in the airplane for blockage and sent the fuel pump to a specialist to be dismantled and inspected. Nothing! No contamination of any kind could be found in the fuel system. My opinion was that the cause was a vapor lock resulting from the hot temperatures leading up to the takeoff. Tom received an official commendation from the Forest Service for his handling of the event and the Forest Service gave our maintenance records a clean bill of health. We all took note of that particular hay field and remembered that, under certain conditions, it could be a possible haven in an emergency power failure occurring shortly after takeoff.

It paid to pay attention. One hot day later in the summer, I was giving dual instruction to the owner of a 150-horsepowered Rallye. We were shooting touch-and-go's on runway six. The Rallye had short field capabilities partly by virtue of its slats on the leading edge of the wings. They automatically deployed below a certain airspeed. Even so, with 150 horsepower it was underpowered for our altitude on a hot day. The carburetor heat stuck in the full hot position on a missed approach with not enough runway to stop in. The aircraft was unable to maintain altitude and I knew that if I attempted a turn, we would surely stall. We were going to land out there somewhere, so I deliberately throttled back and put it into the same field Tom had landed the 210 on earlier. I had less field to work with though, because they were flooding it in order to urge the hay to grow for another cutting. We stopped safely and walked back to the airport. The next morning Herschel and I went out and fixed the carburetor heat problem and drained most of the fuel to lighten the load. With the Rallye's low wings, it was not practical to tow it back to the airport as we had done with the 210, so I flew it out. It took a forty-five degree turn to the right after takeoff and in seconds I was back on the runway. Good thing, too, because the field was completely flooded by nightfall. If anything had gone wrong, I would surely have been sued, but I just couldn't see leaving that poor airplane in a field, trapped in water.

I was enroute to the Nevada County airport when the Cherokee 180's engine began shaking violently. I "poured the coal to it" (increased the throttle to maximum available power), banked toward Sly Creek Reservoir, and quickly set my transponder to squawk 7,700, the emergency frequency. The engine kept running, but still shaking violently. I called Oakland Center and declared an emergency. They had me on radar instantly. I pointed the nose first toward a manzanita brush field, and then in the direction of the Oroville airport, some forty miles distant. It was a scary twenty minutes to the airport. I was glad that there had been no passengers on board to be frightened, or to add to the aircraft's weight. Once down, I called home and dispatched the other Cherokee and a pilot to pick up the waiting customer. He never knew that we had experienced problems.

Oroville Aviation's shop removed the cylinder and found at least a million cracks in it. The exhaust valve had broken off in a pie-shaped piece that had stuck in the roof of the cylinder and the piston had proceeded to beat the hell out of it. The little four banger Lycoming engine did a good job banging away on only three cylinders with the other one just along for the ride!

I was flying a full complement of Forest Service people on a timber survey with the 210-equipped with recon radios to keep us in touch with dispatch. In the pattern for landing at Oroville, I selected the landing gear "down" position. I expected to see the three green lights that would indicate that the main gear and nose gear were all down and locked into landing position. "Oops!" I groaned to myself. I saw the indication that all retractable gear pilots dread, two green lights instead of three. The nose wheel had failed to lock down. I remembered a funny noise when they were cycling down and I suspected that this problem wasn't going to fix itself. After several gear cycles and a fly-over for someone on the ground to check the gear, I prepared to land. I called dispatch on the Forest Service radio and relayed a briefing of the situation. The passengers were given especially careful "before-landing instructions." I had them throw everything they could into the baggage compartment in order to create a tail heavy condition. I was wishing I could throw one of the Forest Service guys in there, too, but I could see how bad that would look in the report! The idea was to land slowly and avoid damage to the propeller and engine, and the less weight up front the better. I touched down with the fuel selector off, the mixture control at Idle Cut Off position, and the magnetos off. At touchdown, the propeller was barely turning and just nicked the pavement when the nose-wheel collapsed. Once again, we were thoroughly investigated by the Forest Service, and the FAA, who made a complete search of our maintenance records. The FAA was represented by my old acquaintance, Dixie, Al Ewald's A & P student at Shasta College. I tried to tell her that the 210 was operating as a "Public Aircraft" since it was flying for a government agency, but she only laughed at the ploy. It didn't matter anyway because once again we were exonerated by both government agencies. I was issued a letter of commendation from the Forest Service similar to Tom's as to the manner in which I handled the incident.

The next situation popped up when Tom took off at Santa Rosa and the 210's engine began to shake violently. He accomplished an emergency 80-260 degree turnaround and landed in the opposite direction. Tom is particularly good at this maneuver. He and I teach all of our students this procedure during their takeoff and landing stages. The tactile maneuver increases their situational awareness in our mountain environment and adds to the number of landings in a period of time. Also, it is normal at our airport to take off on runway six and land on two four. Since it was a Forest Service flight, naturally they had to know all about the problem.

A local shop investigated the problem and was of the opinion that a cylinder through bolt may have been over-torqued, and had finally failed. They patched us up and we returned in a week to retrieve the 210. The trips across California to retrieve airplane and pilot, plus down time and mechanic bills, were getting costly. The Forest Service official inspector mechanic investigated and decided that if one of the cylinder hold-down bolts could have been over-torqued and stretched, then the rest could have been, too. I flew back to the original overhauling shop and had all the bolts replaced and retorqued. (Of course they weren't about to admit any fault in the matter so I had to pay for it all.) Everything was finally fixed properly. Unfortunately, the 210 was getting a "hoodoo" reputation. Informally, the Forest Service let me know that the guys around the coffee pot were talking; they didn't want to ride in the airplane anymore.

I was crushed because I thought that this was the best handling airplane of its type. I loved it and wanted to keep it as a pet! Well, that was tough luck for me. I had little choice but to sell it. Bob Lockwood always quoted some obscure philosopher about business decisions. For example, "If the right hand becomes useless, *cut it off!*" The minute that I "cut it off," the lessor of the Cessna 182 that I was leasing for Forest Service and charter backup jacked up his price to me. He threatened to pull the airplane out from under me if I didn't comply, in spite of our written agreement. I cut *him* off as soon as possible and resolved that, in the future, I would avoid entanglements that I didn't have full control over.

Damian, a local Native American, was flying several relatives around in one of the 180s. Cherokees only have one door, and for one reason or another the door became unuseable, with Damian and his kinfolk inside. He was forced to clamber over the others to access the tool kit in the baggage compartment. With the screwdriver, he managed to work open the baggage door and the plane full of Maidu's scrambled out that way. Damian laughed and wondered what it must have looked like to people who saw a bunch of Indians climbing out through the baggage compartment after landing, and then enter in the same way to continue the flight. With sly humor he told everyone that just like the "no step" sign on the flap means "do not step here," the "do not open" sign on the door must mean, "do not open this door!"

I received a letter from crop duster friend, Fred Gleason, which included a photo of him standing on the bow of the Navy Seal ship, USNS ZUES T-ARC 7 sailing in the Arctic Ocean. He also sent a baseball cap with the ship's logo on it. What was a man in his seventies doing on a military intelligence ship in the far corners of the earth? God only knows!

A desperate request came for me to drop the computer expert off in Hayfork as soon as possible. The mill was shut down and costing the company thousands of dollars per hour. I looked at the weather dubiously, but said I'd give it a try. There was a big front headed our way. I had to fly "on top" for most of the hour and a half flight from the Sierras, across the Sacramento Valley and into the coastal range. The loran and VORs accurately led me over the top of the piled-up clouds to my target. Luckily, there was a small hole right over the airport, and I spiraled down into the little valley. Just before beginning the descent, I could see to the northwest what looked like a tidal wave of menacing weather heading our way.

As I dropped the passenger off, weather closed in and rain began to fall. The base of the clouds had dropped to about twelve-hundred feet above ground level; they merged into the surrounding mountains that rose almost five-thousand feet above the airport on all sides. I used the loran to "barber pole" in a spiral up from the center of the airport. I figured that if the engine failed, or I iced up, I could descend using the same technique. Around and around I climbed, maintaining a left-turning mile arc around the airport waypoint. Gradually, the ADF pointed toward Redding and the VORs tuned to Red Bluff and Redding began to twitch. At least my ability to navigate seemed assured. As I continued to climb, I watched the outside air temperature indicator needle crank counter-clockwise toward the dreaded freezing level. If I accumulated too much ice, and my barber pole scheme didn't work, I might become a statistic. At nine-thousand five-hundred feet, I broke out under a high cirrus cloud layer. The tidal wave of weather was now frighteningly close in the west, reaching to engulf the comparatively- frail plane. I hightailed it in the other direction, toward home. Much to my relief, the area clear of clouds was still there. I dodged multiple stratus layers of clouds and rainstorms until I was finally able to descend into Gansner Airfield. The storm lasted for weeks and broke records in terms of rainfall. It virtually wiped out Highway 70 in the Feather River Canyon and isolated Hayfork for some time!

Mark Tarloff, (d.b.a., "Ice Cap Productions") was in town producing a movie called *White Water Summer,* starring Kevin Bacon and Sean Astin. We became responsible for their air trans-portation between Quincy, one of their shooting sites at Fall River Mills, and the Bay Area. Most of the crew and cast were from the Los Angeles area and needed their city fix every so often. We flew them to San Francisco and waited all day. The pilgrims returned with all sorts of packages filled with things unavailable in the hick, mall-less village of Quincy. Tarloff's production had a budget of around a million bucks to produce his movie. That amount was considered paltry in Hollywood circles; to us, it was pretty impressive. When they rented a huge building at the fairgrounds to shoot night scenes in the woods, half the town was there to ogle at the Hollywood stars. We felt like big shots with our special invitations. Larry Rappaport, the assistant director, was constantly sent off on errands that didn't suit a city boy very well. One day he was supposed to find a beaver dam, so off he went in his brand new Jeep. Judy and I followed him, fully expecting him to get lost in the mountains. After following for miles and miles, it was clear that he didn't have even a remote chance of finding a beaver dam. We overtook him and had him follow us to the nearest beaver architecture. Larry was grateful for our help, and it made him look good.

Finally winter arrived and the time for a wrap-up party was long overdue. The snow was flying and it was pitch black as the string of production vehicles, including a semi-truck, pulled out enroute to Bally's Hotel Casino in Reno. Judy and I followed in our beat up old Jeep Wagoneer. West of Portola and on exactly the site that Marilyn Monroe made famous in the movie, "Bus Stop," the troupe semi-truck jackknifed in the treacherous snow. When we arrived on the nightmarish scene all the crew were standing around and Larry Rappaport was running around frantically trying to do something, but he didn't know what. A California Highway Patrol officer sat in his car with the red lights on. warning oncoming motorists. I noticed that the collective alcohol breaths of those present would have knocked you into next week! I asked Larry if I could help and he shivered as he said, "Yes, yes, anything!" Snow was beginning to accumulate on the curly black hair he wore piled high on his head. I hooked a chain up to the front of the truck and requested that the driver slowly add power while I tried to drag him straight with my four-wheel-drive Jeep. It worked and the truck straightened out! The Highway Patrol Officer waved and the pilgrims continued to make their way to the Mecca of the bright lights, more slowly now.

When we arrived at the designated banquet room at Bally's, everyone else had already been seated. Larry jumped up, pointed at me and yelled out to all those present, "It's Johnny Moore, make room for him and Judy, Johnny saved our lives tonight!" I blushed as we joined the party; hell, it was no big deal! Larry tried to insist that we spend the night, all expenses paid. Frankly, I couldn't imagine spending a whole night with that crowd, fun as they were, and we went on home in the snowstorm. As it turned out, they were all trapped in Bally's for several days because the airlines were shut down due to the severe storms. It must have been quite a drunken free-for-all for a while; I'm glad we missed it!

The instructor brought his boss to me for a Private Flight Test. The candidate wore gold chains around his neck, an open-necked, Hawaiian-type shirt and carried an attitude. In his mind, the flight test was a mere formality, of course, and we had to be quick because he was soon off to Europe on business. Also he wondered out loud why he was bothering to fly this little 172 when most of his operations would be in the King Air or the Lear. The instructor rolled his eyeballs and shrugged, and we got on with the test. The failure was complete. He possessed little knowledge of the maneuvers to be performed. He was unable to perform the easiest task, and was annoyed because "I expected so much of him." Rarely have I seen such self-deception and arrogance.

His instructor pulled me aside and grinned, "Do you realize that you've just flunked a billionaire?"

Have you ever had a friend ask you to fly the family airplane during his absence, in order to keep things oiled and charged up? Sounds like fun, huh? Well, here's what you can get involved with by volunteering to do a good deed—Lt. Col. Dick LeFrancis (retired), owned Skylane Delta Foxtrot, a handsome bird with sunlight glinting off its pampered hull. One day I was giving our mechanic/pilot, Herschel, dual instruction. As we taxied onto the runway, my headset and every other conceivable pilot aid was properly adjusted for takeoff. Throttle advanced, we were thundering down the runway when I had one of those gut feelings that something wasn't quite right. I throttled back and aborted the takeoff. As the 182 slowed down, an uncontrollable nosewheel shimmy commenced, in spite of full-up elevator and no brakes being applied. We discovered that the shimmy dampener was missing. Yeah, simply not there! The absentee owner was outraged when I called him about the situation, and requested that I look into it. After a few investigative phone calls and three-way conversations, it turned out that "Shop South" had performed the last Annual Inspection. They agreed to supply a new shimmy dampener free of charge since they had missed the absence of the part, and had sent the aircraft out in an unairworthy condition. The shimmy dampener arrived in a timely fashion, and I volunteered to take time out of my busy schedule to remove the cowling and install the unit. The shaft of the component had been inserted backwards. Herschel and I disassembled the shimmy control device, turned the shaft around, poured some of my valuable hydraulic oil in its cylinder and reassembled the thing. The unit then fit fine. If you've ever removed and reinstalled a Cessna 182 cowling, you know what a hassle it can be. We completed the procedure and taxied out in order to test our work. With Herschel in the left seat and me giving him instruction, down the runway we roared, that is, until the takeoff was rejected due to one hell of a nose shimmy! Remove cowling, check dampener. Seals are leaking hydraulic fluid. Unit declared "inop."

Exasperated, I called Shop North, the folks who did the Annual Inspection before Shop South did. They said the part we had was not the correct one for the airplane because the hydraulic neck should be right-side up when installed, not upside-down, as ours was. Next (again, on my nickel and precious time) I called Shop South who said the part number was correct and that they would send us new seals to install. (Holy liability!) True to their word, the seals arrived via U. S. mail. That was the good news; the bad part was that they were the wrong parts. Meanwhile, throughout all this rigmarole, I'd been trying to explain to the vacationing Dick why his baby Delta Foxtrot hadn't been getting its exercise as promised. As for the wrong seals, Herschel said that the only thing to do was send the unit back to South Shop for reworking. He also said that he'd take care of the shipping, which was mighty nice of him since he was really busy with his own business and was receiving no pay for this mounting headache. I waited and waited and waited, and finally after making another long distance call to Shop South, I found that the damn thing never arrived. During a search of Herschel's shop, the accursed metal/oil/neopreame contraption was located in a corner partially-assembled with status unknown, and Herschel was out of town on a ten day vacation! I arranged to fly the partially assembled thing to Shop South to be checked out with the latest known facts regarding the physical universe in mind; i.e., filler neck must face up, shaft must face aft. The aircraft and pilot waited for the job to be accomplished and returned to home base. My attempt to reinstall the unit failed again since the shaft was assembled backwards again. I screamed and turned purple in frustration.

I waited for Herschel to return from his vacation, refreshed, I hoped. He dismantled the unit, reversed the shaft, reassembled it and serviced it with more of my hydraulic fluid. This time *it fit!* On went the cowling and we taxied out onto the ramp. This time we didn't even get to the runway. There was no tension on the rudder pedals. I wasn't certain what system the Skylane had, but I knew that it probably had rudder springs. If this was the case, could the violent shimmy have knocked them off? I really didn't have the time or the inclination to tear into this airplane to find out. Meanwhile, the enraged owner was on the phone to Shop South, who had performed the last annual, and to Shop North who had done the one before that. Shop North agreed to make the trek over to our airport to find out what the matter was in order to avoid further trouble. Upon inspection by Shop North, it turned out that there were no rudder springs, but there was a broken steering arm, and it had caused severe damage to the tunnel in which it resides. With this ominous revelation, and the possibility of litigation, Shop South requested that I please ferry the aircraft to them, where they would repair the damage free of charge. That's good; except that I now have to ferry the damn airplane to an airport an hour away and then figure out how to get back.

The recently-returned LeFrancis, who was to be the pilot, was out of a biennial flight review. There also was the matter of a Ferry Permit. At last we accomplished the BFR and the ferry flight to Shop South. The retrieval of LeFrancis was accomplished free of charge by orchestrating a pick-up via a student dual cross-country flight. South Shop claimed that they could locate no damage except for a few pencil marks on the aluminum! Somehow Delta Fox got ferried home again. I sorta forget how. This whole thing was getting to be a blur! When the inspector at Shop North was informed of Shop

South's findings he cried, "B.S., I'll show you!" The aircraft was ferried to Shop North (about a half hour flight) and as he promised, the cracks were pointed out in the lower section of the tunnel. This little slice of life draws to a close with Shop South repairing the damage free of charge. There's an old saying, "Don't volunteer to walk a friend's dog or fly his airplane!"

During August, Dick LeFrancis arranged for Tom and me to go on a VIP ride in a KC-135 out of Beale Air Force Base. The Strategic Air Command mission was three-fold: to refuel an SR-71 "Blackbird" over Montana, to train a cute new female navigator, and to impress a bunch of local important people. The military had hopes that the numerous sound barrier explosions caused by the SR-71 would be forgiven. Tom and I hogged more than our share of time in the cockpit, where we observed the crew working with their sophisticated inertial and omega navigation systems. While over Montana, Tom glanced out the window from about 30,000 feet and identified a lake he was familiar with. The captain shot a sharp glance at the navigator trainee and asked if Tom was right. She maneuvered her WAC chart, plotter and E6B computer around in the old fashioned way and announced, "Believe it or not, he's right!" The crew looked at Tom with new respect.

It was a fantastic, eerie sight as the Blackbird suddenly showed up, seemingly out of nowhere. You could see both pilots' faces in the rare, tandem-seat trainer. It eased up to the winged refueling nozzle. The crew member in the tanker flew the proboscis-like tube to the craft's refueling port located behind the rear cockpit. The event was over in just a few minutes. The pilot in the forward cockpit saluted us as we peered through the refueling windows and he smartly peeled off to his right, disappearing almost instantly.

It was midsummer when Merlin blasted into town in the Cessna 337 Skymaster that he was trying to sell to J.L. He flamboyantly rolled to a stop with both engines shut down. Next, he slid out of the cockpit, dragged his ice chest over to a picnic table and slammed it down. I was watching with interest from our upstairs office. He and J.L. sat there and palavered awhile. Merlin downed one beer after another. J.L. definitely drank his share of booze, but never in an airplane, or before flying. He didn't fly today; Merlin did. They loaded the cold box and jumped in. Both engines started simultaneously and the push-pull twin Cessna charged out to the runway without benefit of a warmup, runup, or even a look out the window! The moment the wheels broke ground they were retracted and the drunk pilot yanked the Skymaster into a steep right turn, rapping with maximum power and just missing the rooftops of downtown Quincy. I got on the Unicom and yelled at Merlin in my most official airport manager voice, "Don't ever come back you son-of-a bitch!" He probably didn't have his radio on anyway.

In the fall, I spotted a deal in Trade-a-Plane. It was a low-time 1975 Cessna TU206 for a terrific price in Tuscalusa. I called Buddy Tingle, light bulb magnate, who promised that he'd hold it for a couple of days while I traveled there. I was fortunate to have a friend (not Metzker this time) who would loan me the money on short notice at reasonable interest; no strings attached. Buddy Tingle turned out to be a real character. His real money was in light bulbs, but he liked to dabble in aviation. He needed money to buy a fleet of 172s for his new academy of aviation. The 206 was a beauty. Not only was it in good shape, but it had a RAM conversion that boosted its horsepower from 285 to 310. Apparently, Buddy needed the money in a hurry, or didn't know what he had, because this was a fabulous deal!

Ferrying the 206, soon to be known as "Rambo," I traversed the to south, tiptoeing around thunderstorms. I landed at Tupelo as the weather closed in. The air below me was like a transparent river because the humidity was so high. I didn't feel comfortable with visible rivers of air and, anyway, I was ready to tour Elvis' hometown. Surprisingly, the weather opened up again, and I took off in the direction of Memphis with Air Route Traffic Control holding my hand. I informed them that I definitely was *not* capable of filing IFR. I thought to myself, "Strange airplane, I don't know what works, unfamiliar country and weather, no Instrument Low Altitude Charts, only a wrinkled WAC chart, gotta stay VFR at all costs!" Center assured me that it would be possible to remain VFR to Memphis, but I was still wary of air that looked like a river.

A couple of things were bothering me. The first one I had a cure for, I closed the vent that was blowing my map around. The second one was more difficult, tiny ants kept biting me! Before I knew it I was between cloud layers and all the while ATC assured me that my destination weather was OK. Soon, though, the story changed, and the weather changed rapidly to a brooding, broken-to-overcast condition. When I arrived over the city, there was one little hole left and I dove through it. Underneath the clouds, my confidence increased and I proceeded to follow a highway north to Jonesboro, Arkansas. That night the thunder and rain were horrific, and a Cessna was lost in the storm.

The advice at the local airport was to avoid stopping at any out-of-the-way Ozark strips for the night or I might find out more about some backwoods preacher than really I wanted to. Remembering the movie *Deliverance,* I heeded that advice and flew nonstop to Tulsa. I was able to get in on a Special VFR clearance while the airlines were stacked up all over the place due to adverse weather.

After a fuel top-off, it was on to Oklahoma City with the help of the Automatic Direction Finder. Although there were towering thunderstorms, it was possible to wind my way between them, and it seemed like every little berg had its own standard broadcast station that the ADF would point to. It would also point to intense lightning activity and its needle remained extremely nervous throughout Oklahoma. Finally, I made it through to the Tradewinds Airport in Amarillo. I saw that it hadn't changed much since I had inadvertently made off with their tiedown clip, banging on the skin of my Luscombe, twenty-eight years ago. By gosh, they were still using those same clips!

At last! Rambo and I made our way home by routing through Flagstaff and Truckee. The first thing I had to do was fumigate the airplane to get rid of those pesky ants that had been driving me crazy enroute. They had swarmed on a lollypop we found under an inspection plate in the belly. Was the mechanic sucking lollipops? The next necessity was to prepare the big Cessna single to meet the requirements of FAR 135 for charters and qualify it for Forest Service use.

FAA inspector Woods and I got along fine, but he was here to do his job. The turbocharger on Rambo had recently been overhauled, but a couple of "yellow tags" (overhaul tags that officially approve the unit to be returned to service) were missing. I asked him, "What can I do?" All the while I knew the answer.

He replied, "No problem, just don't fly it commercially until you can produce the yellow tags." That meant I had to completely overhaul the almost-new turbo system, at considerable cost. But what the hell, that's the way the game is played!

I was climbing over the piled-up clouds on the way from the Sacramento Valley and the newly overhauled turbocharger system was operating superbly. I was thinking that it was going to be fun to climb right over the top and descend into the Quincy area, which often opened up in a "rain shadow" hole. Usually I was forced to sneak up the treacherous Feather River Canyon under the clouds and that was always risky in unstable conditions. Rain or snow squalls could trap you with nothing but granite on all sides. I smugly reached for my oxygen mask with the comforting thought that I had filled the built-in cylinder behind the baggage compartment just a few days ago. Then my heart sank as I noted that the oxygen pressure gauges' needle rested solidly on zero. There must be a leak in the valve; so once again it was necessary to sneak up the treacherous canyon while trying to avoid the familiar hazards. The next day I pulled out the entire, heavy, oxygen system, in favor of having a more useful load! The "useful load" includes fuel, passengers and cargo. (Nothing less useful than an empty O2 bottle!)

For years the #2 avgas pump had been showing up to a three-tenths of a gallon discrepancy between the meter reading and the gallonage readout on every gas sale, and this was being caused by a foot pump slippage. Since we had been paying for this error since 1978, I thought it was about time we got compensated for it. I showed officials that for a period of seven days it came to 41.2 gallons. The county fixed the slippage problem, but no rebate was granted to us.

During the summer of '89, Jeff Meinel was one of the most interesting students we had trained in a while. His opted to take his required long solo cross-country flight across several states to Prescott, Arizona, where he checked out Embry Riddle Aeronautical University. He planned to attend there in the fall, entering as a sixteen year old *Sophomore*. After graduation he planned to enter the military, achieve a meteoric rise to the rank of colonel and be among the first group to colonize Mars!

Sugarpine Aviators played a vital role in the filming of *A Cry In The Wild* starring Jared Rushton, Ned Beatty and

Pamela Sue Martin. About 4:00 a.m. on a cold 1989 October morning, Herschel and I were in makeup at the airport office. I was to play Ned Beatty, who was portraying the slob of a pilot that was flying a mixed up adolescent to visit his divorced father in Canada. Herschel was wearing a wig so as to look like the kid played by Jared Rushton. The story was based on the novel *Hatchet.* On the way to Canada the pilot gave the kid a few rudimentary lessons in controlling the Cessna. The flight lessons were necessary so that the pilot could leave the controls and grab his coffee. The kid wasn't particularly interested. Shortly thereafter the pilot had a fatal heart attack, leaving a very frightened youngster churning off into the unknown with no clue as to his whereabouts. He tried to call out on the radio and talked briefly to someone on the ground (played by Judy) but was soon out of range. Finally, the story went, the airplane ran out of fuel and he crashed it into a nameless lake in the Canadian wilderness. He survived the splash-in and then had to survive the wilderness for a month and a half with very few supplies and among them a hatchet.

Jake, the director, summoned me to the top of a hill where an old 206 fuselage, painted to look like our "Rambo," was suspended from a tall cherry picker. Parts of the movie taken in the cockpit simulated flight with the proper camera angles. Beatty and Rushton were busy making takes. I was there to get my hair done. First, the hairdresser shaved the top of my head and then put my hair up in uncomfortable curlers to simulate the back of Ned Beatty's head. I was to leave the curlers in for twenty-four hours until the next day's shooting in the airplane. The only trouble was that I had a Forest Service recon flight in the meantime, and riding along was Mary Colombe, the supervisor. She was amused when I offered my explanation. It seems like anything goes when you are making a movie!

The Sardine Lakes lay in the shadow of the Sierra Buttes, a huge, saw-tooth mountain whose southern face plunges thousands of feet into the North Fork of the Yuba River. The north face breaks up into spectacular, fractured, vertical granite cliffs that drop into the Lakes Basin. From the Sardine Lake Resort the view is surrealistic and breathtaking. To simulate the crash into Upper Sardine Lake, it was necessary to break over a higher ridge at Young America Lake with full flaps, and the airspeed near stall. With Herschel in the right seat and the camera person in back trying to keep his breakfast down, I banked steeply to the right and left in order to lose altitude rapidly. A helicopter attempted to follow us for filming purposes, but was unable to. Finally, to drop straight down to the small lake's surface, I rolled inverted and retracted the flaps. As we began the free fall, I slowly increased the power on the heat-sensitive turbocharged engine while rolling back to a wings level attitude. The result was a spectacular pull up right *at* the surface of the water, and a great show for the Sardine Lake Resort's guests. They said it was awesome to watch us shoot out over the lake's outlet and plunge down past them into the canyon below. Cameras filmed the event from different angles. It was necessary to repeat the stunt seven or eight times. I didn't care; we were getting paid by the hour!

On a different film run, Herschel had the assistant director with him in "Bucko." We set up a near midair collision, and that took some tricky timing. The giant Aussie in the back became nauseated and asked Herschel what to do (since there were no barf bags to be found). Always a quick thinker, Herschel shouted over the noise, "Use your boot!" With no alternative the poor guy filled up his new Wellington boot with puke! Tom was busy flying other filming runs around the county.

At the Beckwourth Airport Pamela Sue Martin kissed her

screen son Jared Rushton and then Jared and Ned climbed into Rambo to simulate the engine start up. Herschel and I were back at the tail and were ordered to shake it to simulate the engine starting. We started shaking and shortly after Ned yelled, "Clear!" I yelled, "Cut!"

Jake, the director, rushed over and stuck his face close to mine and said, "What the hell are you doing, you don't say cut, *I* say cut!" He calmed down when I explained that you should yell "clear" *before* starting the engine, not afterward.

Suddenly in October, Skip Kobel's airplane disappeared and so did my tiedown chains! Finally at a court hearing in December, Kobel demanded that the county pay his electric bills. Thanks to his attorney, Michael Jackson, he would have won if there had been even a sliver of a case. In the end the court ordered him out. A few months later I got a call from Rick, who has an avionics shop in Nevada, wondering if I knew a weird guy by the name of Skip. Rick had hired him. I laughed and said, "Look out, Halloween has come to your town!"

Pete, in 1979, was a young man-about-town and quite a promoter of himself. You could see that he was a character just by the wild look in his eyes. He blew into the area from New Jersey, where he had quit pre-med at a university and had gotten divorced all at the same time. Although he arrived penniless, homeless and not knowing a soul, he refused public assistance. He managed to work as a bartender, a cook and a gold miner, all jobs with which he was unfamiliar. He parlayed his cooking jobs into chef positions. He had curly black hair and wore it in various styles with mustaches and beards. He claimed that he was a close friend of Floyd Patterson, the heavyweight champion boxer. Pete held a black belt in the Kodenkan Jujitsu system, the same one that I had studied in Chico.

Pete soloed our Cessna 150 in March, and soon afterward was

taking dual instruction in the more expensive Skylane. We took an airborne look at gold lands in Nevada for a wealthy investor from the east, who rode along. The easterner was dripping in gold around his neck and on his wrist and fingers. We landed in Winnemucca where he filed on several thousand acres of land for mining. The cost was considerable. Within a few weeks Pete was out in the wilds of northern Nevada digging up tons of ground with a D-8 Cat. Later, back in Quincy, I, along with him, I took time out to accept an interesting invitation. We were naked except for playboy bunny ears, shorts and a bunny tail, and we served as cocktail waiters. The occasion was an "all girls" party at the Stone House Bar where the girls enjoyed a male stripper and purchased "toys." Boy, was that interesting!

Unfortunately, the gold fields didn't yield a dime, so eventually Pete changed occupations and went to work for Lakeshore Lodge at Bucks Lake. Pete had become a muscle building freak. He was often seen early in the morning running next to the lake while working out with a heavy iron rod. He looked pretty wild, bulging out in his bikini swim trunks, with his long Italian hair contained by a colorful bandanna. Judy and I skied into the resort. Pete was now in charge of security for the place. We poked our heads in to say "Hi." The interior of the place was dim because of the snow banks and boards; blocking the weak winter sun, except from the windows that viewed the lake. It smelled of stale tobacco and spilled whiskey. The chair and bed arrangement in front of the fireplace had the air of a rat's nest. Pete looked like a real mountain man with his open-necked red shirt and muscles bulging out everywhere. His long curly hair hung to his shoulders and he wore a full beard. He had a .45 belted to his waist. They now called him "The Grizz." His eyes were also bulging from the steroids he had been using, and he told us how he was going to win titles for bodybuilding.

The Grizz scored a better job and went to work for a wealthy Bucks Lake homeowner and health enthusiast. His impressive body and quick mind had caught the businessman's attention. The Jujitsu training was an asset, too, because a house guard was needed. It seemed to be the perfect job until one day someone accidentally backed over him with a pickup truck. It would have killed an ordinary man, but due to Pete's extraordinary muscle development and the knowledge of "Kiai," the martial arts' use of one's inner strength, he survived. Insurance paid off big time and Pete had struck his gold mine, except his body shrunk to normal size during the very long recovery time without the benefit of heavy exercise and steroids. After getting run over by the pickup, Pete (formerly The Grizz) got married. He spent most of his insurance money and returned to the East with his family, now a very ordinary looking person.

On a snowy day in February of 1990, the snowplow broke down again; this time the problem was serious, with the rear end blown and the axle lying on the ground. Once again the county refused to fix the plow or otherwise come to our aid to clear the runway. Finally they got an emergency call from the National Guard who were searching for lost skiers. They wanted to use the ramp to land their helicopter. The road department came out with a grader and plowed an area on the ramp just big enough for helicopter operations, but the rest of the ramp, hangars, taxiway and the runway stayed buried. I called the director of emergency services to see if there was any plan in place for directing county resources toward the opening the runway in the event of a heavy storm or an emergency. In a word, he said, "No."

Smitty passed his Private Flight Test with flying colors in June. I considered him one of my good students and casual friends; however, little things began to go wrong. Although he swore that he'd quit drinking, we wondered. He would come back from flying chewing a lot of gum and avoiding conversation. Sometimes he would just fly around going nowhere, accompanied only by his dog, and wouldn't return until everyone had gone home for the day. One day Smitty reserved a Cherokee for an overnight flight to Truckee, and mentioned that he might practice at South Shore Tahoe. I told him not to fool around at the high altitude South Shore airport in the middle of a hot, windy day until he had more experience. A couple of hours after Smitty took off, the FAA Tower supervisor at South Shore called me and wondered if I knew anything about a Cherokee from Quincy. When he revealed the "N" number I knew Smitty had disobeyed my direct orders. I told the Supervisor all I knew about the situation. He related how Smitty first called in, much farther away than would be considered normal procedure. As he approached from over the lake for landing he kept talking, apparently trying to seem professional and flippant. He mostly succeeded in sounding ridiculous. He finally landed and pulled up in front of the FBO and ran for the bathroom. While he was taxiing in at high speed toward the tiedown area, the tower operator had been watching with his binoculars. He saw the dog in the right seat and something that looked suspiciously like a Budweiser can in Smitty's right hand. After using the bathroom facilities at the FBO, Smitty called the tower on the telephone and wondered what runway was in use. The FAA person thought this was strange since that was usually done via aircraft radio. He asked him from where he had departed and what his destination was. Smitty indicated Quincy for both questions. When the tower manager told me that he had asked the police to meet Smitty at Quincy to check for inebriation when he landed I said, "No, no, he's going to Truckee." By the time the cops got to the Truckee Airport, the Cherokee was tied down and Smitty was nowhere to be found. When Smitty returned the next day, I confronted him about landing at the South Shore Airport. He was a smooth talker and tried to tell me that he thought that I had only warned him to be careful if he decided to fly there. I inspected the airplane and found a large dent on the stabilator that wasn't there before. It looked just like a full beer can had been jettisoned out the storm window and had struck the leading edge. Of course, he denied everything, but that was the end of our relationship, business or otherwise.

While perusing Trade-a-Plane, I spotted a 1965 Cessna U206 in Rockford, Illinois, with a very attractive price tag. It was cheaper than comparable 182s that I had looked at and a *lot* more airplane. Even though we already had a TU206, I couldn't pass it up. I reasoned that since it was not turbocharged, it would be rentable, like a 182. (Turbocharged engines are much too easy for the average renter to over boost and shock cool.) I made the call and was soon on my way to meet the folks at Courtesy Aircraft. Commercial flying to Chicago was lengthy. The wait at the bus station at Chicago O'Hare Airport was an assault to one's senses, with horns blaring and sirens screaming non-stop! The endless bus ride west to Rockford was exhausting and I arrived late at night.

The next day, after the usual minor haggling, the purchase was made with a cashier's check. Courtesy Aircraft kindly threw in a set of new headphones. My route home took me north, around heavy weather, to Sioux City and on to an overnight stop in Valentine, Nebraska. The people there were nice enough to let me drive the state-owned airport loaner car into town. Not that I wasn't grateful, but I looked dubiously at the tires. Driving the thing gave me an insecure feeling, so I went straight to the hotel room for fear something would come apart on the car. The next morning I drove a couple of blocks to a diner and had a scrumptious Nebraska breakfast. When I returned to my loaner I was

disappointed to see that one tire was flatter than the pancake I
had just eaten. I dragged out the spare tire and tools and went
about the job of changing the ancient tire, getting filthy in the
process. The next disappointing event happened while driving
up the little hill to the airport. Another tire blew, and I had to
hoof it the rest of the way. I informed the FBO of the situation
and he didn't seem at all surprised. I returned to the car with him
while he installed another bald tire.

Anxious to get in the air, westbound, I reached into my
pocket for the 206's key and found it empty! "Eeech," I felt a cold
shiver, "may I use your phone and call the motel?" No luck, no
key there. "Can we find a locksmith on Sunday?" I asked the
FBO. He found one, and he came right out.

I was expecting a horrendous bill, and you could have
knocked me over with a feather when he said, "No charge, fella,
we Nebraskans aren't out to screw anybody!" I couldn't believe
it; there were still a lot of nice people in this world! I forced
twenty bucks on him in spite of his objections and gratefully
took to the air. I was bound for Rock Springs, Elko, and then
finally home. The new bird needed immediate work to get it
ready for the FAA inspector's 135 check.

To my delight, my old high school mate, Mickey, began
taking flying lessons. (He's the one who slipped me the $20 so
that Judy and I could stay for the New Year's celebration.) One
day I stopped in at the Patio Bar for a beer. Occupying the bar
stool next to me was a mill worker from the plant where Mickey
worked. The employee was complaining to his boss how Mickey,
a black person, had filed complaints about racial prejudice. I
listened to him run Mickey down for a while and finally, hearing
more than enough, I turned to him and grabbed him by the
neck. I said with fire blazing in my eyes, "Mickey is a good friend
of mine and I don't want to hear another word or I'll knock you

off that stool!" The boss laughed out loud, and although red-faced, the worker shut up.

I decided to try using auto gas in Bucko. It was a lot of work to pump the fuel into a barrel, drive it out to the airport, and then pump it in the airplane by hand. Nevertheless, we saved a lot of money. There is a placard on the fuel selector that says, "SWITCH TO SINGLE TANK OPERATION IMMEDIATELY AFTER LEVELING OUT AT ALTITUDES ABOVE 5,000 FEET." It means business especially when you are burning auto fuel! I was giving Mickey cross-country dual. We were climbing out of the hot Sacramento Valley on course from Red Bluff to Quincy. The very moment we leveled out and reduced power, the engine quit cold. My heart quit cold, too, as I grabbed the controls and reversed course toward the valley. I switched from "Both" to the left tank, enriched the mixture and pumped the throttle. The engine would give out a staccato "berrrip" and quit again. I switched to the right tank and finally the engine started again and ran as though nothing happened. The whole episode lasted about forty seconds. A few days later, Mickey had the same thing happen to him while flying solo, but he knew what to do and saved the day! I soon discontinued the use of "mogas."

Bucko had a long run for us; we flew him some 7,000 hours before a ground incident thrust him into the hands of the insurance company. Our renter pilot, Ronnie, as he prepared to start up, conscientiously decided that his preflight hadn't been complete. He reasoned that the aircraft had been sitting all day and it was cold. He carefully chained each wing, but not the tail. He pulled the propeller through by hand with the mixture rich, in order to get the engine well primed. It worked like a charm except that Ronnie wasn't in the cockpit when the engine suddenly bellowed into life; he was diving to one side to keep from being hacked to pieces by the propeller. He had left the magnetos in the "ON" position, and the throttle was advanced enough for the engine to run pretty hard. It ran hard enough to shake loose a tiedown on one wing. Like a crazed mustang, 'round and 'round Bucko went, bucking wildly, with Ronnie in trail trying to get the damn door open. Alas, he was on the side that was locked! Finally, he ran for his life as Bucko shook loose the other chain and lunged straight into a Beechcraft Baron. The twin was a pretty cruddy looking derelict that hadn't flown in a long while; but to its owner, it suddenly became the most expensive aircraft of its species in the world! For many years I had chanced it and turned the money I had saved by not paying hull insurance back into paying for the airplanes. In this case, Bucko was only underinsured, as opposed to uninsured, but the insurance company held off paying anything for a while. The fine print on the coverage stated that *there must be* a qualified pilot or mechanic at the controls when the engine is started. Thankfully, they backed off from that statement and paid up, but they also exercised their option and took Bucko, which was worth more than it was covered for.

It was a nasty summer day with lots of whirlwinds and invisible air roaring up and down. The pilot of the 182 was taking off to the west as I watched him from our tower office where we had an excellent view. He flew into a vertical air current that suddenly increased his airspeed and pitched his nose up into a deadly stalling attitude. I shouted over the Unicom, "Get your nose down!" He leveled out and continued to struggle around the small valley while I told him exactly where to go to avoid the most severe turbulence and down-drafts. I shuddered later at the thought of us getting sued if *anything* went wrong while I was advising him. The pilot returned another day and thanked me profusely. He swore that I'd saved his life because, during the incident, he had been locked into an unreasoning blind panic.

My dream of a fly-in campground finally came true in the summer, sort of. For years I had waved pictures and financial figures in front of the Board of Supervisors trying to show them how successful the campground had been at Columbia Airport. I related to them how we had camped under our wings to attend several Luscombe fly-in's. I described how the hotels and motels of Columbia and Sonora were packed with visitors, and that the grocery stores and camping supply stores were sold out. Thousands of people attended, and a hundred Luscombes, along with many other airplanes, flew in from as far away as Texas. People drove to the event, too. I asked them to imagine the positive financial impact on our area when wave after wave of aircraft organizations chose Gansnser Airfield as a destination to camp and play. All we needed were some facilities and advertisement. Years had gone by with no response from the county and I had almost given up. Finally, as a project, the Rotary Club installed fifteen tiedowns along the taxiway near the pond. They also added two barbecue stands and four picnic tables. By this time the willows, cottonwoods, and pine trees had grown considerably, and the wildflower seeds that volunteers had spread around were blooming and spreading. Unfortunately, there was no water or sanitary facilities, and the camp saw little action.

Amelia, our beloved jet-black mongrel who accompanied us to the airport for seven years, was dead! In her inimitable fashion she had attacked an invading German shepherd in our back yard and went down in defeat. We had lost an important member of the family and I sobbed as I dug her grave in the hard clay next to the pond. We buried her with the stick she had been chewing just before the fight and hoped there was a doggie heaven.

I made a great aircraft purchase. In Trade-a-Plane I spotted a "Superhawk" for sale, located not too far south of us. This Cessna 172M boasted of a "Mike Kelly Conversion" consisting of a 180 hp O-360-A4A Lycoming engine with a fixed pitch propeller. It was perfect for our operation, and the price was cheap, in spite of the fact that it had a complete major overhaul. I called, and we made a deal. The seller said that he would even knock off $500 for my travel expenses if I flew right down and bought it. He couldn't bear to see his pride and joy around any longer. His tale of woe was that he had just retired and his spouse was making him sell the airplane so that he could take her on a world cruise. What a heartbreaker! I wondered how long the marriage might last after that?

I sent the following message to *Flying Magazine:*

> May 30, 1991
> J. Mac McClellan, Editor,
> *Flying Magazine*
> 1633 Broadway
> New York, New York 10019
>
> Dear Editor:
>
> A majority of small FBOs teeter on the brink of extinction, but still plug along because of their love for aviation. Not to be different, I was elbow deep wrenching on one of my greasy aircraft engines over at Nervino's shop, dreaming of the time when I could afford to hire a mechanic.
>
> I've always wanted to be a writer. This was still true when the phone rang on May 22nd. The deep voice,

accented with a slight southern drawl, said, "This is Len Morgan from *Flying Magazine.*" "Big deal," I thought, "another damn subscription salesperson."

Politely, I replied as the phone slid around in my oily hand, "Yes, I'm Johnny Moore. What can I do for you?" (At least the guy didn't ask for the owner.)

Len said in a powerful tone, "Somehow we got ahold of your book on crop dusting and all of us thought it was great! If half of this stuff is true—" Ego stroking references were made about how gutsy I must have been to have lived through all of that.

"We've done a background check on you and know about the articles you've published, as well as getting your ATP jerked for awhile." In a confidential tone Len continued, "We couldn't care less about that 'cause we have our own hassles with the FAA." I thought he must be referring to the LAX TCA alleged infringement resulting in a sixty day suspension of my certificate.

The voice went on and I held my breath. "Based upon what you have already written, *Flying Magazine* is willing to pay you a very large sum of money for each article accepted. Furthermore, we will supply you with a word processor and a fax machine. We'd like to have you write in the areas of crop dusting and aerial fire fighting."

Images already danced around in my mind. I pictured an all-expense-paid trip to where my old Sky Park student, Ed Herzog, was spraying mosquitoes around Kodiak in his Thrush Commander. Great interview! How bout me sitting thirty feet off the tarmac in the cockpit of a C-130 Herk or a P-3 Orion fire bomber? I could describe the sun glinting from the

354 | JOHNNY MOORE

hundreds of gauges, the pungent smells of oil, fuels and the feel of hot aluminum. I could remember, on paper, some of the days when I thundered down deep canyons in some of aviation's great air classics!

Actually, the Alaska thing would be out for now. I suddenly remembered what Al Ewald had told me about Ed. He had been operating a fish camp. One fateful afternoon he was taking delivery of a Thrush Commander to be used in the operation to haul fish. His partner had made landfall ahead of him in the 185 and was in contact with him on the radio. The base of the clouds was now lowering to meet the icy waters and the sun was going down. Ed tried to follow but it was too late. They never found him or the Thrush Commander, and it was assumed that he was still strapped in the cockpit about 280 feet down on the ocean floor. Ed would be unavailable for any interviews with his earthly friends. I shook the image and continued the conversation. Instead, I imagined telling at least a thousand of my closest friends that *Flying Mag* was about to become a major contributor to my income. I began making plans as to how to compensate for the coming required absences from my company duties.

The voice shouted out to someone else in the room, "Hey, when can we get over there? Next Thursday?"

Len turned his voice back to me, "Johnny, next Thursday I'll fly-in with five or so people—you know, an attorney, a photographer, and so on. We'll be there 'bout lunch time. Please have your attorney present when we review the contract."

While I was talking I was thinking, "Hummm, not too far fetched." I'd published an article in *Flying Magazine* back in May of 1977, entitled "Goosed," and another called, "Crop Dusting By Starlight," that appeared in the AOPA Pilot in January 1976. Both pieces related to crop dusting experiences. The book Len was referring to was a thing I'd written in early 1975 of some 143 pages. Its title was, "Breaking Into Agricultural Aviation."

Much of the greatly anticipated day of Thursday had come and gone, but Len and his entourage failed to arrive. The reserved lunch table was used by a much smaller group than had been expected. My attorney was in her office awaiting my summons to review the contract that would change my life. Judy and I had even dressed up for the occasion. Nearing late afternoon, I began a telephone search. Earlier I wondered what kind of fabulously expensive twin Len would arrive in with his five or so passengers. Now I wondered what might have gone wrong? Overwhelmed by my conversation with Len, I had forgotten to get a call back number. After traveling by telephone from New York to Connecticut and God knows where else, I finally ended up at Len's home phone number in Georgia. I let it ring but there was no answer. "Good," I reasoned, "they must be enroute to our airport in Northern California." So, we waited.

Time to try the phone again. Maybe someone will be there and can shed some light as to why Len and company are so late. Hopefully, they didn't ice up in the Rockies or something! I could see wings on all those big bucks I was about to earn. The ringing stopped. "Yes, this is Mrs. Morgan. Oh! Heavens no, there must be some mistake!" She called out, "Len, pick up the other phone!" My gut tightened up and my ears began to burn. I knew something was very wrong. My understanding of reality began to crumble. "No," the familiar voice said, "I've never heard of you!" I tried to relate to him our very important telephone conversation. The more I talked, the more it sounded like I was attempting to pull some sort of scam. After a lengthy conversation, I sensed that Len Morgan and his spouse were very nice people, and were horrified at the notion that someone had used Len's name to perpetrate this cruel hoax.

Having said all of this, Mr. McClellan, I'm enclosing a copy of my book, and a couple of stories from my logbooks. Who knows, maybe dreams really can come true!

Sincerely,
Johnny Moore

September 18, 1991, in a return letter from J. Mac McClellan, Editor-in-Chief, he said that after receiving my package they sent it to Len Morgan. He continues, "After receiving your letter dated September, we contacted Len who said he had spoken with you at some length. Unfortunately, we have no place for your article. at present, but we appreciate your thinking of *FLYING*—Good luck with the placement of your story!"

Former Airports Coordinator and Plumas County Fair Manager, C.W. Adams, was jailed in Los Angeles for grand theft, probation violation and failure to appear in court. This was the result of his earlier employment with a fair in Missouri, and later charges of embezzlement and falsifying accounts of public funds while serving as manager of a fair in Southern California. This was pretty tough stuff, but even so, C.W. had guts. After he got out of stir, I saw him running a booth at the Plumas County Fair; apparently not a bit troubled by his speckled past, or his considerable descent in social status. He shook hands with me as though I was a long lost friend and tried to sell me a hot dog!

I guess I just love to buy and fix up airplanes. By May our fleet consisted of five fine airplanes, but I wasn't satisfied and wanted a low-budget airplane. I also wanted to preclude any probability of low-budget competition. It looked like the right one in Nampa, Idaho. It was a dead ringer for our old 47S that we had sold to the insurance company. I thought that, even though we had been without a two-place Cessna for seven years, people would like the sport and economy of a low-horsepowered and low-cost airplane. Not so, because even after adding a STOL kit, few did. They had grown to like a lot of horsepower. One renter was horrified when I told him he couldn't take a passenger up in the middle of the day on a windy, hot afternoon. I explained to him truthfully, that the performance was just too marginal in those conditions. He retorted angrily that he didn't believe we should have a dangerous airplane like that around! I thought about how I used to instruct in a 150 out of the high altitude Tahoe Valley Airport and thought, "I've got 'em all spoiled." I spoiled everyone with nice avionics too. I made sure all the airplanes that needed refurbishing got new upholstery and paint as well.

One of the instructors commented, "What if our customers go some where else to rent an airplane, won't they be disappointed?"

I replied, "I hope so!"

At the age of eighteen, former star student, Jeff Meinel, graduated from Embry Riddle University with a B. S. and all the flight ratings up through Certified Flight Instructor-Instrument. This was accomplished in the two years after he left us. He wrote to us, "—as an instructor you teach your students the things you were taught and I find myself doing just that, quite a bit—.

From John I remember many low crop-duster turns, and instilling the proper relationship between pitch, power and performance, spins, as well as fingertip flying. From Tom I remember being drilled on engine out, high volume traffic areas, and cross-country planning as well as the pilot flying the plane, rather than vice versa. (Do whatever you have to!!) I appreciated it, guys."

During the summer, we hired Jeff to instruct for us and fly fire patrol. Winter came and he went south. Later an article was written by him and published in *The Feather River Bulletin:*

PILOT OWES LIFE TO FLIGHT INSTRUCTORS

Possibly the greatest tribute a flight instructor can receive is to be lauded by one of his former students acknowledging him as the one who saved the student's life, and other lives as well.

Area flight instructors Johnny Moore, Tom Rahn, Dan English all have that distinction from Jeff H. Meinel of Pasadena, California.

In a letter to The Feather River Bulletin, Meinel wrote, "I'm writing you to compliment local veteran flight instructors (previously mentioned). For I learned to fly from these awesome aviators. I thank them for the emergency procedures they instilled. Their careful instruction probably saved the lives of all on board. It is much appreciated."

On Dec. 22, 1992, while returning from a day trip in Bishop with his father, grandfather and father's friend, Meinel, piloting a Cessna 172 RG encountered difficulties.

Meinel wrote, "On approach to Burbank (over the Santa Clarita Valley-Magic Mountain area) at 8,500 feet, I lost the connecting rod on the No. 4 cylinder of the Lycoming 0-360 engine on the Cessna. An oil mist immediately covered the windshield as seven quarts of oil and I left acquaintances. (The block was found to be pierced in three locations.) The engine seized up and came to a violent stop. After an air start proved fruitless, I declared an emergency and glided at near-gross weight through the Newhall pass. By now, at 3,500 feet, I knew Van Nuys and Whitman (airports) were not options. I selected a (small) soccer field one mile north of San Fernando reservoir. The field looked good from the air, but as we got lower, two sets of powerlines over the approach end, several soccer goalies, only 200 feet of grass, and girls practicing at one corner of the field came into view. After gear down and clearing the powerlines by inches, braking as we touched down hard, and under heavy braking the nose gear collapsed. Our ground roll over a sixty-foot obstacle was under sixty feet. There was no post-crash fire. We got out of the plane quickly without even a scratch."

The County Supervisors were having another crisis. Engineering consultants to the county continued to insist that the county would clean up financially if they owned *all* the hangars. I told county officials that their ideas were too socialistic. The county purchased a set of hangars at Nervino Airport at Beckwourth that were the shabbiest structures at the airport. They were not well occupied at the price the officials expected to rent them. Finally, one outfit gladly paid the going rate until airport manager, Frank Nervino, happened to peek through a crack and saw them filming porn movies!

One day I picked up the telephone and heard a ghost from my Alaska adventures of some twenty-five years ago. The familiar voice said, "Is this the same Johnny Moore that flew for Interior Airways?"

"My God," I exclaimed, "I thought you were dead, Joe!"

He said, "Naaa, that was one of my pilots that got into weather trouble and ran out of luck." He said he was in Reno for a short stop and thought he'd call and say "Hi!" Joe Felder was one of a kind and I hope he stays lucky!

In January of '92, John McMorrow was appointed as Interim Airport Coordinator. I suggested to the board that, due to his position as county Planner, he was the perfect person for the job.

It was a gloomy damn winter. In February I was desperate for something productive to do. I decided that it was high time that I added an Inspection Authorization onto my A & P Mechanic Certificate. With dread in my heart, I jumped into our little Dodge Colt, and headed for another school near the Long Beach Airport. This time I had a little more money than the previous visit to the inner city and could afford to stay at a sleazy motel. My temporary home was on the Pacific Coast Highway within the Signal Hill city limits. The outline of the former name, "Travel Lodge," still remained where the sign had been ripped down.

Each day there was at least eight hours of concentrated study, mostly on airworthiness-related regulations and guidelines. The IA exam was the only FAA test that didn't have the questions published. It was a deep, dark secret, and the feds had just produced a brand new test. Lots of work lay before me in order to be able to pass it. An absolute minimum of time was spent on the necessities of life such as eating. I kept a cold box at the motel from which I fished out a banana, some juice and vitamin pills each morning for breakfast. I would arrive at the school as early as possible to get started. I didn't intend to stay in this hole any longer than absolutely necessary. I did, however, enjoy a few early morning minutes of conversation with the owner, a pleasant blond woman, and her husband, before getting started with the battery of exams. The husband was a large-sized, jolly, black gentleman, who called himself "The Enforcer." He showed me the .357 Magnum pistol he packed around in a holster hidden in his Wellington boot. After school I drove to the intersection where only one car during each green light could make a left turn. That was the one that jammed itself into the middle of the highway on the previous green light. Finally, after navigating that one left turn onto the Pacific Coast Highway, I was "home." Once safely locked in my motel room, I dug out some fruit and nuts and a bottle of gin to mix with Tab, and settled down for a little more study.

One evening on the way back to the motel I decided to go another direction to pick up supplies for the cold box. It got dark and started to rain. I stopped at a service station to ask directions and a Hispanic guy headed me off in the wrong direction. (My fault for not speaking Spanish—got to remedy that someday.) Soon I was cruising up and down the inner city barrios totally lost in the night and rain. I was thankful that the little Colt had plenty of gas and that the door locks worked. Eventually, I crossed the Pacific Coast Highway again and made my way back to the motel, exhausted.

Finally it was over and I met Judy at John Wayne-Orange county Airport. She wanted to keep me company during the long twelve-hour drive back home. It began to rain cats and dogs up the Grapevine. The little Colt was in danger of being washed off the highway by the big trucks throwing out streams of water in their wake. Across the San Joaquin Valley in the darkness, huge tumbleweeds were spinning across Interstate 5 in the westerly gale. Trucks were just creeping along and the tiny Dodge was on two wheels most of the time because of the powerful wind gusts. The lights were out all over the area. We finally located a motel and gratefully crawled into bed by the light of a candle.

Within the week I presented myself at the Reno FSDO for the Inspection Authorization examination. Inspector Woods was pleased when I passed the test with flying colors. I evaded the little trap he had set for me. There was a brand new Airworthiness Directive that applied to the aircraft I had been assigned to research. It showed up only in the microfiche Biweekly AD Supplement. As I drove home to Meadow Valley with the IA ticket in my pocket, I felt that I had come a long way. I recalled that embarrassing time at Charlie Jensen's strip when I had cut the capillary tube on my Luscombe's oil temperature bulb just so I could get the nut off easier!

In March, the steel on the front of the snowplow got bent when the blade caught on concrete hidden under the snow. I asked that it be repaired (estimated cost was $300) but it left the airport never to return. From then on, by decision of airports coordinator, McMorrow, the snow was removed by a contractor operating a backhoe and a grader. The cost was astronomical.

I feel good when I hear good things about my friends. Remember Larry McNutt, "The Arctic Fox," the high school classmate who joined me in Alaska in 1965? In the past several years, Larry had become interested in gymnasiums and their equipment, and in muscle development. At the age of fifty-three he attained the bodybuilding title of "Mr. Nevada!" Other old friends were doing well, too. I saw that Steve Miller's Hillside Aviation had gotten bigger and bigger with several cargo contracts requiring multiengine aircraft. His single- and multi-engine charter, flight instruction, and shop endeavors were all busy, not to mention the café upstairs. Steve's laid-back hippie brother, Paul, was now head of several departments at Peterson Tractor. The other brother, Dave, won *first place* at Oshkosh with a Swearingen SX300 that he built himself.

Disaster struck in January '93, when a renter decided to make the short flight to Chester in the Superhawk and failed to check the local Notices To Airmen (NOTAMS). Rogers Field at Chester was buried in fifteen feet of snow. The snow blower had made a path not much wider than a wingspan when the pilot made his approach. Have you ever landed in a narrow white canyon? That's what it was like when I flew over to view the wreckage the next day. A tire had struck something that caused the high wing to swerve to the left. The left wing was crumpled, and then in rapid succession, the nose and the tail hit the white wall as the aircraft spun around. The new airport manager and FBO, Dan English, found himself with a nice bit of winter mechanical work!

Virginia Rutter seemed like a nice old gal. She had flown up from the valley in the family 150 and had done a pretty good job on her Private Flight Test. Far better than the macho cop from the same area a couple of days before, who had left in a rage because I failed him. Problems developed when Virginia's husband, Melvin, arrived for his flight test a couple of months later in their family 172. (They had two family airplanes because while they were students they couldn't fly together except in formation.) She had indicated that since she had passed her test it was necessary that Melvin pass his too. The underlying impression was that Melvin was the kind of jerk that couldn't stand it if a woman was to out-achieve him.

Melvin came in the office with his application while Virginia remained in the 150. He had brought the 172. When I invited her into the office, she declined and said that she was going to pray for Melvin. Melvin smelled like stale cigarettes and urine. First he told me what a rotten, unfair son-of-a-bitch the previous examiner, who had flunked him, was. Then he gave me a crooked smile as he handed over the examiner's fee, and slyly suggested that at that price he expected a *guaranteed pass*. I treated it all as a joke and hoped that his flying was better than his personality. In spite of Virginia's fervent prayers, his flying was pretty lousy. When I informed Melvin that he would have to return for several items listed in the Practical Test Standards, and that we should try to complete the oral portion, he became surly. He said, "Forget it, this is the end of my flying."

Virginia was present and her personality changed dramatically. She said, "If he can't fly, I won't!" Nothing I could say would calm them down.

A few days later I got a call from the Reno FAA FSDO Chief who said, "What the hell are you doing over there, Johnny? To hear these people talk you are abrupt, impolite and are terrorizing everyone!" I responded with the truth and he laughed and said, "I thought it was something like that, sour grapes! Carry on!"

I heard news from my old duster partner, Jim Lister. He had gone to work in Bakersfield and was flying turbine powered Thrush Commanders. He had located an old 1957 classic Cessna 310 in bad shape and fixed it up. The home end of his daily commute was often fogged in at San Luis Obispo, and waiting at the other end was a short, wired-in strip. Jim's multi-engine, instrument and short field techniques had been kept sharpened. He said that, while crop dusting he strapped a camcorder up in the windshield and videotaped some routine day and night spray jobs that took him under power lines and around steel towers. The results had been shown on the television program, "American Adventure."

It was fun pretending to be a celebrity for a few minutes. Here's what happened. George, the mill superintendent, and Dan, who supplied steel for various building projects, partied together a lot! I flew them and their women to Reno for a bash. Dan was trying to impress the girl's mother, who he hoped would be his future mother-in-law. Since I knew I would be sitting around a lot while standing by, I called John Metzker, now president of the corporation that owned Fitzgeralds, Harold's Club and the Nevada Club Casinos. John said, "As a matter of fact we are having a family dinner at the restaurant on the fifth floor of Harold's Club. Why don't you come and join us?" I said that I would.

It was afternoon and everyone was already feeling pretty good when I loaded the champagne and the five passengers into

Rambo. Dan and George kept asking me how much the flight
would cost and I replied that I wouldn't know until we got back.
Every so often one of the guys would make a big production of
waving a hundred dollar bill around and stuffing it in my shirt
pocket asking, "Will this help?" I assured them that it would. A
long, white limousine picked us up at the Reno airport and we
cruised over to South Virginia Street. The limo's wet bar was
fully equipped, but of course I had to stick with Diet Coke. Dan
had the driver pull up to the side door of Harold's Club and told
him to "standby until further notice," and slipped him a C note.
They bragged that they were going to dine in the fanciest restaurant in town right after winning a fortune in the casino.

George asked me condescendingly, "Where are you going
to eat?"

I pointed to Harold's Club and replied seriously, "With the
owner." They all roared with laughter at the joke and headed into
the gaudily lit casino. There were ringing bells and Buzzers indicating payoffs and jackpots at the slot machines. Lights flashed
everywhere and the whole place Buzzed with excitement. I rode
the elevator to the fifth floor to the "fanciest restaurant in town."
Once inside, I spotted a very large table populated with members
of various generations of the Metzker family and was welcomed
into the group. Meanwhile my charter bunch became tired of
gambling and made their way to the fifth floor, were ushered in,
and were seated. Dan and George noticed me sitting over with
the Metzker's and wanted to be introduced to my "friend." So I
introduced John to them and Dan insisted that he wanted to buy
him dinner.

John replied, "You can't buy me dinner in my own place. I'll
buy *you* dinner!" After the meal my charter group partied on
while I eventually retired to the limousine. The driver was
standing on the sidewalk; he suggested that I relax and watch

some television. I popped open a Coke and flipped on the TV. You could just barely see inside the tinted windows from outside with the illumination of the TV screen. People would stream out the door of the casino and stare through the window curiously, wondering which celebrity I was!

I was getting bored and decided to spice things up. What we needed was a tail dragger to train all those pilots out there who lusted to perfect the macho pilot skills demanded by old fashioned flying critters equipped with "conventional gear." I set out to find a nice Cessna 120 or 140, but instead found a 170B, owned by an old Enterprise Sky Park friend. He was willing to part with the aircraft that he had hangared, loved and cherished for years, but had hardly flown.

I advertised on the West Coast and nationally offering advanced tail wheel instruction, and basic Ag Pilot flying techniques. Unfortunately, I couldn't find any power lines that anyone would let me fly under for the Ag stuff. There were a lot of calls but not many takers.

The 170B is more of a handful than one might think. Look at that little round vertical stabilizer way out on the end of that long fuselage. It spells *no control* in certain situations. The huge fowler flaps can complicate things too. In the tail up, tail down exercises, the would-be tail dragger experts explore the situations that cause "no control" events. During one learning technique, I let them work the rudders and yoke while I put them in the worst possible predicaments with the throttle. With various flap settings, they would then work the throttle while I worked the controls, and vice versa. Each combination offered different insights. It was best for us to travel to long runways and thick air for these maneuvers.

In April the contract was let for an above-ground storage tank, fuel island, and self serve credit card fuel dispenser. The dispenser was the cheapest the county could buy. Even so, the thing cost $83,446 and it only held 6,000 gallons. Later the runway and ramp paving began and lasted most of the summer. I had to beg, plead with, and bribe the construction bosses to let us slip in and out on flights. Part of the time we had to move our fleet to Beckwourth and Chester.

I received a promotional package from Citibank that claimed that I could earn one mile of free air travel on American Airlines for every dollar spent on their Advantage Master Card. This sounded very interesting since I was paying all my bills with checks, including county avgas bills that were as high as $8,000 per month. By paying by check I was saving the county about three percent on my purchases. I explained to the Airports Coordinator's secretary how patriotic I was being by saving the county the credit card charges. She seemed confused and asked, "Why are you telling me all this, will it make my job any easier?"

A little miffed, I explained the same thing to McMorrow, expecting a reply something like, "We certainly appreciate that," or anything akin to appreciation. Instead he merely looked perplexed and shrugged his shoulders. The warm fuzzy patriotic feeling was gone. That very day I sent for my Citibank Aadvantage Master Card.

The group of good ole boy drinking buddy pilots had decided that we were doing entirely too well. After all, we had all those airplanes and a couple of new cars. A pattern of antagonism was becoming obvious, and escalating. One of the group told me that he and his friends didn't think my contract as airport manager with the county was at all legal. He believed that I could be dismissed at will. These were people whom I had been giving advice to, loaning tools to, helping and serving faithfully for fifteen years. They had been keeping in close touch with the Airports Coordinator with their viewpoints. I was alarmed at the increasing boldness and, what I thought were, inappropriate official suggestions concerning work that I should have to do. I decided to think on it long and hard.

The runway was being resurfaced and the new fuel facility and automatic dispenser was being constructed. In a letter to McMorrow I suggested that as an incentive to buy at home, all fuel users should be allowed a discount according to the volume that they purchased throughout the year. I thought that one cent a gallon for every thousand gallons purchased would be appropriate. There was no answer from him.

Terry Reeson had his 1958 Cessna 172 for sale. A beauty it was, with its orange and white paint scheme. It was just one year newer than "Bucko," I couldn't stand seeing it sit there with a for sale sign on it any longer. I bought both the airplane and hangar. The location of the hangar was perfect, right across from our hangar/office. There was a sentimental value too. The hangar had been the site our first office back in 1977, unheated and unlighted as it was. The problem was that I was left with too many airplanes. The 170B had flown 500 hours in a year, but it was performing a lot of work a 172 could do. It also carried with it a strong potential to be wrecked by some renter pilot who had gone too long between recurrent flights. I stripped the 150 and the 172 of all their expensive radio gear and sold them cheap. The 150 buyer was a gambler. He said, "Tell you what, let's flip a coin and if it's heads, I'll pay $10,500, if it's tails I'll pay $9,500. I let him flip and, of course, I lost the toss. The happy gambler flew the 150 away without even noticing the hail damage on top of the wings. I heaved a sigh of relief, not feeling that I had really lost! The expensive equipment was then installed in the "new" 172 and our financial situation staggered back into balance.

It was a fine day in August of 1994, when Judy and I stepped onto the American Airlines MD80 for an adventure-filled vacation to Maine. The flying was free thanks to our Advantage Master Card. To hell with saving the county its three percent! After arriving in Boston, we drove north to Patten, where my Grandpa Rogers' pioneer family had settled the "Down East" country in and around Baxter State Park. Grandpa's brother, Lori, had retired from a distinguished career as a bacteriologist. (He has a wing of the University of Maine named after him.) He had built a working model of an early Down East sawmill that had been operated by Grandpa and his father, L.B., and other members of the family. Every year the community put on a celebration at the sawmill museum called "The Beanhole Feed," in which they buried beans in big pots surrounded by hot coals. Later the Rogers family had a special get together of their own on the north side of Shinn Pond, accessible only by boat or four-wheel drive. That night I witnessed a scene that I regret having missed all these years. Fifty or sixty related people gathered around the bonfire in the Rogers compound; the kids were burning boxes decorated like houses and telling ancient children's stories. The tradition was started by Grandpa's mother, Mary Elizabeth, who had written a moving account about the settling of Down East Maine. It was a truly memorable vacation all made possible by the County of Plumas paying an extra credit card processing fee!

After returning from our rare summertime getaway, I took a close, hard look at my relationship with my tight group of opponents on the airport. Again, I thought with disgust; these people are the same ones we had worked so hard to please for so many years. I had thought, until recently, that we were friends. As long as we were perceived as peons, or servants, everything was fine, but when it seemed that we were doing well financially, jealousy rose its ugly head. One of them even said to me, "Someone is going to cut you down to size!"

Bob, our beloved Manx cat, died of feline leukemia. I buried him near Amelia, the dog. Both of them had been dear family members and we cried.

Chapter 14

I Quit!

I was sick of being a county whipping boy who was becoming less and less certain of what his job duties were, exactly. For example, one day McMorrow asked me to climb the tall tower on top of Hospital Hill and fix the rotating beacon. I said that was best left to a trained electrician.

Diary: 10/1/94
Enough of this bullshit, I quit! (Last entry.)

I more-or-less traded my resignation as airport manager for a rewritten Fixed Based Operator contract to cover us for another ten years. We moved out of the county office over the restaurant and into the shop in the big hangar. I stepped more lightly now, my spirit soared!

On October 15th, in a newspaper interview, McMorrow referred to my departure; "In the past, he's only basically piled snow and pumped gas. We can pile the snow, and the gas is now distributed through a credit card pump."

On October 19th, *The Feather River Bulletin* offered this editorial:

THANKS JOHNNY

"With Johnny Moore's recent resignation as manager of Quincy's Gansner Airport, the county lost a dedicated county employee who served the aviation needs of the area for the past 16 years.

But local aviators need not worry since Johnny will continue as a fixed based operator at the local airport.

With growth of his aviation business, he now has a staff of pilots and a fleet of six aircraft for rentals, charters and flight instruction—outstanding for a small town and impressive if you consider he and his wife Judy started with a small two-seat Cessna 150 for flight training in 1977. Since starting (at Quincy) he has trained about 250 people to fly—nearly all finishing the program to go on and receive a pilots license.

Overall, he operated the rural airport for the county with great effectiveness. With antiquated equipment he did a good job keeping airport runway and apron areas open during winter. All told, the county's relationship with Moore has been a good marriage over the years. Both sides greatly benefited from it during nearly two decades. He built his business while helping the county maintain the badly needed airport.

Moore has deep flying roots here. His father John Wesley Moore was a local pilot, flight surgeon in the service and credited with founding Sky Harbor airport, which was located in East Quincy behind Holiday Market. His mother Francis Gail Rogers (Moore) was killed at Sky Harbor in a plane wreck nearly 50 years ago—one day before she was to take a test for her Commercial Pilot's license.

Moore's resignation was greeted with little more than a few yawns by county officials, some of whom made rude comments about his performance. But we believe Moore should have been afforded more respect. He's earned it."

Letters To The Editor popped up; one that referred to a newspaper article saying that I could not be reached for comment. It says, *"From that statement it is obvious that no effort was made to reach Johnny as he is normally at the airport eight to 10 hours a day, six to seven days a week."* Another said, *"Moore was more than an airport manager as he welcomed me each day, assisted in securing my airplane, provided fuel, oil and a clean windshield when needed. In addition, he was a wealth of information regarding community events. He was aviation's spokesperson for Plumas County. He was usually the first person you talked with, by radio, and the first person you met when you landed. He was always service oriented——. From the first call to Quincy when arriving by air to the call for "traffic," when departing Quincy, Moore took good care to see that the visitor and the local aviator were treated with courtesy. He was Plumas County's aviation ambassador in Quincy. He will be missed in that role."*

McMorrow still had a little trick up his sleeve. Acting on my year-old suggestion, he suddenly had our office/ hangar declared surplus property and put it up for sealed bid. The ordeal ended with me digging up 25k to secure our future operation, I hoped, without any farther outside interference or antagonism. It was necessary to sell the "Superhawk" for exactly $25,000.

Even with the loss of the county revenue and benefits, and minus the Superhawk, it was like a great weight had been lifted from my shoulders, and Judy's too. It was hard to imagine not having to run for the gas pump every time someone pulled up— and otherwise being responsible for the county facility. I hoped that my ex-"friends" would enjoying dragging that dirty gas hose around.

Chapter 15
Back to Business

In the spring of 1995, a "hundred-year" snowstorm blew through Plumas County causing damage at the airport. Snow removal and repair costs were high, and I was no longer in a position to help. It felt strange to be on the sidelines after all those years of battling snow on the airport with an ancient snowplow. Federal emergency funds were held up because Plumas County had no emergency plans that included airports (I had tried to alert county officials about that). To highlight my memory of this storm, Jim Lister told me that he was flying into South Lake Tahoe for a wedding ceremony when the storm hit. It was IFR all the way from San Luis Obispo but there was a small hole over the lake. Jim decided to make the approach in his trusty old Cessna 310. His landing into the high mountain airport went OK, but within half an hour four people died nearby at Pollock Pines when their light aircraft iced up and crashed. Sometimes timing is everything!

The FAA decided that all Pilot Examiners must undergo surveillance and I was no exception. In October the big day for the monitored flight check came, and I made the mistake of arranging a three-way intercom to allow the Inspector in the back seat to monitor the conversation. Now in the air, as the candidate increased the wing's angle of attack to produce a power on stall, there came a loud puffing sound from the back seat and the whole airplane shook. The shaking was not from any stall buffet, but from the Inspector's foot bouncing nervously on the floor. He rasped, "You don't *have* to do a *full* stall you know!" He seemed terrified and it was distracting the applicant. To make a long story short, the student remained a student awhile longer. The FAA inspector's boss at the Flight Standards District Office asked me how the surveillance went, and I complained about his handling of the matter. I said that I didn't consider him a peer and that he should be transferred to be in charge of an airline or something. Instead of transferring him, they put him in charge of our charter operations too!

In a book written and copyrighted in 1993, by Jim Magoffin entitled, *Triumph Over Turbulence,* he claims to be "the luckiest bush pilot in Alaska." If that's not true, he must be the smartest. He had the vision to invest in North Slope oil and the Sagwon bush airport site that later became a hub of excitement and commerce. Interior Airways became Alaska International Air; and more recently, a big scheduled airline called MarkAir. Magoffin makes his point loud and clear throughout his book that the biggest obstacles blocking his successful operations were government induced. I sent him a letter of congratulations on his great book and decided to send him a rough draft of my chapter on Alaska to see what he thought about it. I received a letter of encouragement followed up by a telephone call that, for me, seemed to melt away thirty years. I could picture him as though I still was working for Interior Airways in 1965. I asked him how my memory served me in my writing and he replied that my recollections of those times and events were excellent!

Some people thrive with government involvement, and some don't. For example, Al Ewald's former student mechanic and former owner of a topless bar, Dixie, is now the Manager of an FAA Flight Standards District Office, and doing fine. On the other hand, Roy Reagan, former chief pilot of Aero Union Corporation, was implicated in a seventy-million-dollar scam. The scandal involved the selling of military C-130 Hercules aircraft that had been exchanged by the government for old, outmoded (and comparatively worthless) air tankers. The idea was that the Herks were to be modified for fire fighting. Instead, some of the four engine turboprops were sold for profit. Maybe Roy shoulda stuck to flying 'em insteada sellin' 'em.

It was August 1995, Al Ewald's 58th birthday. His A & P students at Shasta College decided to throw him a surprise party. He walked into the lecture room prepared to deliver his usual ho hum discussion of gyro instruments, when he became suspicious, because *all* the students were present at 1:00 p.m. Normally they were at least fifteen minutes late. He turned to step toward the door and noted that one six-foot-five student stood cross armed in front of it nodding, "no." He looked at the back door and another large student guarded that exit. On the blackboard the following was inscribed, "Al, sit down in the chair of honor," and an arrow pointed toward the chair. Al shrugged and sat down. Suddenly out of the back exit burst "Melissa," from "Wishful Fantasies," scattering flower pedals and passing out champagne glasses. Al's eyes widened as he noted her scanty, exotic clothing. Then the music began and out danced "Heidi," who stripped to the waist amid wild cheering and clapping (the clappers included the female members of the class). Heidi danced seductively over to the chair where Al sat red-faced and grinning like an idiot. Then she jumped into his lap, enthusiastically straddling him and beating him in the face with her bare boobs! Al loved it, but all the while he was remembering that the FAA Blue Ribbon team was scheduled to arrive today to inspect his facilities. He hoped they would be late!

We went along with a slightly indecent proposal from Mark, who owned a summer home on the shore of Bucks Lake. His brother was having a birthday party. Mark purchased from a porn shop, several life sized "Swedish Bikini Team" dolls, including all the anatomically correct attachments. Water was poured into their feet for weight and Tom dropped them out of the 206 not far from the shoreline near the cabin. They looked very real as they fell toward the lake feet first. Speed boats from all over the lake made rooster tails as they closed in for the rescue. A hearty laugh was had by all!

More government B. S.! I received a notice from the State of California, specifically from the Council for Private Postsecondary and Vocational Education. They claimed that I was in violation of their rules. On a previously filed Declaration of Exemption I had supposedly failed to submit representative copies of existing media advertising or promotional materials. Furthermore, I had not included a description of the educational services being offered. Furthermore-*more*, they were turning the matter over to their Special Investigator with the Council for further action. For Christ's sake's, people, we give flight instruction and we don't need any "help" from the State of California!

Ronnie Bones flew in the night before and showed up bright and early for his flight test. The little Cessna 150 was sheathed in ice from the frigid night before. He attempted to start it up in order to taxi over closer to our operation on the ramp. I winced as I saw fuel gushing out under the cowling as the little engine slowly turned over in an attempt to start. Fortunately, it didn't even try to fire because a catastrophic engine blaze would surely have resulted. I hurried over and suggested that we let the little guy warmup in the sun while we reviewed his application.

It really irritates me when a flight test candidate starts in with statements such as, "I'm so impressed with your experience," or "I'm such a beginner and I've got so much to learn, and I really look up to you," blah, blah blah! Anyhow, that's how it started. The 150's battery was dead as a doornail from the futile cranking, so we started the flight test with my giving him a hand prop. The alternator began charging and everything was fine. The flight portion of the test went reasonably well too. The problems began with the cross-country flight planning during the oral exam later. When we were walking into the exam room Ronnie's whining began again. He stopped me and said, "You know, I don't drink or smoke and it's a miracle that I've made it this far, but one day I found the Lord and it touched my heart."

I replied lightly, trying to avoid being drawn into some sort of religious discussion, "Well, maybe the Lord will help you with your oral!" He didn't, and it was necessary for Ronnie to retake that portion of the test.

The next flight test was late in starting due to fog. Rudolph, from Redding, circled and circled and finally alighted when there was not a trace of fog left, although he could probably landed twenty minutes sooner. He parked at the tiedown space located at the most distant spot from my office, effectively wasting more time. At this time of year the sun drops below the rugged horizon by 4:00 p.m. After checking his application, I suggested that he do a "quick" preflight and then we could begin our flight. Rudolph painstakingly checked every rivet on the airplane. I nervously followed him around and noted to him that the sun was descending in the southwest and that time was of the essence. He looked at me with suspicious eyes and said, "How do I know that you aren't trying to trick me into being negligent by making me hurry too fast? I'm a man that can't be hurried." I sighed and relaxed as the shadows got longer. The flight was barely acceptable, but Rudolph had to come back to complete the oral. I wrote him a Letter of Discontinuance. He needed to take off right away if he hoped to make it home to Redding before dark. I explained that I didn't want him to have to deal with the inevitable fog that forms after dark this time of year.

My FAA mentor (the one I had complained about) told me that I could *not* give the oral before the flight test. I explained to him that in this mountain community, in the summer, density altitude becomes a problem for a small trainer in the middle of the day. I said that it was better to let an individual takeoff *alone* from this windy hot airport while light on fuel for best performance, rather than to attempt a flight test with two aboard under those conditions, especially when attempting short and soft field takeoffs and landings. The Inspector asked elsewhere for guidance and called me back with the statement that, "The procedure is legal but not recommended, use your own judgment." I assured him that I would.

Since the first of the year I had been negotiating with John McMorrow about the price of fuel and was being more-or-less ignored. To prove my point, I vowed to him that I would not buy any more of the product from the County of Plumas until the price was dropped. I immediately established charge accounts in surrounding areas with operators who gave me an excellent FBO discount. To be effective with the fuel boycott procedure, it required the cooperation of our crew and customers, and thankfully, I got it. It was necessary to use the bigger aircraft as "nurse rigs," and to siphon fuel to containers and transfer it around to the aircraft that needed it at the time. It was hardball poker and if you wanted to be a player, you didn't dare blink. The result was dramatic. McMorrow and I had a meeting. He said, "Without you, I might as well not be in the fuel business." The result was that the price of fuel was lowered by a walloping amount to everyone. Things were looking up!

I was chosen to be on a committee to plan an "Antique Wings and Wheels" fly-in at Gansner Airfield. Among the mover and shaker committee members were some of the "good ole boys." I'm getting to be a regular social butterfly!

The face of Bob Silvera, now thirty-seven, appeared on nationwide television with the nickname of "The Box Car Murderer." He stands accused of beating dozens of transients to death all across the country. He confessed to some forty-seven murders. Judy and I remember him as a soft-spoken, well-mannered fellow who wore long sleeves to cover his many tattoos. C.W. hired him to live at the Chester Airport and assume the title of caretaker, a job that commanded little pay. "After all," Adams reasoned, "any jerk can pump gas, and the county is saving lots of money by not having to pay a Manager." C.W. really knew how to pick 'em!

In December we had our annual Aviators Flying Club dinner at the airport restaurant, and as usual, I received a roasting. Bob, Avail, and Crystal were dressed up in Broadway musical outfits complete with straw hats, canes, and for the girls, sexy black stockings. They called their trio, "Aerotica." While dancing to the background music they chanted the following original score:

> Up on the hangar, reindeer pause
> Down jumps good old Santa Claus
> Skipping past the planes, orange & brown
> A bag of goodies he sets down.

> What do you think he has for *John?*
> A new 210 'cause the other one's gone
> It got off the ground then made some noise
> Scaring to death all the Forest Service boys!

Tom was the pilot and we hear
After the landing they gave him a cheer
But when the ground they touched upon
Everyone on board had to go to the jon!

Ho, ho, ho, who wouldn't go
Ho, ho, ho, who wouldn't go
Up on the hangar, click, click, click
Skipping past the planes comes ole Saint Nick.

The Forest Service tried it once again
This time to Oroville in the 210
Oh *Johnny* tried to put the wheels down
But they just laughed and hung around
So a new 210 is what Johnny needs
Let's hope the next one is up to speed!

(CHORUS – EVERYONE!)

Sometimes, when my schedule permits, I leave the airport early and go home to Meadow Valley and relax out by the pond. I take a sip of my favorite libation and observe the insects dancing on the clear cold spring water. As the sun settles toward the towering cliffs to the west, I release my mind from the tightly-focused thoughts of the day and drift to a more relaxed and, at first, mindless state. The reflections on the water produce a black, luminescent effect. I see the tiny insect struggling on the surface tension of the water, and the trout waiting below for the right moment to strike at the hapless creature. The eagle soars overhead, waiting for a chance at the trout. The scene is timeless and has been repeated every day for millions of years. I thought of the long life of the white rose bush that I had planted under the eaves at the airport when I was first learning to fly. It was still there and flourishing with fabulous white flowers during the spring, and all the while ignoring the raging trials and tribulations of the people around it.

It struck me that I had learned something that I didn't know as a young flier. There was always someone bigger, faster, smarter, a better pilot, and in politics and wealth, more powerful than you. In spite of that, I had managed to do things *my* way, and I had done OK. Not many people can say that. I reflected on the unfathomable nature of the universe and wondered if my ancestors were out there somewhere. There were plenty of religious fanatics only too ready to straighten me out on that subject! I thought about my parents who were cut down so early in their full and promising lives, and wondered how I had been spared, and why. I so often found myself, or put myself, in so many dangerous situations, only to survive. I knew that my will to live and fly another day was strong. I never gave up. I didn't then and won't now. I must fly!